The Wilderness Educator:

The Wilderness Education Association

The Wilderness Educator:

*The Wilderness
Education Association
Curriculum Guide*

*Edited by
David Cockrell*

Merrillville, Indiana

The Wilderness Educator

Printed in the U.S.A.

Published by
ICS BOOKS, Inc.
107 E. 89th Ave.
Merrillville, Indiana
46410

Library of Congress Cataloging-in-Publication Data

The Wilderness educator : the Wilderness Education Association curriculum guide / edited by David Cockrell
    p.   cm.
Includes index.
ISBN 0-934802-19-X : $29.95
1. Recreation leaders--Training of. 2. Outdoor life—Study and teaching. 3. Camping—Environmental aspects—Study and teaching. 4. Survival skills—Study and teaching.   I. Cockrell, David, 1950-
II. Wilderness Education Association (U.S.)
GV181.35.W55 1991
790'.071'1—dc20   90-25774

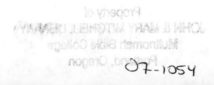

Affectionately dedicated to our WEA instructors for their professionalism and
devotion to duty.

Contents in Brief

CONTENTS

3. ─────────────────────────────────

Group Dynamics in the Outdoors: A Model for Teaching Outdoor Leaders 35
Maurice Phipps

4. ─────────────────────────────────

Environmental Ethics and Backcountry Conservation Practices 65
David Cockrell

5. ─────────────────────────────────

Basic Wilderness Skills 83
Jack Drury, Bruce Bonney and David Cockrell

6. ⎯⎯⎯⎯⎯⎯⎯⎯⎯⎯⎯⎯⎯⎯⎯⎯⎯⎯

Rations Planning and Food Preparation 105
Jack Drury, Bruce Bonney and David Cockrell

7. ⎯⎯⎯⎯⎯⎯⎯⎯⎯⎯⎯⎯⎯⎯⎯⎯⎯⎯

Adventure Skills and Travel Modes 129
Jerry Cinnamon and Ed Raiola

8. ⎯⎯⎯⎯⎯⎯⎯⎯⎯⎯⎯⎯⎯⎯⎯⎯⎯⎯

Wilderness Emergency Procedures and Treatment 149
William W. Forgey, M.D.

9.

Course Administration 169
Mark Wagstaff and David Cockrell

Index 189

PREFACE

Have you contemplated, perhaps with some trepidation, leading a group of people on an extended wilderness outing? Perhaps, as in my case, you have led such trips with mixed results and thought long about what you could have done differently. If your responsibilities or aspirations include wilderness expeditionary leadership, this book is important reading.

The Wilderness Educator and the works it builds upon form the body of knowledge regarded as essential for Wilderness Education Association instructors. Wilderness Education Association (W.E.A.) courses are 28-35 day educational expeditions designed to teach outdoor leadership in wilderness environments. Hundreds of W.E.A. standard courses have been sponsored by universities in remote environments from Alaska to Newfoundland, from the Gila Wilderness of New Mexico to the mountains of North Carolina. In these pages, some of W.E.A.'s most experienced and articulate instructors have crystallized the lessons of over a decade of W.E.A. experience.

Naturally, the lessons have broad application beyond the W.E.A. programs themselves. The W.E.A. curriculum has evolved from the work of scouting leaders, interpreters in natural resource management agencies, Outward Bound and National Outdoor Leadership School instructors, community-based outdoor recreation programmers, Sierra Club outing leaders and many, many others. The topics covered include the major issues faced by any wilderness expedition: judgment and decision making, leadership, environmental ethics, wilderness living and travel, nutrition, emergency procedures and administration. But other books already address many of these issues well. The unique feature of *The Wilderness Educator* is its emphasis on the teaching of wilderness expeditionary leadership.

This is a book designed for educators and leaders of educational backcountry experiences. Each chapter draws together theoretical frameworks from a variety of related disciplines with bearing on the particular issue at hand. Thus, Kelly Cain's chapter on judgment summarizes material from the outdoor leadership literature as well as the decision-making literature in social and organizational psychology to present a framework for the making of quality decisions in the field. Dr. Forgey's detailed discussions of the etiologies of chronic and immersion hypothermia draw from clinical studies and experimental work in medicine and exercise physiology. One should not expect the authors to gloss over the complicated issues here. They do not—from the chemistry of backcountry water purification to the effects of psychological stress on leadership decisions. For each subject the emphasis is on addressing complex or poorly understood issues in some detail and referencing several excellent available publications explaining the basics.

But, again, this is a book for educators, not a technical manual. Each chapter includes a detailed discussion of ways to teach the material at hand. The nutrition and rations planning chapter does include a discussion of the complementarity of vegetable proteins. But it also describes nine specific strategies for teaching rations planning to aspiring outdoor leaders—including a formal lecture on nutritional theory, a week-long rations-planning exercise, actual food selections and purchases, a food-identification class, basic cooking and baking classes, potluck dinners, a rations swap, and a rationing evaluation exercise. Similar strategies are outlined for teaching each of the W.E.A. curriculum areas, from map and compass to conflict resolution.

In these ways the book reflects a basic orientation of W.E.A.: An emphasis on the "whys" behind things and the ways to teach. No rules are presented here—only principles. The "whys" behind each principle are explained as fully as possible. When specific procedures are recommended for field activities or teaching (and they often are), there is a recognition that these represent only one way of doing things. Experience has shown, however, that it is a way that works.

The book goes beyond what you might wish to teach in the field. This is the material that W.E.A. instructors are expected to know. As aspiring outdoor leaders, students in W.E.A. courses will begin to assimilate this body of knowledge, but it is far too much to master in a single "sitting." It will be useful as a text for a semester-long course accompanying the W.E.A. National Standard Program (N.S.P.), a course that we have taught and found extremely enriching. To expedite the process of translating this curriculum into manageable proportions in a field-teaching situation, Jack Drury has developed a detailed set of W.E.A. National Standard Program lesson plans, also available from ICS Books. An ideal application is to use this curriculum guide in conjunction with the lesson plans both in the field and in preparatory or follow-up exercises in town.

There are many people who have contributed in nurturing the current project to fruition. Foremost, the authors who have contributed manuscripts deserve thanks for their perseverance over the nearly four years that this book has been in the making and remaking. Sandra Braun deserves special recognition for the original idea of an "instructor's manual" and the first outlines for the book. Tom Todd and Dr. Forgey at ICS Books have provided patient and thoughtful guidance to the book's organization and presentation. Jack Drury, Bruce Bonney, Chris Cashel, Sandy Braun, Maurice Phipps, Dr. Forgey, Nancy Maylath, and the W.E.A. students of North Country Community College, Virginia Tech, and the University of North Carolina at Wilmington all read and contributed to other authors' manuscripts, enriching them greatly. Frida Ayala, a W.E.A.-certified outdoor leader from Venezuela, provided the illustrations. The clerical assistance of Beth Hartbauer and Kathy Keys was a major contribution. Thanks go to the Wilderness Education Association and the Adirondack North Country Association, who provided support for a concentrated effort on the curriculum guide during the summer of 1988. I would like to thank my family, Jude, Ary, and Neva, without whom all of this would have been done much more quickly but with so much less meaning. Finally, of course, we all thank Paul Petzoldt, who built the foundation upon which all our current castles stand.

David Cockrell
Pueblo, Colorado
December 1990

FOREWORD
by Paul Petzoldt

In 1984, in *The New Wilderness Handbook,* I wrote of a fledgling national effort to educate users of the wild outdoors. There I tried to characterize the damage that I have seen inflicted upon North America's wild lands by well-meaning but uninformed travelers. I suggested that the enjoyment and safety of wilderness outings could be greatly enhanced if leaders were more knowledgeable. I outlined a certification and education program that had been adopted by a number of universities to educate outdoor leaders.

Today it is most gratifying to me to see the progress that has been made by the Wilderness Education Association. Many new universities have joined the ranks teaching our national standard curriculum. But perhaps even more importantly, the curriculum is at last reaching out to the broader audience of wilderness users. In 1989, the Tennessee Department of Conservation became the first natural resource management agency to be accredited to teach the national standard program for outdoor leadership certification. And the Boy Scouts of America Philmont Scout Ranch in New Mexico has adopted W.E.A.'s new Wilderness Steward Program as part of its outdoor leadership training.

As W.E.A. gains recognition and acceptance, it is critical that the curriculum remains abreast of the very best thinking in the outdoor leadership community. Fundamental principles of the curriculum have evolved over twenty-five years of programs through the National Outdoor Leadership School and W.E.A. Many of the basic ideas are summarized in *The New Wilderness Handbook.* But I wrote that for everyone who ventures into the wilderness—from the day hiker to the seasoned outdoors person.

What has been needed for some time now is a book addressed specifically to the expedition leader with instructional responsibilities. The present volume fills that gap. It is not enough for W.E.A. instructors to understand the basics of outdoor leadership. They must now be conversant with the sophisticated theories that are becoming the stock in trade for the outdoor leadership profession.

Kelly Cain's discussion of outdoor judgment and decision making in chapter 2, for example, begins with my ideas about the central role of judgment in outdoor leadership. Based on his doctoral work on the topic, Cain draws in theories from other disciplines and details a conceptual framework for making quality decisions in the field. Also based on his doctoral dissertation, Maurice Phipps' discussion of the elements of outdoor leadership and expeditionary group dynamics provides a logical framework for understanding how groups develop and effective leaders behave.

In chapter 4, David Cockrell updates the standard N.O.L.S. conservation practices based on a review of research, but more importantly he provides specific techniques for teaching lasting environmental ethics. The chapters on rations planning and clothing and equipment are appropriately headed up by Jack Drury, one of W.E.A.'s most experienced and accomplished affiliate instructors. The sophistication of his outfitting skills (he even uses a computer for rations planning!) is reflected in state-of-the-art discussions.

My fundamental philosophies of understanding one's abilities and limitations and avoiding survival situations have been examined and amplified significantly by Jerry Cinnamon and Ed Raiola in their chapter on adventure travel modes. Dr. Bill Forgey's frank and direct approach to wilderness emergencies provides a new appreciation of the complexities of environmental injuries as well as the conceptual tools for applying basic first aid knowledge in the wilderness environment. Finally, in the first and last chapters, Mark Wagstaff and David Cockrell have described the activities of W.E.A., the process of accreditation, and the issues involved in administering a course. This is important, basic information for all W.E.A. instructors, and much of it is adaptable to a variety of outdoor programs.

At the time of this writing, outdoor leadership certification remains a controversial issue, although the controversy seems to have peaked. What sustains W.E.A. and continues to attract students and members is the curriculum. In many ways, this curriculum reflects and embodies my life's work. The present volume is an important milestone in the ongoing refinement of this living body of knowledge.

1.

AN INTRODUCTION TO THE WILDERNESS EDUCATION ASSOCIATION

by David Cockrell
University of
Southern Colorado
and
Frank Lupton
Western Illinois University

The mission of the Wilderness Education Association (W.E.A.) is to promote the professionalization of outdoor leadership and to thereby improve the safety of outdoor trips and enhance the conservation of the wild outdoors. W.E.A. promotes professionalism through several equally important strategies: certification, accreditation, affiliation, membership, program consulting, and research and development.

W.E.A.'s National Standard Program for Outdoor Leadership Certification (N.S.P.) emphasizes experiential teaching and learning of a standard basic curriculum under field conditions. When the N.S.P. is coupled with the student's prior outdoor study and experience, the result is often adequate knowledge and practical experience in leading others safely with minimum impact to the environment. Certified graduates know their limitations and abilities, have the knowledge and judgment to plan and lead trips within their abilities, and the judgment to refrain from accepting leadership responsibilities beyond their abilities. The N.S.P. is taught by W.E.A. certification instructors under the auspices of accredited universities or agencies who have met the qualifications for formal W.E.A. accreditation. N.S.P. graduates and instructors often teach "wilderness steward programs," addressing one or more of the 18 elements in the N.S.P. curriculum. These shorter courses are offered with W.E.A. approval through a variety of W.E.A. steward affiliate institutions.

W.E.A. further promotes the professionalism of outdoor leadership through the administration of a membership program. Members of the association receive many services, including an annual professional conference, a newsletter, regular curriculum updates, equipment bargains, and an employment clearinghouse. W.E.A. members, graduates, instructors and affiliates also provide consultation services for program and curriculum development, instructor referrals, and speakers for a variety of groups. The provision of this forum for professional interchange is encouraging the continued refinement of professional skills and knowledge in the field.

Finally, W.E.A. encourages the generation of new knowledge about education in the wild outdoors through the conduct of field research and the administration of an information clearinghouse available to members.

In this introductory chapter of the curriculum guide, the accreditation and certification processes are briefly described. We then briefly outline five research studies that have been conducted on various aspects of the W.E.A. curriculum so the reader may appreciate some of the successes and challenges faced by the organization. The chapter closes with a discussion of directions for the immediate future.

Wilderness Education Association Accreditation, Affiliation and Programs

W.E.A. ACCREDITED UNIVERSITY

A college or university that offers the National Standard Program for Outdoor Leadership Certification, employing the standard W.E.A. curriculum, evaluation process, and certification procedures. A fully accredited university must employ a certified W.E.A. instructor as a full-time faculty member, provide the necessary administrative support for a major educational expedition, submit an annual accreditation fee, and pay small administrative fees for each student enrolled in National Standard courses.

W.E.A. PROVISIONALLY ACCREDITED UNIVERSITY

A college or university that offers the National Standard Program on a regular or occasional basis by employing a certified W.E.A. instructor as an adjunct faculty member. Other requirements for provisional accreditation are equivalent to those for full accreditation.

THE NATIONAL STANDARD PROGRAM FOR
OUTDOOR LEADERSHIP CERTIFICATION

The National Standard Program is a 28-35 day "expedition" based on the W.E.A. 18 point curriculum and taught by a W.E.A. instructor at an accredited college or university. While it is felt that the above is the ideal means to teach the N.S.P., the W.E.A. will grant approval for programs that address all components of the core curriculum in one of the following formats:

A. At least three weeks of continuous wilderness travel within the context of a longer course(s) to be completed within one academic year (the 3-1 option).

B. Two wilderness field trips of two continuous weeks within the context of a longer course(s) to be completed within a two-year period (the 2-2-2 option).

C. A two-week continuous wilderness field experience with two additional continuous wilderness field experiences of one week each within the context of a longer course(s) to be completed within one academic year (the 2-1-1 option).

WILDERNESS STEWARD AFFILIATE ORGANIZATIONS

Educational, resource management or social service organizations who offer W.E.A. Wilderness Steward Programs and wish to be promoted through W.E.A. advertising and publications. Steward Affiliates pay an annual $50 affiliation fee, and $15 introductory membership fees for each steward course participant.

WILDERNESS STEWARD PROGRAMS

Programs taught by W.E.A. certified leaders and instructors that include one or more of the 18 components of the W.E.A. curriculum. A Wilderness Steward Program may be authorized in two ways:

A. A certified W.E.A. instructor may offer a W.E.A. Wilderness Steward Program by providing notice to the executive director prior to the course, along with such information as dates, location, topics to be covered and costs.

B. A certified W.E.A. leader can offer a W.E.A. Wilderness Steward Program by submitting an application to the executive director prior to the course.

Wilderness Steward Program participants who submit an application and a $15 introductory membership fee will receive all W.E.A. membership benefits as well as a certificate of participation listing the course title, topics covered, the number of hours of participation and the course instructor's signature.

LEVELS OF W.E.A. CERTIFICATION

A. W.E.A. Head Instructor: W.E.A. head instructors have completed an instructor's course (or in rare cases a N.S.P. course), apprenticed on one N.S.P. course and been recommended for head instructor status by the head instructor of the apprenticeship course. Certification instructors have clearly demonstrated the ability to effectively teach the N.S.P. curriculum.

B. W.E.A. Instructor Apprentice: Apprentices have completed a W.E.A. instructor's course. To be eligible for an instructor's course, a candidate must be 21 years old, hold current Red Cross Advanced First Aid/C.P.R. certifications, have completed a Bachelor's degree (usually an advanced degree), and have substantial outdoor leadership training and experience separate from W.E.A.

C. Certified Outdoor Leader: To become certified, a student must complete a N.S.P. and demonstrate an ability to:

a. Teach others how to use and enjoy the wilderness with minimum impact;

b. Safely lead others in the wild outdoors;

c. Exercise good judgment in a variety of outdoor environments and conditions; and

d. Demonstrate a basic standard of outdoor knowledge and experience. The certification is not an unconditional guarantee of the graduate's present or future leadership effectiveness. It is based on an observation of the individual's performance in a specific time and place. However, not all students who complete an N.S.P. course are routinely certified.

D. The Wilderness Steward Certificate: This certificate of participation is granted upon successful completion of a Wilderness Steward Program or N.S.P. course. Normally, students are expected to demonstrate an understanding of one or more areas of the W.E.A. curriculum. The curriculum areas addressed by the course and the number of hours involved are indicated on the certificate.

Figure 1-1

Requirements and Steps in the Accreditation Process

In order to become accredited to teach the N.S.P., a candidate institution must prepare a curriculum plan explaining details of how the N.S.P. curriculum will be incorporated into the institution's program and staffing. The curriculum plan is evaluated by the W.E.A. Board of Trustees at one of their biannual meetings. The plan will either be approved for accreditation, rejected (rarely), or returned with recommendations for revision (more commonly). Because revisions may be requested, it is advisable that the curriculum plan be submitted for consideration at least six months prior to the first planned N.S.P. course offering (e.g., the October Trustee's meeting for course offerings the following summer).

In order to be accredited, the curriculum plan must meet each of the following standards:

1. The adopting institution must teach the N.S.P. curriculum as summarized in the curriculum outline and detailed in this curriculum guide with accompanying lesson plans. The preferred format is a single course consisting of 28-35 days of field experience in a wilderness setting. However, as described above, the 3-1, 2-2-2, and 2-1-1 options are acceptable substitutes for institutions in which a single long course is not feasible. The curriculum plan should include a course syllabus (or syllabi) clearly indicating how and when the 18 N.S.P. curriculum areas will be addressed.

2. The adopting institution must document that they can provide adequate equipment, supplies and logistical support for a major educational expedition.

3. A W.E.A. certification instructor must teach the course. For full accreditation, the certification instructor must be a full-time faculty member. For provisionally accredited institutions, an adjunct faculty member may teach the W.E.A. course. W.E.A. coordinates a network of certification instructors, most with graduate degrees, and can refer candidates for either adjunct or permanent faculty positions. W.E.A. instructors brought in as adjunct faculty exclusively to teach the W.E.A. course must receive compensation comparable to that of other faculty of like rank for equivalent credit load responsibilities. W.E.A.-referred instructors will arrive at least three days prior to the beginning of a course to ensure quality planning and communication.

4. Standard W.E.A. evaluation and certification procedures must be employed. The course evaluation process is described in detail in chapter 9 of this curriculum guide, and all written evaluation instruments described there must be filed with the W.E.A. office within one month of the termination of the course. The decision to certify N.S.P. students rests solely with the W.E.A. instructor(s) based on his/her understanding of the criteria for quality outdoor judgment and leadership. Students who wish to appeal a certification

decision may do so by presenting written testimony to the Board of Trustees. However, certification decisions made by instructors are usually regarded as final, and instructors may not make certification contingent upon completion of postcourse assignments. Likewise, while the course grading system should reflect the standard W.E.A. evaluation process, the assignment of grades is the prerogative of the institution. W.E.A. recommends that the usual distribution of grades for the adopting institution be fully employed on the N.S.P. course.

5. The adopting institution must pay an annual accreditation fee and a small fee for each N.S.P. student for administrative expenses associated with provision of curriculum materials, diplomas, membership services and the maintenance of permanent records. The student fee applies regardless of whether the student becomes certified and is due at the beginning of the N.S.P. course along with a completed diploma order form. For institutions offering the N.S.P. through a multicourse format, the student fee is due at the beginning of the sequence and is not refundable for students not completing the sequence.

6. The adopting institution must agree to allow W.E.A. representatives to visit or otherwise monitor the N.S.P. program at a time and by a process mutually agreed upon.

Also, as part of the accreditation agreement, W.E.A. contracts to provide the following services:

1. W.E.A. will provide the standard 18 point N.S.P. curriculum, along with regular updates. Accredited institutions are exclusively provided with the curriculum outline, standardized handouts on rations planning, equipment, water treatment, and other selected topics, and standard evaluation forms.

2. W.E.A. will administer a nationally recognized certification system. N.S.P. graduates receive diplomas, membership cards and full W.E.A. membership privileges. A permanent file is maintained on each certified graduate containing registration forms, ability assessment forms and student evaluation forms, and these are made available to prospective employers at the request of the student.

3. W.E.A. coordinates a national outdoor leadership communications network. Accredited institutions receive the monthly "Trustees and Affiliates Briefing System" (T.A.B.S.), W.E.A.'s quarterly newsletter "The Legend," access to a computerized job-referral service for graduates, and periodic updates on the W.E.A. curriculum. In addition, each accredited university and affiliate institution receives a copy of the W.E.A. curriculum guide and the W.E.A.

curriculum lesson plans. W.E.A. also sponsors an annual national meeting for accredited institutions, affiliates and members. Finally, W.E.A. promotes accredited institutions' programs through a variety of national marketing efforts, including brochures, magazine advertisements, conference participation, and so forth.

Recent Research and Current Trends in W.E.A.

As W.E.A. has grown in stature and evolved over the past decade and a half, the important emphasis of the organization has clearly been the N.S.P. curriculum. As one talks with graduates and instructors, it becomes apparent that certification is not so important, perhaps only a vehicle for professionalism. A standard line in W.E.A. is that the W.E.A. way is only one way (out of many possibilities) but it is a way that works! Interestingly, the W.E.A. "way," or the process and content of the curriculum, is itself in a constant state of evolution. As new information emerges on how to teach leadership styles or treat hypothermia, the curriculum is adapted to accommodate it. This is possible primarily because the emphasis is not on the "correctness" of practices in the backcountry, but rather on the quality of judgment and decisions.

As might be expected, a number of W.E.A. instructors and associates have conducted research on various aspects of the curriculum. Five such studies are summarized here briefly to give a sense of the level of ongoing inquiry that molds this "living" curriculum.

Cockrell and Detzel (1985) and Cockrell, Detzel and Braun (1986) reported results of the first follow-up study of certified W.E.A. graduates through 1983. Two hundred sixty-one of the 648 graduates (41%) completed questionnaires. The mean age of this sample was 27.4 years, and 74% held at least a bachelor's degree. Fifty-three percent reported that they had been involved in formal outdoor leadership responsibilities prior to attending a W.E.A. course. Graduates were largely quite satisfied with their courses. They felt most of the objectives had been met, rated their instructors favorably, and felt they had been evaluated fairly. Ratings by graduates with prior leadership experience tended to be higher.

This study focused especially on the effectiveness of the courses in teaching safety and backcountry conservation, and on standardization of the curriculum nationally. Knowledge levels of graduates concerning standard safety and conservation practices were only moderate. Reported postcourse evacuations and rescues per participant/day were lower but not significantly so. The self-rated influence of W.E.A. on graduates' subsequent safety and conservation efforts was 3.08 and 3.48 respectively on 4.0 scales. In regard to standardization, graduates reported implementing a mean of 4.54 of the 18 W.E.A. curriculum areas into their subsequent programs due to the W.E.A. experience. The authors concluded that W.E.A. was most influential in the curriculum areas of expedition behavior, travel techniques in the wild outdoors, judgment and rations planning. The conservation curriculum was judged more effective than safety-related curriculum elements, although neither of these curriculum areas was adequately standardized across courses. While supportive of many of the unique aspects of the W.E.A. curriculum, this study pointed out the need to monitor N.S.P. courses closely and standardize the training sequence for W.E.A. instructors.

Another large-scale survey research study by Sakofs (1987) compared W.E.A., Outward Bound and National Outdoor Leadership School instructors (n=184). Sakofs found 60% to favor the idea of certifying outdoor leaders and 60% to support a nationally accredited outdoor leadership curriculum. While there were no differences in support levels for certification across the three schools, there were profound differences in support for a standardized curriculum. One hundred percent of the W.E.A. instructors supported a standardized curriculum, while only 46% and 50% of the O.B. and N.O.L.S. instructors respectively supported standardization. Interestingly, Sakofs found no significant difference across the three organizations in importance levels assigned to various curriculum topics.

Several investigators have focused directly on the process of teaching leadership on W.E.A. courses. Phipps (1986, 1987) has developed and tested a group dynamics teaching model for use on W.E.A. courses. The model is underpinned by Hersey and Blanchard's model of situational leadership and Jones' model of group development. The teaching model involves teaching nine basic "units" of leadership competence in a systematic order and assessing changes in students' leadership behaviors and group interaction patterns. In comparing 56 students on six W.E.A. courses, Phipps found improved leadership behaviors and attitudes as well as more positive group dynamics on those courses using the teaching model. Phipps explains his model in detail here in chapter 3 of the curriculum guide.

Cashel (1986) has initiated an intriguing investigation of instructor and student behaviors using the Flanders Interaction Analysis System, a method for recording and categorizing specific teacher actions and their impact on desired student learning responses. In her initial investigations, she filmed three instructors on two W.E.A. courses to assess differences in their instructional styles, and changes in style across curriculum areas. She found, for example, that two instructors integrated information and expanded on student ideas much better in skills classes than lectures. The effects on students included more initiative, less dependence in their responses, and less time spent in silence and confusion.

Finally, a recent dissertation by W.E.A. instructor Kelly Cain (1988) examined the opinions of 26 North American experts on the development, evaluation and documentation of judgment and decision-making ability in outdoor leaders. Three rounds of questionnaires in this Delphi study led to considerable consensus regarding these controversial issues. There was 100% consensus that judgment/decision-making ability can be developed (a fundamental presupposition in W.E.A. courses). The most favored methods for teaching judgment included "experience in a variety of environments and seasons, with varying conditions of intensity" and "realistic opportunities for students to lead peers in stress and non-stress situations." There was also a 100% consensus that judgment and decision-making ability can be evaluated. Mentor evaluations, self- and peer evaluations were among the favored methods.

Cain found slightly less agreement about whether the quality of judgment/decision making could be documented or whether this would be beneficial. Finally, he found little agreement about whether judgment ability is tied to specific outdoor activities or is an independent quality and no agreement concerning the preference of certifying individuals or programs. Thus, while this study showed broad-based support for the underlying foundations of W.E.A.'s approach to outdoor leadership training, it mirrored the field's continuing ambivalence about certification as a mechanism for professionalism.

Figure 1-2

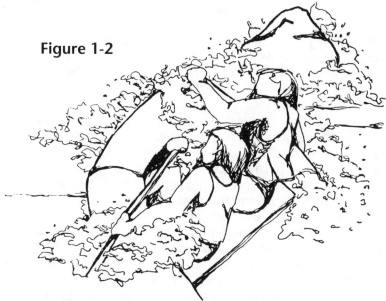

Some Directions for the Future

As was indicated in the beginning of this chapter, W.E.A.'s fundamental commitment is to the enhancement of the profession of outdoor leadership. In a discussion of certified public accounts, Gregory, Mueller, and Tabor (1976) identified five essential elements for an occupation's admission to the status of "profession."

1. A specialized body of knowledge with a high degree of intellectual content;

2. A recognized educational process for admission to the profession;

3. A self-imposed code of professional conduct;

4. A motive for service oriented to the public interest taking precedence over personal gain and self-interest; and

5. A recognition of status by persons outside the profession.

An outdoor leadership certification system provides a potential standard for admission to the profession and some recognition of status by various publics. Such a system seems presumptuous, however, unless it is developed in conjunction with the other elements of the profession.

A specialized body of knowledge is emerging in outdoor leadership with a grounding in social science theory (Ewert, 1987). Much of the current professional knowledge base pertaining to wilderness expedition leadership is summarized in the remaining chapters of this curriculum guide and taught on N.S.P. courses. It is critical, however, that W.E.A. remain abreast of current developments in the profession, and modify the N.S.P. curriculum accordingly. To this end, W.E.A. has activated a curriculum advisory committee consisting of instructors, representatives of accredited institutions and other recognized experts to continuously update and monitor all aspects of the certification curriculum. Continuing research on the processes and outcomes of adventure programming is also needed to advance this element of professionalism. W.E.A. actively promotes research in its courses and by its associates. A W.E.A. research policies committee is beginning to screen proposals and to recommend policies to the trustees for the promotion of legitimate research.

New university-level programs for the preparation of outdoor professionals are emerging at a steady pace. Efforts at curriculum coordination and evaluation may best be undertaken by an independent national organization with professional advancement as its principal concern. Enlarging the network of W.E.A. accredited colleges and affiliated organizations continues to be a high priority for the organization. In addition, a standard course monitoring system assists each affiliate in maintaining quality, and a re-certification procedure is being considered. Smaller-scale versions of the curriculum are also in review to broaden its versatility.

Finally, W.E.A. hopes to facilitate the development of service motives and a professional code of ethics through the communications network it sponsors for members. Advanced-skills seminars for graduates, several levels of newsletters, an annual conference and a job-search service are in place now with growth anticipated.

Clearly, the path to fulfillment of W.E.A.'s original urgent mission has been long and is far from completed. W.E.A's approach has always been controversial and the organization has evolved greatly over its short history. But the thousands of lessons learned through struggling with the W.E.A. curriculum on hundreds of courses have been rich, rewarding experiences. Many of these lessons are encapsulated in the remaining pages of this book by some of W.E.A.'s prominent leaders. Read on, and may your future wilderness adventures be enhanced accordingly!

REFERENCES

Cain, K. D. (1988). A Delphi study of the development, evaluation and documentation of judgment and decision-making ability in outdoor leaders of adventure education programs. Unpublished doctoral dissertation, University of Minnesota, St. Paul.

Cashel, C. and Gangstead, S. (1986). Outdoor leadership under a microscope: A look at teacher effectiveness. Paper presented at the second national conference on outdoor recreation, Davis, CA.

Cockrell, D., Detzel, D. and Braun, S. L. (1986). Certified wilderness trip leaders: Their knowledge levels, safety records and opinions of certification courses. *In* R. C. Lucas (Ed.), *Proceedings—National Wilderness Research Conference: Current Research.* U.S. Forest Service InterMountain Research Station Gen. Tech. Report INT- 212. Ogden, UT, 297-304.

Cockrell, D. and Detzel, D. (1985). Effects of outdoor leadership certification on safety, impacts and program standardization. *Park Practice Program Trends, 22*(3), 15-21.

Ewert, A. (1987). Research in experiential education: An overview. *Journal of Experiential Education,* 10(2), 4-7.

Phipps, M. (1987). Experiential leadership education. *Journal of Experiential Education,* 10(2), 22-28.

Phipps, M. (1986). An assessment of a systematic approach to teaching outdoor leadership in expedition settings. Unpublished doctoral dissertation, University of Minnesota, St. Paul.

Sakofs, M. (1987). The field instructor's orientation toward certification. *Journal of Experiential Education,* 10(2), 40-42.

2.

JUDGMENT AND DECISION-MAKING ABILITY

by Kelly Cain
University of Wisconsin
- River Falls

One aspect of outdoor leadership is absolute and unquestionable; a leader must be able to make quality decisions, decisions that are based on good judgment, that work, are safe, protect the environment and accomplish the purpose of the outing (Petzoldt, 1984).

Introduction

The feature of the W.E.A. curriculum that distinguishes it the most from all other outdoor leadership development programs is its emphasis upon theoretical and experience-based judgment and decision-making ability as the necessary foundation of all outdoor leadership competence. As the core is to the apple, so is judgment and decision-making ability to outdoor leadership. Not only is it the foundation, but the on going evolution of the W.E.A. curriculum has been continually based upon the premise that sound judgment and decision-making ability can be developed, evaluated and documented in students and practitioners alike.

For the context of this chapter, the terms "judgment," "decision making," and "experience-based judgment" have been combined and abbreviated as "J/D-M" (unless otherwise noted). There are three reasons for this. First, their usage is often interrelated, substituted and implied in previous literature. Second, by definition, they are mutually dependent. And finally, experience-based judgment (a contemporary usage of this concept in the field) is considered as the applied sense of the common theoretical base.

Judgment and decision making are combined here and used in the context that it represents not only the "glue" but also the cumulative measure of all outdoor leader competence and action. Or in other words, J/D-M is the synthesizing, catalytic agent by which all other competence is expressed, acted upon, and consequently evaluated.

Besides the premise stated above, there are three fundamental postulates that underlie the discussion that follows. First, an outdoor leader's responsibilities include, but are not limited to, three fundamental issues. First, he/she must positively facilitate the educational benefit of perceived and/or real risk while minimizing the odds for injury or death to students and staff. Second, the leader must maximize the quality and the enjoyment of the experience in relation to the goals of the curriculum, the collective group, and its individual members. Finally, he/she must maintain, if not improve, the condition of the environmental resources being used.

The second postulate is that, as a leader, every specific situation is a unique one due to the infinite combination of factors possible. Even though a leader might recognize various similarities to other situations he/she has previously encountered, they will not be identical to the one at hand. Thus, each judgment or decision made to maximize goals at any particular moment will vary across specific situations as well. As an old Petzoldt axiom goes, "Rules are for fools." Or in other words, blanket laws and policies, in place of leader judgment, are often the factors that needlessly limit the students' gain of experience-based judgment and the overall educational benefit of any particular situation.

As the infinite number of situational interactions surface within and between the leader(s), the group member(s), the environmental setting and the logistical conditions, it is primarily the leader's J/D-M ability that will be relied upon to accomplish the holistic management of factors. This does not preclude that groups should be called upon to make the judgments and decisions as often as possible, but it is the leader's judgment and decision-making ability that determines when it is in the best interest of the group for this to happen.

The final, but equally important, postulate is that when considering leadership development, it is important to distinguish between leadership "training" and leadership "education" or "teaching." The distinction is made here because training tends to denote how something should, or even must be done, as in a recipe, as opposed to education, which denotes how it can be done, why it is done in this way for this situation, and a means by which it might be adapted to future situations. After all, judgments and decisions are the essence of "why" a leader takes any particular action. The above distinction should compel W.E.A. instructors to emphasize leadership education as a process by which students are encouraged to and actually practice making judgments and decisions on both a cognitive and physical level. The student's experience would be based upon adapting their practical skills, technical knowledge and previous experience to immediate course situations. They will hopefully be made aware of the value of this whether in the wilderness or in their normal everyday life.

W.E.A. recognizes and encourages its instructors to nurture this holistic educational potential available to every individual who comes into contact with its curriculum, especially in terms of the J/D-M ability that can be transferred to every facet of a participant's life. As Hunt (1984, p. 21) puts it,

> There is something strange and incongruent about an educational movement that espouses responsibility, initiative, and freedom and then turns around and does everything it can to minimize the presence of these very values in the means by which they teach. This conflict of values is the root of my concern. My assumption is that the instructor judgment, situational approach to decision-making is more in line with the fundamental values of a total learning process than is the legalistic rule-based approach.

In applying these three postulates, consider the degree of leader-based J/D-M ability that is required of W.E.A. instructors in order to integrate:

1. Maximizing the quality and enjoyment of a uniquely specialized outdoor educational experience with the development of J/D-M ability as its central focus while:

2. Coping with the infinitely variable combination of goals, needs, opportunities, problems, conflicts and dangers that will arise; and

3. Conducting formal evaluations ultimately aimed at certifying the basic J/D-M ability of each program participant in other outdoor programs and environmental settings.

A tall order to say the least, but not an impossible one.

A theoretical basis for defining the J/D-M framework within the W.E.A. curriculum is presented here in three parts. Part I describes the theoretical foundation and definitions for "judgment and decision making" as applied to the W.E.A. curriculum. Part II focuses on the detailed description of the J/D-M process and its application in the field. Part III centers on the application of the J/D-M process to the W.E.A. curriculum.

Theoretical Foundations and Definitions

Although the theoretical foundations for general leadership-based judgment and decision making have been well documented in the literature and research of a number of fields (Cattail, 1946; Fiedler, 1967; Simon, 1976; Stodgill, 1948; Reitz, 1977; Macgregor-Burns, 1979), it is relatively new in outdoor leadership (Easther, 1979). The primary theoretical basis for this chapter, and ultimately the W.E.A. curriculum, lies in the synonymity of leadership and the J/D-M process.

For it is the hundreds of judgments made and executed by the leader every day that are collectively the physical manifestation of the leadership responsibility that he/she holds. So it is essential to remember throughout this discussion that J/D-M is not just the crucial element of a "safe" versus "unsafe" experience, it is ideally the essence and driving force of every word, gesture, and action performed in support of fulfilling W.E.A. goals.

So, on a theoretical level, how do we get at the guts of leadership and decision making? Reitz (1977) explains that when a judgment or decision must be made, there are basically two major factors that should be considered. The first is to determine who the decision-maker will be. The second is to determine what process the decision-maker or makers will use.

Rich (1980) expresses that leaders are individuals who have learned and practiced the behaviors of influencing others. These behaviors, referred to by Rich (1980), would typically include goal setting, decision making, motivation, communication patterns, and change strategies, but the most important of these is leadership style.

As is well documented in voluminous literature, there are three predominant basic styles of decision making—autocratic, democratic (participating), and laissez-faire. While there is no one "best" style of leadership for all situations, some portion of the success of a decision will ultimately be measured by the leader diagnosing and selecting the most appropriate style. The degree to which the leader shares the judgment and decision-making power with the group over an indefinite period of time distinguishes the leadership style that he/she can come to be known by—a reputation of such.

It is obvious that the leader is historically always assumed to be the decision-maker, which reflects the autocratic style and is exemplary of the "classical theory" of leadership. As is quite apparent in contemporary times, leadership has evolved to more often include those being led in the decision-making process—"the humanistic approach"—reflecting the overriding importance of the group or the participating and laissez-faire styles. This facilitates a socially equal and harmonious atmosphere where each group member is tapped for his/her particular talents and is able to establish her/his identity and self-esteem within the group.

Participating leadership moves beyond the leader's power to recognize the follower's power (Webber, 1975, p. 173).

All three of these have found their place in the outdoor leadership field and each has its appropriate place in the W.E.A. curriculum, but that's a different chapter. For the context of this chapter, I define outdoor leadership as the continual series of judgments, decisions, actions, and evaluations executed by a leader in the interest of maximizing a group's goals in relation to an adventure education pursuit—in this case, a W.E.A. course and the comprehensive goals of the W.E.A. curriculum. This definition implies both the classical and the humanistic contexts since it is common practice, and in my opinion preferable, for W.E.A. instructors to delegate the judgment and decision-making process to individual students and/or the entire group whenever possible. After all, how can we expect students to develop the improved J/D-M ability that we profess to teach if they have not actually practiced in "real" situations with constructive, yet empathic, feedback—a facilitative role rather than a dictator. Therefore, the theory of the J/D-M process itself, as applied to every experiential application in the field, becomes the central importance.

As is the case with leadership, voluminous amounts of literature are available on the theory of judgment and decision making (Hersey and Blanchard, 1982; Macgregor-Burns, 1979; Reitz, 1977; Rich, 1980; and Simon, 1976). Decision making implies that there is a choice to be made among alternative courses of action. The process of making choices requires judgment, which is only one aspect of the decision-making process.

The deliberation over what is or is not "quality" or "sound" J/D-M ability has raged for some time and will probably continue. Regardless, to define J/D-M ability as such, outside of a very specific and definable context (e.g., a legally documented case study), leaves the definition open to unending criticism. Therefore, as pointed out in other literature (Cain and McAvoy, 1989), we are left with defining them in the context of "humane idealism" and the "spirit of excellence." As such, it is appropriate to consider "quality" judgment and decision-making ability as two distinctly different, but mutually dependent, entities.

"Quality" judgment is the measure of a leader's mental and physical ability to, and process by which he/she anticipates and recognizes needs or opportunities for some degree of action in relation to the group's collective goals and in relation to the priorities of his/her responsibilities. These needs or opportunities are characterized by the situational interactions of what they perceive, observe, and know about themselves, the group, and the circumstances of any specific situation (Cain and McAvoy, 1989).

"Quality" decision-making ability is the measure of a leader's power and essential capacity to consistently make decisions based upon their judgments that maximize attainment of the group's collective goals and performance in his/her leadership responsibilities (Cain & McAvoy, 1989).

As an example, a leader may gain the reputation of having "sound judgment" in general because he/she rarely has evacuations off of courses in which he/she is involved. Another leader may gain a reputation for "poor judgment" solely because of one serious accident for which that leader was ultimately responsible even though he/she was not directly involved. Regardless of whether a leader's J/D-M ability is termed "sound" or "poor," it can and often does imply the total combination and series of leadership judgments, decisions, actions and evaluations made during a particular day, course, or throughout a career.

As Rich (1980) points out, the process of making decisions becomes most important after specific goals have been established. Therefore, the setting of goals becomes a decision-making process in itself.

In order to achieve the goal, decisions must be made relating to personnel, policies, procedures, resources and organization. Decisions occur at all levels of organizations and become the lifeblood of success (Rich, 1980, p. 140).

Decision making implies that there is a choice to be made among alternative courses of action. The process of making choices requires judgment, which is only one aspect of the decision-making process. Quoting Simon (1976, p. 4), who is considered to be one of the founders of decision-making theory,

> In so far as decisions lead toward the selection of final goals, they will be called "value judgments" so far as they involve the implementation of such goals, they will be called "factual judgments."

There has been a development of various kinds of decision making processes over the years (Rich, 1980) that incorporate and/or can be applied to "value judgments" and "factual judgments." While there are certainly a number of hybrid models in the outdoor leadership literature (Ewert, 1987; Priest, 1987), the one I have chosen, due to its simplicity, yet comprehensiveness and adaptability to the outdoor leadership field, is the "Normative Model" as outlined by Reitz (1977, p.187).

The Normative Model is divided into seven steps:
1. Setting Objectives
2. Recognizing a Problem
3. Evaluating the Problem
4. Searching for Alternatives
5. Evaluating Alternatives
6. Choosing among Alternatives
7. Carrying Out, Following Up the Decision

As the reader can see by comparison of this model to the one outlined in the next section of this chapter, I have adapted and redefined Reitz's Normative Model of the decision-making process. The basic model has, for the most part, been left intact except for the setting of objectives, which is a decision-making process in itself. It is obvious that goals and objectives are necessary to measure the direction and success of the decision-making process, but a new set of objectives is not established each time the process is carried out.

The theoretical need for sound judgment and decision-making ability is also well founded in the outdoor leadership literature in the United States. Paul Petzoldt (1974, 1984) is generally regarded to be the primary originator of its importance in this country. Rankin (1987) quotes Petzoldt's explanation of the application of judgment to the goals of N.O.L.S. in the early 1970s.

We not only develop techniques, we develop judgment and that, in the outdoors, is most important (p. 319).

Since then, the concept and importance of judgment as the "glue" by which all competence is expressed in outdoor leadership has been pointed out by a large number of writers in the field (Buell, 1983; Cain, 1985; Cousineau, 1977; Ewert, 1987; Ford and Blanchard, 1985; Green, 1981; Hunt, 1984; McAvoy, 1980 and 1987; Miles, 1987; Priest, 1987; Simer and Sullivan, 1983; and Swiderski, 1981).

Prior to the U.S. emphasis on judgment in outdoor leadership, a solid foundation for it had already been established in Britain and Canada. John Jackson, former director of the Plas y Brenin National Mountain Leadership Training Centre for Britain is often credited with the earliest associations of judgment and decision making to outdoor leadership.

There is plenty of room for an individual approach and each good leader will solve problems in his or her own way, but THE DECISIONS MADE AND SOLUTIONS TO PROBLEMS WILL OBEY CERTAIN BASIC RULES AND WILL BE DETERMINED BY THE INDIVIDUAL'S ABILITY TO MAKE SOUND JUDGMENTS BASED ON KNOWLEDGE AND EXPERIENCE. (Jackson, no date)

The right person
Having the right people
In the right place
At the right time
With the right knowledge
And the right equipment
(Jackson, 1973)

As an outgrowth of Jackson's influence, as well as of the certification issue in Canada, Rogers (1979) developed the theme of "objective judgment" in his well-respected monograph, "Leading to Share—Sharing to Lead." He then based sound leadership on the integration of five broad areas with objective judgment as their mediating factor. The five areas are the environmental, physiological, safety, sociological, and technical forces that are inherent in any situation. He holds that outdoor leadership development should be accomplished through a "symbolic relationship" between two separate schemes. The technical outdoor skill training (i.e., rock climbing, canoeing, etc.) could be obtained from certifying groups, while leadership de-

velopment (i.e., communication skills, group process, etc.) should be provided through separate and specific leadership education curriculums. He
maintains that it is only through a long individual growth and maturing
process that objective judgment can emerge as a natural leadership skill and
be based on more than facts and knowledge (Rogers, 1979).

A more recent framing of the judgment and decision-making theory in
outdoor leadership that I would encourage the reader to explore is "The Role
of Judgment, Decision Making, and Problem Solving for Outdoor Leaders"
by Priest (1988). This piece presents a very elaborate dissection and schemat-
ic that differentiates much more stringently between J/D-M and problem
solving, while I prefer to see them as one and the same thing in most situations, depending on how one defines the terms.

The literature review section could go on and on in trying to be fair to
every person who has written in this area (see Bibliography). But from my review and my own personal experience over the past ten years, the most recent and what I consider to be an excellent treatise of the J/D-M dilemma in
outdoor leadership has come from Dr. John Miles (1987). Although he focuses his arguments primarily on "good" and "bad" judgment as it relates to
safety, and not on the academic understanding of the J/D-M process, his description of the collective personal attributes that constitute judgment is
worth noting here.

Knowledge—of the hazards peculiar to the [environment]
• of self and one's skills in performing the activity involved
in the situation.
• of the capabilities of the group.
• of past experience in similar situations.

Skill—ability in the activity involved in the outing. To judge the capabilities of others to handle challenges and difficulties of terrain
and other factors requires that the leader be expert in doing so.

Self-confidence—a belief that whatever choice is made, it is the
right one because it is based on the leader's knowledge and experiences.

Selflessness—whatever decision is made is based on concern for the
welfare of the group (including the leader) with minimal concern for
the reputation and possible repercussion to self.

Commitment—the leader is committed to his or her role, willing to
face the consequences of making a decision regardless of the outcome. He or she is also committed above all else in the situation to
the health and safety of the group.

Expedition (as with promptness and speed)—alternatives are reviewed and the decision made quickly, without hesitation, but not too quickly. The old saw, "She who hesitates is lost," might be quite literally true in an outdoor leadership situation. The key element in this is "deliberate speed," no rushing to judgment, but no vacillation either.

Experience—What did I do last time in this situation? What have others done in this place and what have been the consequences (Miles, 1987, p. 505)?

Dr. Miles points out that the one ingredient most commonly identified as essential to judgment is knowledge, but it alone, as he further states, is insufficient for "good" judgment. Obviously someone with massive academic knowledge of whitewater kayaking but poor self-confidence and no experience is "an accident waiting to happen," especially if he/she accepts responsibility for leading others in such an activity. In W.E.A., we have historically embraced all of the attributes pointed out above, but the one always given the most credence because it is the hardest to attain is selflessness. For if a leader's "cup runneth over" with all else, but they are selfish in their decisions, . . . well, you fill in the rest!

As such, the list of attributes above represents the collective maturity that is required to consistently make and execute "quality" decisions. It is this maturity that causes a leader, in most cases, to err on the side of prudence, if they err at all. The mature leader with "good" judgment will not accept responsibility beyond his/her abilities.

The Judgment and Decision-making Process

It is the intention of this portion of the chapter to provide a way by which the J/D-M process in the W.E.A. curriculum might be understood and improved. As such, the process presented here is generically a process that has been adapted from other areas of leadership (Reitz, 1979) as discussed in the Theoretical Foundations. It should be noted that, insomuch as I have presented here what I consider to be a good, but generic, process; the reader is encouraged to redefine and elaborate on the process in any way that he/she feels is valuable to themselves and their students.

The seven basic steps are:

STEP 1
the observation and recognition of a need or opportunity to act on behalf of maximizing individual and group goals;

STEP 2
the collection of all available information that describes the conditions of the need or opportunity;

STEP 3
the identification and analysis of potential options for action that can be executed to satisfy the need or opportunity based upon the observations and collection of information;

STEP 4
the identification of potential consequences that may be incurred by execution of each individual option or combination thereof;

STEP 5
the selection of one or any combination of the most appropriate options;

STEP 6
the execution of that decision; and

STEP 7
the evaluation of the outcome and consideration of subsequent decision-making and action if necessary.

It seems impossible, to me, to suggest that any one step of the process has more significance than any other for failure to pay attention to any one of them while exercising total prudence in the others will, more often than not, result in a negative outcome. These negative results could vary from a participant's hurt feelings to damaged equipment, to serious injury, to a lawsuit. On the other hand, if the instructor begins to consistently and critically "think" through the process for each of the hundreds of decisions that he/she makes each day in the field, the results will more likely be smiles, a sense of achievement, group cohesiveness, no serious injuries, no damaged equipment, and so forth.

Hopefully, with practice, this process of "critical thinking" brings the instructor, and just as importantly the students, to the point that it becomes the natural way that they think. Granted, all other personal attributes (social, emotional, or physical), time constraints, group participation and environmental conditions will contribute to the successful use of the process, but it cannot be over stressed that attention to detail of the entire process is paramount. Therefore, the following detailed description of each step is provided as a guideline.

Step 1:
A leader is often flirting with a social and/or physical disaster if he/she doesn't have the ability to observe and recognize the need or opportunity to act on behalf of the group's collective goals or on behalf of his/her own inherent responsibilities.

In many situations (and necessarily so), it is the group members who are the observers/recognizers and the ones who are compelled to act on behalf of the group, which includes the leader. This action may be in several forms, but will generally include informing the leader of a situational need or opportunity, or taking action themselves.

Regardless of who determines the need to act, the motivational force has to be the determination that there is actually *something* to act upon. This *something* is any situational interaction that characterizes a need or opportunity to act. This may range from simply choosing words to respond to the question of a participant about the identity of a bird, to where to pitch a tent, to choosing what to fix for breakfast, to choosing an appropriate climbing site for a group, to allowing the group to determine the next day's agenda, to recognizing the potential for emotional breakdown of a participant in a stressful situation, to the final "yes" or "no" determination of certification for a participant, to. . . !

The pertinent question that must be considered here before any of the above scenarios can be addressed is, What are the generic ingredients that produce a specific situational interaction in the outdoors that calls for action based on sound J/D-M ability? To answer this question, consider the four main factors of variability in any leader/group relationship that collectively contribute to these situational interactions: (1) the purpose of the outing, or in this case, the specific goals and objectives of the W.E.A. curriculum; (2) the collective characteristics of the group which includes the leader; (3) the unique environmental setting for the course; and (4) the logistical conditions under which the group is operating. I think it's valuable to take a little closer look at each of these.

While the goals and objectives of the W.E.A. curriculum are considered at length in other areas of the text, it is important to note that the primary influence and benefit to the participant is the improved J/D-M ability derived from the detailed delivery and practice of the 18 category curriculum over a standard five-week-wilderness-course format. The student generally cannot help but have a clearer understanding, and thus improved J/D-M ability regarding wilderness behavior, from having actually experienced, for example, how climate, time, and energy control, expedition behavior, or simply minimum impact camping affect virtually every J/D-M process. The detailed understanding, delivery and practice of the entire curriculum is the backbone of thousands of judgments/decisions that will be carried out and evaluated by the group.

The group (leaders and participants) brings to the collective situation many personal influences that feed the interactions. These individual and personal variables will generally include varying degrees of education, experience, physical ability and health, technical skills, moral values, personality, and emotions, just to name a few. They also bring with them their own personal goals and expectations for the outing or experience that may or may not complement those of the W.E.A.

The leader and the group also bring to the situation some role-specific characteristics. The leader him/herself adds the specific variables of that leadership position such as legal/professional responsibilities and specialized leadership skills and knowledge. Besides their individual personalities and traits discussed above, group members collectively establish a group personality that is evident through some degree of cohesiveness, morale, empathy and motivation, all of which are integrally affected by the quality of leadership, or in other words, the quality of the collective decisions made in their behalf.

The environmental setting can be divided into a variety of ingredients. This would specifically include weather conditions, topography/geology of the area, and the soil, water, flora and fauna that might be encountered. Weather might range from sunny, blue skies with a temperature of 80 degrees Fahrenheit to blizzard conditions with minus 100 degrees wind chills. Topography/geology, soil, water, flora, and fauna can also have the same varying extremes of condition.

The environmental setting might also include human influences external to the group such as local inhabitants, nonrecreational or commercial users of the same resource, other recreational users, resource owners/ managers, or any human manipulation of the resource being used that could affect any aspect of the situational interactions. Human alterations could be anything from broken glass to an old logging road to an entirely bolted route up a remote climbing site.

The final category of influences to any specific judgment/decision-making moment is collectively referred to as logistics. Logistics, in this case, refers to the specific supportive goods and/or services that are desired or needed for an experience and which are initially determined by judgments of the leader and the physical setting from which logistical support will be carried out. The logistics list in this sense would generally include, but not be limited to equipment, clothing, rations, lodging, transportation, insurance, permits, emergency response information, and so forth.

The awesome responsibility for leadership of a W.E.A. course, or outdoor program in general, is incomprehensible until one considers the exponential number of combinations of situational interactions that could arise at any particular moment, and which may or may not be anticipated or even recognized by the leader. In general, the quality of a leader is measured by his/ her ability to anticipate and to minimize unnecessary or counterproductive situations before they occur. Obviously, some of these types of individual J/ D-M processes would be carried out before the course even begins and might include screening participants, predetermining the route, or ordering specialized equipment to name a few.

Step 2:
The collection of all information that describes the conditions of the need or op-

portunity to act involves surveying and compiling the specific circumstances that define a realized need or opportunity.

This collection of information may be accomplished by the leader individually or collectively with the group members. It might involve asking one essential question of an individual student to round out what is already known, or it could require a group meeting lasting an entire morning.

Obviously, the information should be as complete and reliable as possible. It should also represent a cross section of the various factors of variability as described in Step 1 (i.e., W.E.A. goals and curriculum, group characteristics, environmental characteristics, and logistics). The significance of this step should not be overlooked, as a common mistake in the J/D-M process is to make judgments before one is fully aware of the reality of the situation.

One other caution regarding the informational stage is the confidentiality factor. Depending on the problem at hand, making information available to the group that in your judgment should not or legally cannot be released can be a very awkward situation if they are involved in the decision-making process. This is especially true in cases of personal medical histories and confidential statements made to you by group members.

Step 3:
Step 3 involves the analysis and identification of all potential options of action that can be executed to satisfy the need or opportunity for action, based upon the observations and collection of information.

Once again, the ability of a leader to be able to identify options of action, based upon the circumstances of a particular situation, is greatly dependent upon: (1) past experience of having done so in similar situations: (2) technical knowledge and/or skill related to the situation at hand; and (3) some degree of natural analytic and innovative ability.

Obviously someone who has all of the above except for actual experience is at a disadvantage. But given that the individual is not under a time or environmental constraint that is life threatening, he, in my opinion, has as much potential for arriving at a sound set of options as someone who has the experience but lacks technical knowledge and analytic ability.

Identification of all potential options is much like a brainstorming session from which a leader will hopefully have as many choices as possible. This pool of options is likely to range from the most conservative/low-risk type to the very liberal/high-risk type, for it is within this spectrum that a leader will hopefully find an option that fits two conditions: (1) that execution of the option is within their own and/or the group's level of expertise/ability: and (2) that the option maximizes the group and/or individual goals, especially safety.

Step 4:
This step involves the anticipation and/or identification of all potential con-sequences that may be incurred by execution of each individual option or combina-tion thereof.

It is at this step that a leader and fellow group members may find that the short-term consequences are quite obvious. But it is often the unobvious, long-term consequences that an inexperienced leader or group will fail to notice and from which they may potentially suffer.

Step 5:
Step 5, the selection of one or any combination of the most appropriate options is the culmination of all the information-gathering efforts of the first four steps.

The selection process or decision process is left to the discretion of the leader just as has been the rest of the process in terms of the degree of par-ticipation group members are allowed to exhibit.

Based upon the information and situation at hand, the leader may him/herself be the sole decision-maker as to what option will be selected, thus carrying out an autocratic decision. The leaders may allow a vote among the group as to the option they wish, thus exercising a democratic process. The leader might otherwise require that all group members unanimously agree upon one option that exemplifies a consensus style. Finally, a leader in some instances might impose no decision structure on the group, accepting what-ever process and decision emerges from a laissez-faire style.

Since a detailed discussion of these various styles is presented in chapter 3, it is not essential in this chapter to reevaluate the benefits and con-sequences of each of these. Suffice it to say that one decision that a leader generally makes alone is the decision as to how much power he/she will al-low a group to have in deciding any particular situation for themselves. This decision will be influenced by group maturity, safety implications, organiza-tional policies, time availability, etc. This decision is one of the most crucial when considering the enhancement of leadership development and ability in others.

Obviously, the final results of the J/D-M process must be measured in real terms, which generally means the outcomes of one's actions or the lack thereof. But even if what is considered to be a safe and workable decision is arrived at, if it is generated in a style inappropriate to the educational benefit of the moment, it lacks the sense of "quality" that we strive for in outdoor leadership development.

In contrast, the failure to decide on a course of action is in essence a de-cision not to act, but it is still a decision and an action, and one that is often met with a loss of credibility as the leader. On the other hand, a common pitfall is when the leader decides to let the group decide without any con-straints or limitations on their options and then is not willing to allow them to carry out that decision. Again, there is a loss of trust and respect. Only when a judgment is made and action begun, with maximum allowable participation of the group in all steps of the process, can a leader honestly begin to realize the quality of his/her leadership. It is only then that he/she begins to know whether or not he/she needs to reevaluate and redirect that action in a more goal-fulfilling manner, even if it means changing his/her mind.

Step 6:
Step 6 involves the execution of any option or combination of options selected in Step 5.

The carrying out of a decision requires that a leader, depending on the circumstances of the need or opportunity, be able to: (1) effectively communicate directions or instructions; (2) delegate power to other individuals; and (3) if necessary, act, without interference to the delegated leader, in the capacity of a regular group member in carrying out the decision.

The communication of instructions may take several forms. It may be to communicate instructions directly, delegate responsibility to another group member(s) for delivery of instructions, or in very simple situations, it may take the form of a simple nonverbal response or gesture. The classic issue here is inevitably that someone in the group, or some portion of the entire group, will not understand and carry out the directions in a counter productive manner. Obviously, this is especially important in dangerous or stressful situations.

Step 7:
The final step involves evaluation of the result of the first six steps and considers the need for subsequent decision making and action if necessary.

This evaluation is concerned with not only satisfying the original need or opportunity but also determining whether the quality of the final decision could be improved for the sake of the group and individual goals. An even more basic consideration is to determine whether or not new needs, and/or opportunities, have been created through the process.

The evaluation should be an examination of the objective and subjective effects of the process on the leader(s), the group member(s), nongroup member(s), the environment, or logistical concerns.

The process, with the completion of the seventh step, becomes a spiral—ongoing and cumulative. It does so by continually reevaluating and reacting in relation to the constantly changing circumstances of the course over time. It is an analytical and cognitive means by which a leader may take mental inventory and react accordingly.

In many instances, evaluation and completion of the first six steps of the process may become a simultaneous occurrence. This is due to the interlocking complexity of a situation, the limited time available to use the process, and the quality with which it is carried out. These conditions may radically compress the process into a mere intuitive reaction upon which immediate action is taken. An example of this is easily realized if one imagines a quick and possibly angered response by a leader to a student's seemingly insulting/insensitive remark, or in more physical terms, a leader's instinctive move to prevent a careless student from falling from a rappel site.

To direct the wholehearted development of leadership, especially in others, is an awesome task. The example that a desirable leader sets must be one that allows the student(s) to see that the leader is not infallible. It allows the student to see that self-critique, flexibility, and improvement of one's own judgment/decision-making ability is a constant requirement of every quality leader. The student *should not* be led to believe that a leader must always make the wisest decision the first time (although this may be a life-threatening necessity in some instances). The student *should* be led to believe that only through being allowed to experience and make tolerable mistakes can he/she expect to grow and improve to the point that he/she can make the more serious choices.

This is a very important point in W.E.A. courses due to the daily assigning of a student as "leader of the day" who assumes as much responsibility for comprehensive decision making as possible. If the instructor is not willing to subordinate himself, except in cases of safety and in the context of long-term implications of the course, then the student-leader's decision making becomes a farce and a negative experience. A classic dilemma on our courses is how much power to give up in any particular situation to student-leader and group decision making.

Applications of the Process to the W.E.A. Curriculum

Throughout the J/D-M process described above, including action and evaluation, the greater the degree of participation by the student/group, the greater the opportunity for J/D-M enhancement in those individuals. The leader who allows the group member(s) to contribute and take responsibility for completion of each step of the process allows those individuals an insight into the decision-making process that, in traditional terms, has often been an unshared secret of the leader's mind.

Encouraging group members to participate in the process compels them to be intimately connected with the consequences of it, good or bad. It compels them to be observant for needs and opportunities related to the group. It compels them to be aware of information, both technical and situational, related to those needs or opportunities. It compels them to generate unobvious options and logically consider the consequences of those options if put into action. It compels them to participate in making decisions for the benefit of themselves and others. It compels them to respond to directions or take action themselves. It compels them to evaluate the reasons for their own actions within the group and ask themselves "why." And ultimately, it gives them solid ground for making well-informed decisions in their everyday lives.

The continual evolution of methods by which we have historically taught J/D-M in W.E.A. courses is the backbone to our curriculum. As expressed by Bonney and Drury (1988),

> Participants should understand that the decision making process itself is a system of thought which can be applied in any situation regardless of circumstance.

The conceptual and academic approach to doing this has centered on teaching each of our curriculum topic areas by having the students express what they would consider to be the judgment factors for that particular topic.

For a simple example, we do not teach that a latrine must be a specific size, depth, and distance from water and camp. Rather we ask the student to express what consideration should be given to the digging of a latrine for the entire group and then fill in the areas that they do not adequately consider, such as soil type, privacy, managing agency regulations, estimated need, long-term care, etc. By doing this, we empower the student to critically and logically *think* for themselves rather than to rely totally on memory.

After demonstrating and then having them actually perform a certain task for themselves on numerous occasions over the course of the field program, they typically have mastered that and any other curriculum topic taught in similar fashion. This is especially important in teaching the subject of judgment and decision making itself.

W.E.A. relies very strongly on a number of techniques for facilitating the development of J/D-M ability in students. These typically include:

1. A formal decision-making theory presentation;
2. Instructor example on a continual basis;
3. Leader of the day (LOD) designation and self-critique;
4. Daily journal entries;
5. Daily debriefings;
6. Instructor observation and feedback; and
7. Peer evaluation and feedback.

Each of these plays a significant role.

Through each, the primary concern is to have the student constructively critique the quality of not only every significant decision on the course but also the quality of the process by which that decision was derived regardless of who made it. The structure for this critique obviously follows the prescribed J/D-M process be it in verbal or journal form with conclusions drawn from both an individual and group effort.

Following the formal J/D-M theory presentation, the instructor's verbalization of the decision-making process used in their own daily actions from the beginning to the end of the course is an extremely important detail. Obviously the students will be looking for any errors that the instructor may make in the process, whether it is in the sequence or a missed piece of information. If the proper tone has been set with the group from the beginning, the instructor will have gained the student's respect and will not have to be worried about any loss of credibility due to small oversights. The experienced and shrewd instructor will learn to purposely leave out pieces of information to the explanation of a decision in order for the student to demonstrate a growing proficiency.

This type of tone is invaluable for the rest of the course and the students' confidence in being able to express themselves and their mistakes without fear of rejection, especially as they begin to take turns with being the *leader of the day (LOD)*. I have personally found it very productive to always give the designated LOD the opportunity to identify their own perceptions of their daily performance before anyone else, including the instructor(s), is allowed to speak. By doing so the student is better able to build and maintain self-respect. They will also be able to demonstrate a level of maturity that they may not otherwise get the opportunity to demonstrate.

There can obviously be some very uncomfortable situations when a student is blind to their own behaviors. They may make consistently poor quality decisions, gloss over various steps of the process, and/or express unjustifiable rationales. This must be managed very carefully during LOD discussions and daily debriefings where peer evaluation and feedback can sometimes be unpredictable depending on the personality of the group. One other pitfall is the potential for disagreement between students as to what was or was not a "quality" decision (i.e., the LOD acted on a different priority than someone else or the rest of the group felt should be first). Reference to the group dynamics chapter will help considerably in this regard.

Journals provide the student with an insight into his/her own thinking that he/she may not otherwise even consider or devote time to. There is considerable documentation of its value in the experiential education field and in psychology. Journalizing is especially helpful to the instructor for evaluating a student who possibly is one of the best in the group at mastering and incorporating the J/D-M process into their thinking but who has a difficult time verbalizing it under the pressure of public scrutiny. It also provides the instructor with another major means of assessing the quality with which a student carries out the J/D-M process on other major decisions within the group for which he is not directly responsible. Finally, the journal provides the student with an historical record that he/she can generally look back on with great pleasure and further insight into his/her own personal development in years to come.

Last, but proverbially not least, is the responsibility of instructor evaluation and feedback regarding each student's J/D-M ability. Not a pleasant responsibility in some cases! Without extremely careful attention to detail about each student throughout the course, and close scrutiny of all of the above evaluation tools, certification can easily become a mockery of professionalism within our field. The evaluation that an instructor makes on a student's J/D-M ability is in essence a judgment about that student's maturity as a leader and as a person. The ease and legitimacy with which this can be accomplished again depends most heavily on the tone of the course from the first day, and the daily consistency thereafter with which the instructor can candidly, objectively, and compassionately critique a student's progress. Nothing is more distasteful or embarrassing than a student who at the end of the course thinks that he/she has done a good job with the course and with mastering the spirit of the J/D-M process only to find out that the instructor(s) do(es) not agree.

The very subtle, but common, theme that runs throughout the entire curriculum process is the explanation of why any action should be, is, or was taken, why it was performed in the way it was, and in what way might that action be improved now or for similar situations in the future (Petzoldt, 1984). This theme provides the leader with a framework through which he/she is able to provide, for the student, an explanation of his/her own decisions and actions. It's an example for the student which stresses that if he/she does not know why something should be done or why it should be done in a particular way, then he/she risks taking an action for which the potential consequences are unfamiliar, especially in terms of safety.

A leadership curriculum with teaching techniques centering on the explanation of why is very time consuming and demands excellent management and communications skills from the instructor(s). However, the realized benefit of relevance that the student experiences through this technique is far superior to a rote learning method that is more likely to yield rote results in a world of nonrote situations. Again, "Rules are for fools."

The complex nature of J/D-M makes it a difficult skill to teach, but not an impossible one. It, like any other skill, will have its share of students who cannot seem to gain any proficiency at it, but there will be more who can.

The fact that much of the adventure education field views the certification of J/D-M ability as crude at best requires that every effort be made to carry through with prescribed methods. I agree that certification cannot "guarantee" the long-term future J/D-M ability of an individual, but it can certainly act as an indicator of predictable behavior. The legitimacy of the W.E.A. certification, in my eyes, hinges on the acceptance that we and our graduates have a sound, basic outdoor leadership ability necessary to safely meet the needs of most adventure education programs in the country, as long as the student has the technical skill required for both specific adventure activities or "special populations" not covered in their W.E.A. course. The W.E.A. certification is based upon observable judgment and decision-making behavior in the field, and not that graduates are 5.9 climbers or Class IV paddlers.

The future responsibility of our graduates is to accept outdoor leadership

duties only within their strengths and arenas of good judgment as they develop over the years. It is the instructor's responsibility to see that the student knows what his/her strengths and limitations are at the time of the
course's ending, and that the credibility of the certification based on the
strengths and limitations of each participant is maintained in every case.

As many respected professionals in the outdoor field have pointed out,
the development of leadership judgment is a long-term process involving
the attainment of experience, technical knowledge, practical skill and individual maturity. But as March (1985) and Petzoldt (1984) point out, the
importance of developing a prudent leadership attitude with which to tem-
per one's judgment cannot be overstressed. After all, the leader whose judgment is fueled by arrogant technical competence may be the greatest of all
outdoor leadership dangers.

References

Bonney, B. & Drury, J. (1988). *Decision making lesson plan.* Saranac Lake,
NY: North Country Community College. (Unpublished manuscript).

Buell, L. (1983). *Outdoor Leadership Competency.* Greenfield, MA: Environmental Awareness Publications.

Cain, K. D. (1985). Wilderness education association certification. In J.
Miles and R. Watters (Eds.), *Proceedings of the 1984 Conference on Outdoor Recreation* (pp. 53-61). Pocatello: Idaho State University Press.

Cain, K. and McAvoy, L. (1991). Experience-based judgment. In J. Miles
and S. Priest (Eds.), *Adventure Education.* State College, PA: Venture Publishing.

Cattail, R. (1946). *Description and measurement of personality.* New York:
Yonkers on Hudson.

Cousineau, C. (1977). A Delphi consensus on a set of principles for the
development of a certification system for educators in outdoor activities. *Dissertation Abstracts International*, 38A, 4472A. (University Microfilms No. 77-
30810)

Easther, R. (1979). *Assessment and selection of adventure activity leaders: A
comparison of methods.* Unpublished master's thesis, University of Oregon,
Eugene, OR.

Ewert, A. (1987). *Decision-making in the outdoor pursuits setting.* Paper presented at the national conference of the Association for Experiential Education, Port Townsend , WA.

Fiedler, F. E. (1967). *A theory of leadership effectiveness.* New York:
McGraw-Hill.

Ford, P. and Blanchard, J. (1985). *Leadership and administration of outdoor
pursuits.* State College, PA: Venture Publishing Inc.

Green, P. (1981). The content of a college level outdoor leadership course
for land based outdoor pursuits in the Pacific Northwest: A Delphi consensus. Doctoral dissertation, University of Oregon (University Microfilms
No. DEO 82-01832)

Hersey, P. and Blanchard, K. H. (l982). *Management of organizational behavior: utilizing human resources, (4th Ed.).* Englewood Cliffs, NJ: Prentice-Hall, Inc.

Hunt, Jr., J. S. (1984). Opinion: The dangers of substituting rules for instructor judgment in adventure programs. *Journal of Experiential Education, 7,* 20-21.

Jackson, J. A. (No Date). *Notes on party leadership.* Unpublished manuscript.

Jackson, J. A. (1973). *A few thoughts on party leadership.* Plas y Brenin N.M.C. (Unpublished manuscript).

Macgregor, Burns, J. (1979). *Leadership.* New York: Harper and Row.

March, W. (1985). Wilderness leadership certification—Catch 22—Assessing the outdoor leader: An insoluble problem? In J. Miles and R. Watters (Eds.), *Proceedings of the 1984 Conference on Outdoor Recreation* (pp. 37-41). Pocatello: Idaho State University Press.

McAvoy, L. H. (1987). Education for outdoor leadership. In J. Meier, T. Morash, and G. Welton (Eds.), *High adventure outdoor pursuits: Organization and leadership* (pp. 459-467). Columbus, OH: Publishing Horizons, Inc.

Miles, J. C. (1987). The problem of judgment in outdoor leadership. In J. Meier, T. Morash, and G. Welton (Eds.), *High adventure outdoor pursuits: Organization and leadership* (pp.502-509). Columbus, OH: Publishing Horizons, Inc.

Petzoldt, P. K. (1974). *The wilderness handbook.* New York: W. W. Norton and Co.

Petzoldt, P. K. (1984). *The new wilderness handbook.* New York: W. W. Norton and Co.

Priest, S. (1987). *Judgment, decision making, problem solving: Critical trinity for outdoor leaders.* Paper presented at the national conference of the Association for Experiential Education, Port Townsend, WA.

Priest, S. (1988). *The role of judgment, decision making, and problem solving for outdoor leaders.* Journal of Experiential Education. *11(3), 19-26.*

Rankin, K. (1987). 35 Days in the Wyoming Wilderness. In J. Meier, T. Morash, and G. Welton (Eds.), *High adventure outdoor pursuits: Organization and leadership* (pp.319-323). Columbus, OH: Publishing Horizons, Inc.

Reitz, H. J. (1977). *Behavior in organizations.* Homewood, IL: Richard D. Irwin, Inc.

Rich, D. W. (1980). *Leadership training handbook.* Published Doctor of Education project in lieu of dissertation, University of Northern Colorado, Greeley, CO.

Rogers, R. J. (1979). *Leading to share—sharing to lead.* Monograph. Ontario, Canada: Council of Outdoor Educators of Ontario. (ERIC Document Reproduction Service No. ED 178 234).

Simer, P. and Sullivan, J. (1983). *The National Outdoor Leadership School's Wilderness Guide.* New York: Simon & Schuster.

Simon, H. A. (1976). *Administrative behavior.* London: The Free Press.

Stodgill, R. M. (1981). *Handbook of leadership.* New York: The Free Press.

Stodgill, R. M. (1948). Personality factors associated with leadership: A survey of the literature. *Journal of Psychology,* 25, 35-71.

Swiderski, M. J. (1981). Outdoor leadership competencies identified by outdoor leaders in five western regions. Dissertation Abstracts International, 42, 3753A.

Webber, R. A. (1975). *Management: basic elements of managing organizations.* Homewood, IL: Richard D. Irwin, Inc.

3.

GROUP DYNAMICS IN THE OUTDOORS: A Model for Teaching Outdoor Leaders

by Maurice L. Phipps
Western State College of Colorado

Groups in the outdoors often experience conflict. In an expedition setting, where there are few ways to "escape" from the group, feelings become intensified and incidents magnified out of all proportion. The success of many an otherwise well-planned trip has been jeopardized by the lack of education in how to deal with such problems. This is compounded by a lack of awareness on the part of group members and leaders in how their behaviors affect each other. Some behaviors are conscious and others are unconscious, but if they are brought out and discussed openly, changes can be made more easily than pushing them "under the carpet." If they are suppressed they will surface later, usually more violently. Making group dynamics an explicit part of the learning experience from the very beginning can relieve many problems that could emerge later. This can even be started at pretrip meetings.

The teaching model described here is intended to be used as a flexible guide as what might work with one group could fail with another. The model has worked well with college-age students. The manner in which it is presented is critical: If the students see the usefulness of learning these communication skills, it becomes an integral part of their leadership. Such a process hopefully will lead us to a team of interdependent members rather than just a group of individuals! With modifications, this model could be used for shorter or longer expeditions.

THE TEACHING MODEL

Cohesiveness is the key to success, so in the course introduction, introduce a "we" feeling and stress teamwork. Explain the goals of the course and the group clearly to ensure that everyone is aware of the goals and can work towards the same ends. Include an ice-breaker and brief individual introductions.

As outdoor courses involve many different educational aspects, the group and people skills need to be tailored at the right moments. For example, including "expedition behavior" early is a good idea as this clarifies behavioral norms and brings an awareness into the group that these civilities do exist. Teaching group roles is often best left to an opportune time when some of the behaviors have been exhibited and roles are unfolding. It can have the advantage of stopping some negative behaviors just by giving them labels. There is no best order of teaching, but a logical sequence is as follows:

1. Group development
2. Expedition behavior
3. Giving and receiving feedback
4. Conflict strategies
5. Conflict resolution
6. Group dynamics
7. Role functions in groups
8. Defense mechanisms in groups
9. Group dynamics questionnaire

The teaching style can involve lecture, discussion and experiential work directly applied to situations that occur from time to time, as well as exercises and role plays.

It is important to realize that any group is made up of individuals, so a strong recommendation is to get to know the individuals more intimately. A 15 minute introduction from each person distributed over the shakedown period of the course will often reveal information that could be helpful in understanding problems later. It also opens people up and increases communication in general. Frequent one-on-one student-leader meetings also reduce tension produced by poor communication.

An understanding of the following elements of group dynamics will enable the students to increase their knowledge of the internal workings of the group and give labels to behaviors. This will make changes more possible when needed. Simply the awareness of them will eliminate many dysfunctional roles that often appear. It would be a recommendation to include at least the first five of the nine elements of this teaching model in the shake-down period of the course so that they can be applied early.

Group Development

Groups go through an initial period where rules, roles, and rewards are all in flux. Cohesive groups are often noisy, they joke around, have disagreements, arguments and overrun time limits. Noncohesive groups are often quiet, boring and apathetic. They seldom disagree and deal quickly with important issues including little discussion.

Tension is always initially present and can be dealt with through smiles, laughs or jokes, or can be dissipated by humor, direct comment, or conciliation. Positive behaviors can be established by their being supported and eventually becoming norms. Norms are the common beliefs of the group, giving expectations of behavior. They help interactions by specifying the responses that are expected.

In group development, there is both a human component, establishing and maintaining relations, and a task component, the job to be done. Anticipating the kinds of group interaction problems that are predictable enables the leader to avoid being caught off guard and landed with a surprise situation. As the stages of group development are predictable, they can be controlled. For example, good organization and the correct leader style can ease the group through the conflict stage. The two dimensions, personal relations and task functions, combine at the different stages of group development. Four stages of development are suggested by Jones (1973), as summarized in Table 3-1.

Jones' Model of Group Development

STAGE	PERSONAL RELATIONS	TASK FUNCTIONS
1.	Dependency	Orientation
2.	Conflict	Organization
3.	Cohesion	Data-flow
4.	Interdependence	Problem-solving

Table 3-1

Initially, personal relations show dependency on the leader who sets the ground rules. At this stage the parallel task function is orientation of individuals to the work involved. Individuals will be questioning why they are here, what they are going to do, how it will be done and what the goals will be.

Next, conflict develops in personal relations, and organization emerges as a task function. The conflict may be covert but it is there. Conflicts are normal expectations. Johnson and Johnson (1975) suggest that, "it is not the presence of conflicts that causes disastrous and unfortunate things, it is the harmful and ineffective management of conflicts." Conflicts come from contention for leadership, task, influence and popularity. They are complicated by our own (leaders' and followers') unresolved problems with authority, dependency and rules. At this stage the group has emerged through orientation and is feeling less dependent on the leader. A desire from the group emerges to organize both tasks and relationships that creates conflict as different ideas clash.

If the group resolves the interpersonal conflicts, a sense of being a team is achieved and the cohesion enables data-flow to take place efficiently. Ideas are shared with feelings and feedback is given. There is sharing of information related to the task and people feel good about belonging to the group. There could be a period of play unrelated to the task, an enjoyment of the cohesion.

Interdependence is not achieved by many groups. There is a high commitment to activities related to the common goals. Experimentation with problem solving is supported and there is collaboration and competition that is functional. Members of the group can interact with each other as a team. They are more than just cohesive, they have no fears in sharing points of view as they respect each other's expertise. Divergent thinking is accepted and encouraged within the group. The members are interdependent and not reliant on a specific leader unless the task changes to something unfamiliar.

Sharing Jones's model with groups enables insight into what may be expected and it also gives a goal to aim for—interdependence and problem solving. It is useful for the leaders as a predictor of group behavior. For the group members, it acts as a reference for certain norms. An example would be the conflict stage. If conflict is expected, then followers will be less anxious when the group starts to experience it. Jones' model also corresponds to Hersey and Blanchard's (1984) Situational Leadership model, which enables better judgment in the choice of leadership style according to the stage of development that the group may be in.

Expedition Behavior

Paul Petzoldt (1984) maintains that "expedition behavior is a basic teachable skill." He brings out the point that conscious control can be lost in situations that seem desperate, such as storms, accidents and especially when food runs short.

Petzoldt devotes a chapter in his book *The Wilderness Handbook* to expedition behavior, spelling out in detail positive and negative behaviors. Time taken to do this at the beginning of a course or expedition helps to set positive group norms during the orientation phase of the group's development. A comprehensive session that facilitates everyone's involvement will lay cooperatively set ground rules (group norms). Expedition behavior as defined by Petzoldt (1984, p.168) is:

An awareness of the relationship of individual to individual, individual to group, group to individual, group to other groups, individual and groups to the multi users of the region, individual and group to administrative agencies, and individual and group to local populace. Good expedition behavior is the awareness, plus the motivation and character to be concerned for others in every respect as one is for oneself. Poor expedition behavior is a breakdown in human relations caused by selfishness, rationalization, ignorance of personal faults, dodging blame or responsibility, physical weakness and in extreme cases, not being able to risk one's own survival to insure that of a companion (p. 168).

An effective way to teach expedition behavior is to explain Petzoldt's concepts, "individual to individual, individual to group," etc., then divide the group into smaller groups of three or four to discuss what would be acceptable behavior for this group using all Petzoldt's subheadings of expedition behavior. After this has been thoroughly discussed, combine all the smaller groups to cooperatively lay down the group norms together, with the instructors facilitating and adding information that the students may not be aware of. If the group norms are set cooperatively in this manner, the members will be more likely to follow them than if they are imposed rules. Some examples are: sharing food and equipment, respecting personal space in tents, courteousness at group meetings and being on time for meetings. Petzoldt gives many more examples in his chapter on expedition behavior.

Giving and Receiving Feedback
When group norms are overstepped or problems occur, feedback has to be given for behavior to change. Often an evaluation of the "leader of the day" is done as a group process in a review of the day. When reviewing the day or addressing behavioral problems, some individuals receiving feedback can become defensive. Defensiveness should be discouraged by giving feedback in as positive a manner as possible and sometimes feedback concerning expedition behavior could be given in private. It should be equated as far as possible with "support" throughout the course at all times and is more easily accepted if the communication climate of the group is positive.

Feedback done "one-on-one" with students, two or three times or more during the course prevents such problems as misguided goals. For example, students sometimes think that they are on an Outward Bound-style course and as such should be traveling more than W.E.A. groups generally do. Feedback for the leader of the day is often done by the group as well as the instructors. In this situation, asking the student leader first what he/she would have done differently in hindsight reduces defensiveness as he/she can often see his/her mistakes as he/she made them. It is all the better, too, that students are encouraged to evaluate themselves in this way as this completes the reflection part of the experiential learning cycle.

Giving feedback requires accuracy, objectivity and clear communication. Focus feedback on:

1. Behavior rather than the person
2. Observations rather than inferences
3. Description rather than judgment; in terms of more or less, rather than either / or Rather than "You are a . . . !" it would be more appropriate to say "When you did this, it made me feel . . . !"
4. Behavior related to a specific situation rather than abstractions
5. Sharing of information and ideas rather than giving advice
6. Exploring alternatives rather than answers
7. The value it may have for the recipient not the kudos or release for the giver
8. The amount of information that the person can receive

Give feedback at the right time and place. Excellent feedback presented at an inappropriate time may do more harm than good. For example, if a person is angry and emotional, then it may be better to wait until they have calmed down. Feedback enables the learning to take place more effectively after the experiential leadership situations. Some groups attack when giving feedback, while some do not really give any; just generic positive statements. Both these styles need to be monitored. Both attacking styles and non-constructive feedback need to be discouraged by using good communication skills to develop trust between group members so that they understand that feedback is part of the learning process. Once trust develops and if the above guidelines are followed, students accept feedback as a useful learning situation. Positive feedback is far more effective than criticism.

Conflict Strategies

We assume from the group development section of this model that conflict is going to appear even though we have laid ground rules (group norms) through discussing expedition behavior. It is essential to be able to discuss specific conflict behaviors in feedback and review sessions, so analysis of such strategies is needed. Describing and labeling conflict strategies enables recognition and helps considerably in conflict resolutions. Conflict strategies should be viewed here as behaviors consciously chosen because of their importance to the individual.

Johnson and Johnson (1982) describe an exercise they call "Stranded in the Desert," which initiates controversy and conflict. This is one of many conflict/consensus exercises. The group has to resolve a hypothetical situation of survival in the desert in which there are alternative solutions.

The exercise should be given to the group to resolve as if the solution is important, without them being aware that its primary purpose is to uncover conflict styles.

Give a copy of the exercise that explains the situation to each member of the group and give a time limit of one-half hour for them to resolve it by consensus (voting will destroy any discussion, controversy, conflict, and learning). Small groups of around six would be preferable to a large group, to enable more interactions.

STRANDED IN THE DESERT EXERCISE

Situation: You are one of eight members of a geology club that is on a field trip to study unusual formations in the New Mexico desert. It is the last week in July. You have been driving over old trails, far from any road, in order to see out-of-the-way formations. At 10:47 a.m. the specially equipped minibus in which your club is riding overturns, rolls into a 15 to 20 foot ravine, and burns. The driver and the professional advisor to the club are killed. The rest of you are relatively uninjured.

You know that the nearest ranch is approximately 45 miles east of where you are. There is no other place of habitation closer. When your club does not report to its motel that evening you will be missed. Several people know generally where you are, but because of the nature of your outing, they will not be able to pinpoint your exact whereabouts.

The area around you is rather rugged and very dry. You heard from a weather report before you left that the temperature would reach 110 degrees, making the surface temperature 130 degrees. You are all dressed in light-weight summer clothing, although you do have hats and sunglasses. Before your minibus burned, you were able to salvage the following items:

Magnetic compass
Large, light-blue canvas
Book, *Animals of the Desert*
One jacket per person
Accurate map of the area
A .38 caliber pistol, loaded
Rearview mirror
One flashlight
Bottle of 1,000 salt tablets
Four canteens, each containing two quarts of water

The group needs to make two decisions:
(1) to stay where it is or to try to walk out, and
(2) to hunt for food or not to hunt.

To make these decisions, it will be necessary to rank the salvaged items in order of their importance. In making the group decisions, your group must stay together.

The correct answer is not the issue at stake here, and giving one could reinforce the competitiveness of some of the students. When the time limit is over, get everyone together and give an explanation of the following strategies as outlined by Johnson (1981).

1. **The Turtle—**
   withdraws from the conflict.

2. **The Shark—**
   forces and tries to make opponents accept his/her solution.

3. **The Teddy Bear—**
   smooths and avoids the conflict in favor of harmony.

4. **The Fox—**
   compromises, giving up part of his/her goals and persuades others to give up part of theirs.

5. **The Owl—**
   views conflicts as problems to be solved, confronts, seeking solutions that will satisfy both parties.

Drawing the turtle, shark, etc., in notebooks provides for some amusement and lowers any tension produced by the exercise. It also paints mental pictures so students tend to use the terminology frequently after it has been introduced.

Ask the students to write the names of the others in their group on small pieces of paper and on the other side of each piece write the conflict strategy that best fits their actions in this exercise. Then pass the pieces of paper to the members of the group. Each member should receive pieces of paper containing his/her conflict styles as seen by the other members. This enables a perception check.

At different times, all of these styles are appropriate; however, good judgment is necessary in choosing the appropriate style at the right time. The style chosen may be affected by the necessity to keep good relations, achieve personal goals, or by safety factors.

Conflict Resolution (Johnson, 1981)

Johnson suggests a progression of definite stages in defining and resolving interpersonal conflicts. These stages are as follows:

I. Define Conflicts Constructively

A. Define the conflict.

B. Define the conflict trying to describe the other person's actions towards me.

C. Define the conflict as a mutual problem.

D. Define the conflict to give a specific description of the other person's actions.

E. Focus on describing feelings about or reactions to the other person's actions.

F. Focus on how I create and continue the conflict.

II. Confrontation and Negotiation

In confronting another person and negotiating a resolution to a conflict, the following steps can be taken:

A. Confront the opposition

1. Do not hit and run, schedule a negotiating session.
2. Communicate openly your perceptions of and feelings about the issues involved in the conflict and try to do so in minimally threatening ways.
3. Comprehend fully the other person's views of and feelings about the conflict.
4. Do not demand change.

The skills required are:

1. Use of personal statements—how the conflict affects "me"
2. Use of relationship statements—how the conflict affects us
3. Use of behavior descriptions—behavior reference rather than personal attacks
4. Direct descriptions—be direct and to the point
5. Understanding responses—say how you understand explanations
6. Interpretive responses—enquire further if you don't understand responses
7. A perception check—give a summary of what you perceive
8. Constructive feedback skills—see earlier section on feedback skills.

B. Arrive at a mutually agreeable definition of the conflict

C. Communicate position and feelings

D. Communicate cooperative intentions

E. Take the other's perspective

F. Reach an agreement through negotiation

1. Generate and evaluate possible solutions

2. Decide together, without voting, the best solution

3. Plan its implementation

4. Plan for an evaluation of this at a later date

Teaching conflict resolution is best done in the shakedown period of the course so that the skills can be used in the real situations that will emerge later. An interesting way to teach conflict resolution is to have the group "invent" situations in pairs and role play the resolution in front of the group.

Group Dynamics (Pfeiffer and Jones, 1973)

The group process is the dynamics of what is happening between group members while the group is working on the content or task. Process and content make up all interactions. The group process, or "dynamics" is often neglected even when it causes serious problems. As it emerges, it encompasses morale, tone, atmosphere, influence, participation, style of influences, leadership struggles, conflict, competition and cooperation. An understanding of group process will enable leaders to diagnose group problems early and deal with them more effectively. It can relieve tension in the group by educating the group in group dynamics, showing that this is expected development. Many students naively expect that the group should be always completely harmonious. The four areas that would be usefully covered here are:

1. Communication

2. Task and group maintenance

3. Emotional issues

4. Cohesion building

COMMUNICATION

Without effective communication, a breakdown in the team will ensue. Communication includes getting the message across as intended, but also creating a receptive atmosphere dealing with conflict, effecting motivation and using management techniques. It is obvious that communication is essential and set times to enable this must be made available. A review of the day will enable consolidation of the day's instruction after students have had time to digest material, but will also enable a time to air problems and mon-

Figure 3-1

itor the group process. Some students have a resistance to the specific diagnosis of process. They can be encouraged to become involved through making it one of the duties of the "leader of the day," to analyze the workings of the group and to point out malfunctional behavior, and to praise functional behavior during the review sessions. This provides an experiential way of learning the different roles that group members can play, and it also encourages positive behavior.

Positive communication skills are important in maintaining morale. Incorrect leadership style such as being autocratic at inappropriate times can be very demotivating. A study of *Transactional Analysis* by Eric Berne gives insights into the importance of this. Berne encourages the development of an "I'm O.K., you're O.K.," life position and suggests the appropriate use of adult, parent or child ego states to effect this. Are group members acting positively in a childlike way, such as enjoying, discovering, that is, sliding down a snow bank, or is it negative and dangerous horseplay? As the leader, do you adopt the same ego state and join in, be parental (prejudicial or protective), or adopt an adult ego state and compute a decision oriented towards reality based on good judgment in the particular situation that you are faced with (Bankie et al., 1983)? Immediately acting parental using an autocratic style in a harmless situation would be a crossed transaction placing the students in a one-down situation (the leader in the position, I'm O.K., you're not O.K.). An open communication climate needs to be developed rather than a defensive one. Using the correct transaction encourages positive communication. In general, it is often the case that words alone are very ineffective in communication and experiential learning proves to be necessary. An example is active reviewing where events can be reenacted in role plays.

Communication and participation are not necessarily the same. Someone with little participation may still capture the attention of the group, while some may be verbose and ignored. Influence can be positive or negative; it can enlist support or alienate. The styles of influence can be likened to the styles of conflict mentioned under "conflict strategies."

Communicating feelings is as important as communicating thoughts. It should be a group norm to be able to express feelings and a leader's responsibility to allow communication of feelings from all individuals. It is a good thing to own feelings and not to make excuses for them. Refusal to include this kind of information reduces the individual's sense of worth and belonging. It demotivates, causing bad morale. Expression of feelings may be inhibited, but non verbal communication is often made through the tone of voice, facial expressions, gestures, etc. An effective way to bring out feelings and anxieties is to use the "anonymous note in the hat" exercise. Everyone in the group writes down their anxieties in a note anonymously and places them in a hat. These are shuffled and drawn randomly out of the hat by the group members and read out loud by individuals from the group. Appropriate communication techniques such as effective feedback, conflict management, active listening, paraphrasing, etc., are then required to deal with these anxieties. Active listening is required in a situation like this to communicate to the student that you as the leader are listening with a view to addressing problems, rather than just going through the motions of looking at problems. Active listening involves showing empathy and doing perception checks by restating or paraphrasing (restating in a different way) to ensure that communication is accurate. For the leader, it ensures that you are getting to the heart of the problem. For the students, it creates trust and an understanding that their anxieties are really being listened to.

TASK AND GROUP MAINTENANCE

To maintain harmonious working relationships and create a good working atmosphere, these functions are important. They include:

Gatekeeping (helping others into the discussion or cutting off others)
Clarification of ideas
Evaluating suggestions
Diagnosing problems
Mediating arguments
Relieving tension (by joking or placing the issue in perspective).

The social aspects of the group involvement should not be underestimated. Socializing on expeditions can be done informally or at banquets, which are good social occasions. Combined "cook-ins," campfire style activities, songs and stories all give social outlets not directly related to the task. Specials events such as swimming at hot springs or an arranged special meal at the trailhead with plenty of fruit are unbelievable tonics for group morale. Maintaining group morale in such ways creates an atmosphere that ensures that the task can be done effectively. Organizationally, group task maintenance is effected using functions such as clarification of ideas, evaluating suggestions and diagnosing problems.

EMOTIONAL ISSUES

Emotional issues include power struggles, fears, identities, goals, needs and intimacy. Dependancy, fighting and dominance issues can affect relationships and communication. For example, someone withdrawing emotionally affects the group and pairing up can have negative consequences. Such issues need to be confronted either openly in front of the whole group or privately on an individual basis, depending on the situation.

COHESION BUILDING

Explain that strong feelings and anger are acceptable, but use these tactics to deal with it:

a. Stay in the here and now.

b. Use "I" statements (eg., I feel).

c. Keep words congruent with feelings.

d. Talk directly to group members rather than talk in general terms.

Make it clear that it is not necessary to justify personal feelings; have an expectation of no backstabbing and model it.

Some techniques to meet group needs are (Borman and Borman, 1990):

a. Share stories, this promotes connectedness

b. Assign attainable goals

c. When giving feedback to the group as a whole, give feedback as if the group is a person, using the techniques discussed earlier

d. Identify personal needs and either meet them or acknowledge the impossibility.

Develop cohesiveness by the following:

a. Identify we, our, not they or me.

b. Build a tradition through history, fantasy, and ceremony.

c. Stress teamwork.

d. Get the group to recognize good work.

e. Give group rewards such as fruit or chocolate at resupplies. Give verbal rewards, praising the group for meeting group norms.

f. Treat the group as people, not as machines. People have feelings. Always include time for people to share these and make it an expectation rather than have people bury them.

An atmosphere is created in the way a group works. Individuals differ in the kind of atmosphere they like; some prefer it to be congenial, others prefer conflict or competition. It can change from time to time from work, play, satisfaction and sluggishness to enthusiasm. There can be an air of permissiveness, warmth, or defensiveness. People could be inhibited or spontaneous.

EXPERIENTIAL EXERCISE

A group activity such as a tyrolean traverse or practice rescue followed by a process questionnaire and subsequent discussion illustrates the dynamics. An experiential exercise enables the students to relate directly to a situation instead of struggling with hypothetical concepts. An individual questionnaire ensures that everyone considers the various interplays and makes the facilitation of the process much easier. It also illustrates some different perceptions and perspectives.

Examples of questions are:

1. Did you begin by clarifying the task and making a plan? Explain.
2. Did anyone emerge as a leader? Who?
3. Did anyone else take on an informal role? Explain.
4. Who was the most influential? Why?
5. Did anyone feel left out?
6. Was your group effective? Explain why or why not.
7. How did you feel about your group?
8. How do you feel about your own participation in the group?
   Describe yourself as a group member.
   How do you think the other group members see you?
   How did you try to influence the others?
9. What was most discouraging or frustrating about this whole exercise?
10. Did you ever disagree? How was this resolved?
11. What did you learn about yourselves? Each other? The group?
12. Did any of your group members have any "personal agendas?"
    Explain. Did you? Explain.

Group Roles

Role functions in a group consist of what it takes to do the job and what it takes to strengthen and maintain the group. Jane Warters (1960) in *Group Guidance: Principles and Practice,* describes the roles as follows:

TASK ROLES

1. Initiating activity: solutions, new ideas, etc.
2. Seeking opinions: looking for an expression of feeling.
3. Seeking information: clarification of values, suggestions and ideas.
4. Giving information: offering facts, generalizations, relating one's own experience to the group problem.
5. Giving opinion: concerns values rather than fact.

6. Elaborating: clarifying examples and proposals.
7. Coordinating: showing relationships among various ideas or suggestions.
8. Summarizing: pulling together related ideas and related suggestions.
9. Testing feasibility: making applications of suggestions to situations, examining practicality of ideas.

GROUP-BUILDING ROLES
1. Encouraging: being friendly, warm, responsive to others, praising others and their ideas.
2. Gatekeeping: trying to make it possible for another member to make a contribution to the group.
3. Standard setting: expressing standards for the group to use in choosing its content or procedures or in evaluating its decisions, reminding the group to avoid decisions that conflict with group standards.
4. Following: going along with decisions of the group, thoughtfully accepting ideas of others.
5. Expressing group feeling: summarizing what group feeling is sensed to be, describing reactions of group to ideas.

BOTH GROUP-BUILDING AND MAINTENANCE ROLES
1. Evaluating: submitting group decisions or accomplishments to compare with group standards, measuring accomplishments against goals.
2. Diagnosing: determining sources of difficulties, appropriate steps to take next, analyzing the main blocks to progress.
3. Testing for consensus: tentatively asking for group opinions in order to find out if the group is reaching consensus.
4. Mediating: harmonizing, conciliating differences in points of view, making compromise solutions.
5. Relieving tensions: draining off negative feelings by joking or pouring oil on troubled waters, putting tense situations in a wider context.

TYPES OF DYSFUNCTIONAL BEHAVIOR
This aspect of group roles is very important as these roles can create a negative communication climate. These roles should be discouraged.
1. Being aggressive: working for status by criticizing or blaming others, showing hostility against the group or some individual, deflating the ego or status of others.
2. Blocking: interfering with the progress of the group by going off on a tangent, citing personal experiences unrelated to the problem, arguing too much on a point, rejecting ideas without consideration.
3. Self-confession: using the group as a sounding board, expressing personal, non-group-oriented feelings or points of view.
4. Competing: vying with others to produce the best ideas, talk the most, play the most roles, trying to gain favor with the leader.

5. Seeking sympathy: trying to induce other group members to be sympathetic to one's problems or misfortunes, deploring one's own situation or disparaging one's own ideas to gain support.

6. Special pleading: introducing or supporting suggestions related to one's own pet concerns or philosophies, lobbying.

7. Horsing around: clowning, joking, mimicking, disrupting the work of the group.

8. Seeking recognition: attempting to call attention to one's self by loud or excessive talking, extreme ideas, or unusual behavior.

9. Withdrawing: acting indifferent or passive, resorting to excessive formality, daydreaming, doodling, whispering to others, wandering from the subject.

Such behavior as the above could be regarded as a symptom that all is not well with the group's ability to satisfy individual needs. However, each person is likely to interpret behavior differently. Content and group conditions must also be taken into account. For example, there are times when some forms of aggression contribute positively by clearing the air and instilling energy into the group.

Defense Mechanisms in Groups

Defense mechanisms are behaviors motivated by a personal need to maintain one's position in the group. Defense mechanisms evade conflict by moving away (flight) or toward (fight) the source of the conflict, according to Paul Thorenson (1972). His categorization of these defenses applies to any group as conflict often arises along with corresponding defenses.

FIGHT DEFENSES

1. Competition with the facilitator: This can be an attempt to build personal ego or avoid dealing with a personal problem. It occurs sometimes, for example, on "professional" courses as individuals try to justify their situations.

2. Cynicism: This challenges the group goals through skeptical questioning of genuine behavior.

3. Interrogation: Someone giving heavy questioning may be trying to keep the spotlight away from himself/herself.

FLIGHT DEFENSES

1. Intellectualization: This is a way of evading giving anything away personally or emotionally. It is sometimes done in introductions to avoid any self-disclosure. Self-disclosure done appropriately cultivates trust; intellectualizing evades giving personal or emotional information. Encour-

agement of "I" statements should help to discourage this.

2. Generalization: Impersonal statements about group behavior such as "we think" rather than "I think" means the individual may be speaking for the group without the group's consent.

3. Projection: One person's unconscious needs or behaviors projected onto another, he/ she attributes to others traits that are unacceptable in him/herself (something one doesn't like about oneself that can be seen in another).

4. Rationalization: This is a substitution of less incriminating reasons to try and justify a decision, feeling, emotion, or statement rather than what is probably the correct one.

5. Withdrawal: Members suddenly falling silent are in flight. Individual confrontation followed possibly by group confrontation is necessary to bring such an individual back.

GROUP MANIPULATION DEFENSE

1. Pairing is subgrouping to gain support.

2. "Red-crossing" is a defense of a person under fire to try and encourage mutual aid.

3. Focusing on one issue enables the group to spend excessive time on a person or issue to keep the action away from where it should be.

Generally evasive maneuvering should be confronted using effective feedback techniques.

Decision Making

Decision making is done sometimes by the leader and sometimes by the group, depending on the situation. A good leader makes a judgment about the group, the task and the environment before making decisions. The continuum between leader-centered and group-centered leadership allows some different styles of decision making between the two (Hersey and Blanchard, 1982). Table 3-2 illustrates this.

If a decision is made by the whole group, then it is difficult to undo without going through the whole process. Undoing a group decision with a leader-centered decision will destroy trust. In outdoor leadership a careful balance of decision making is necessary. Some are best made by the group, such as those connected with discipline, making it a group norm and not an imposed one.

An example is the problem of tardiness. If the group decides what to do about it, having arrived at the decision unanimously, then they will re-

Table 3-2

Tannenbaum and Schmidt's Leadership Continuum

LEADER CONTROL CONDITIONS
A. Time factor and urgency to prevent an emergency
B. Emergency
C. Individual knowledge—the leader knows
   what to do, the group doesn't
D. Lack of group skills—lack of understanding
   of group dynamics with an inability to facilitate
E. Expectations of Leader's role—
   the group might expect the group to be leader-centered
F. Legal responsibility

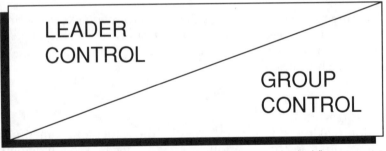

Leader decides, announces decision	Leader decides, sells decisions	Leader presents ideas, invites questions	Leader presents tentative ideas subject to change	Leader defines boundaries, group decides	Group defines boundaries and decides

GROUP CONTROL CONDITIONS
A. No time pressure
B. No emergency
C. Group knowledge regarding the situation
D. Group skills in regard to dynamics with an ability
   to facilitate group discussions
E. Expectation of the group—if there is not an expectation
   to take responsibilty, followers may find it difficult to take it.
F. Freedom of responsibilty
(Hersey and Blanchard, 1982)

inforce it. This will prevent the leader from alienating him, or herself by e forcing a punishment.

The Group Dynamics Questionnaire (Phipps, 1986)

The Group Dynamics Questionnaire consists of both task and relationship questions. If the questionnaire is filled out by each student quoting examples, it gives good instructor feedback on how each student understands the group. It also acts as a barometer of group atmosphere. It often highlights problems that may not be obvious to group leaders. Peers are often aware of undercurrents and if the checklist is kept confidential, these surface and can be dealt with in a diplomatic way. The questionnaire can be administered two or three times during the course to assist the instructor in assessing the stage of development that the group may be in. Without such feedback, the instructor leader might not realize that some aspect of the group dynamics is deteriorating. The Group Dynamics Questionnaire, given as a probe at times can alert the instructor leader to possible problems.

Being aware of the possible negative behaviors in groups and making the group aware of them can enable energy to be spent building a positive atmosphere, eventually pulling the group together into a team. Working through this teaching model should help to bring an awareness of the complex interaction that exists in group dynamics.

REFERENCES

Bankie, B., Bankie, E., McInnes, J., Oelslager, L., Phipps, M., (1983). *A brief review of psychological theories and counseling techniques for outdoor leaders.* Mankato MN: Mankato State University. (ERIC Document Reproduction Service No. ED 244 752).

Berne, Eric. (1968).*Games people play: Psychology of human relationships.* Hamondswoh, Middlesex: Penguin.

Borman, E. and Borman, N. (1976). *Effective small group communication. (2nd. ed.).* Minneapolis: Burgess Publishing Company.

Hersey, Paul and Blanchard, Ken. (1982). *Management of organizational behavoir: Utilizing human resources (4th ed.).* Englewood Cliffs, NJ: Prentice-Hall, Inc., 151-152.

Johnson, David W. and Frank P. (1982). *Joining together: Group theory and group skills. (2nd ed.).* Englewood Cliffs, NJ: Prentice-Hall, Inc., 140.

Jones, John E., (1973). A Model of Group Development. In J. E. Jones and J. W. Pfeiffer (Eds.), *The annual handbook for group facilitators.* LaJolla, CA: University Associates, 129.

Johnson, D. (1981). *Reaching out: Interpersonal effectiveness and self-actualization. (2nd ed.).* Englewood Cliffs: Prentice Hall.

Petzoldt, P. (1984) *The wilderness handbook*. New York: W.W. Norton and Company.

Pfeiffer, W. J. and Jones, J. E. (1972). "What to Look for in Groups." *In The annual handbook for group facilitators*. La Jolla,CA: University Associates.

Phipps. Maurice, L. (1986). "The group dynamics questionnaire." *In An assessment of a systematic approach to teaching leadership in expedition settings*. Doctoral dissertation, University of Minnesota.

Thorenson, P. (1972). "Defense mechanisms in groups." *In The annual handbook for group facilitators*. LaJolla,CA: University Associates.

Warters, J. (1960). *Group guidance: Principles and practice*. New York: McGraw Hill.

OUTDOOR LEADERSHIP: WHAT STYLE?
By Maurice L. Phipps and Cynthia A. Phipps

Much literature pertaining to leadership offers different styles of leadership. These are often the autocratic, democratic or laissez-faire styles. The potential leader is sometimes under the misconception then that a style has to be chosen that best fits one's personality. Another misconception is that leaders are born and that you cannot teach people to be leaders.

Leadership is taught a great deal in management spheres and also in the outdoors through universities, the Wilderness Education Association, the National Outdoor Leadership School, Outward Bound and similar institutions. To be effective, leadership teaching has to be done experientially, enabling practice and feedback for students making judgment decisions. The charismatic or "born" leader may have many followers but may make poor judgment decisions without adequate training. The trained leader must have and demonstrate confidence to effect decisions or he/she will have no followers.

A concept of prime importance is that the leader has to manage people which automatically ensures conflict. Conflict in a group is essential for health and growth. The question then is not the inevitability of conflict but the function of leadership in expressing, shaping and curbing it (Macgregor-Burns, 1979). This management is specific to the leaders' and followers' goals to obtain maximum motivation. Common goals should be the first priority to establish with a group.

Is it the leader's job to "keep the lid on things?" Not according to Mac-gregor-Burns (1979), who suggests transforming leadership. Such leadership occurs when one or more persons engage with others in such a way that leaders and followers raise one another to higher levels of motivation and morality. As leaders we are bound to take into account both human and environmental ethics as a higher level of thinking as well as motivation. Thus, in transforming leadership, the leader's role is to encourage growth in followers and to establish a climate where he/she can grow as well without losing the leadership position. Motivation is a key issue for the leader, particularly in the outdoors where groups are often confined together. Sometimes simply an awareness that a person's seemingly strange behavior may be motivated by totally unconscious needs can help a leader address the behavior empathically. Transformational leadership enables new levels of motivation in both leaders and followers, but should be exercised with care as leadership of a group should not be lost by the appointed leader. The leader has some responsibilities that cannot be delegated. It is important that the leader recognize that the followers may mistakenly view the allowed process as weakness and be prepared to deal with that perception, as in most groups there will be contenders for the leadership.

All groups are different and groups change so the leader must change his or her style to achieve goals in the most effective way. It can be seen then that having one style only could be ineffective. The situation may also determine the style. Hersey and Blanchard (1982), in *Management of Organizational Behavior: Utilizing Human Resources*, give us a situational leadership theory that takes into account the situation and the behavior or mental state of the followers.

Situational Leadership™ (Hersey and Blanchard, 1982).

Situational Leadership™ is based on the amount of direction (task behavior) and the amount of socio emotional support (relationship behavior) a leader must provide given the situation and the level of "maturity" of his or her followers. Group dynamics studies by Cartwright and Zander (1960), the Ohio State University leadership studies (1957), and Blake and Mouton's Managerial Grid, quoted in Hersey and Blanchard (1982) dispelled the idea that task and relationship were either/or leadership styles (that we should use a task- or a relationship-oriented style). Instead, styles tend to vary within leaders (Hersey and Blanchard,1982)

Hersey and Blanchard maintain that research of the past several decades has supported the contention that there is no "best" style of leadership and that any of the four basic styles shown in Table 3-1 may be effective or in-effective depending on the situation. The diagram illustrates the four styles; the curve represents the path along which leader behavior moves as the fol-lowers' maturity (readiness) changes. The styles vary in amounts of task/relationship behavior, which are explained for each quadrant. Maturity level is the ability and willingness (readiness) of individuals or a group to take re-sponsibility for directing their own behavior. Having gauged the maturity level, the leader then decides which leadership style to use: telling, selling, participating or delegating. This management/leadership style is specific to the leadership and followers' goals and to obtain maximum motivation.

The bell-shaped curve (see Table 3-3) in the style-of-the leader portion of the model means that as the maturity level of one's followers develops, the appropriate style of leadership moves accordingly in the model along the curvilinear function.

Tannenbaum and Schmidt's Leadership Continuum

In the Group Dynamics Teaching Model, reference was made to Tan-nenbaum and Schmidt's Leadership Continuum with regard to decision mak-ing (see Table 3-2). This theory is similar to situational leadership, but il-lustrates the different styles on a continuum. It also makes reference to leader-centered and group-centered decisions. It shows how the conditions can help dictate the choice of leader style. An advantage of situational lead-ership is that it enables a method of choosing styles from the middle of the continuum by assessing the followers' readiness and it also takes into con-sideration both task and relationship in decision making. Both theories are useful, however, in determining the appropriate style of leadership as they complement each other.

Situational Leadership and Group Development

An important link regarding the Situational Leadership model and group dynamics is the information on group development by Jones (1973). The four stages of group development as suggested by Jones are shown in Table 3-1.

In this model the stages correspond to the Hersey-Blanchard leader styles and it is an important framework to understand when dealing with groups in expedition settings. The natural development of the group can be en-hanced by the use of the correct leadership style according to the Hersey-Blanchard theory. The awareness of a conflict stage that the group can strive to work through will reduce apprehensions and tensions, making co-hesiveness and interdependence more attainable.

As situations change rapidly in the fluid environment of the outdoors (task functions may change from orientation through to problem solving in a few hours), personal relations also change with this and so the cor-

Table 3-3

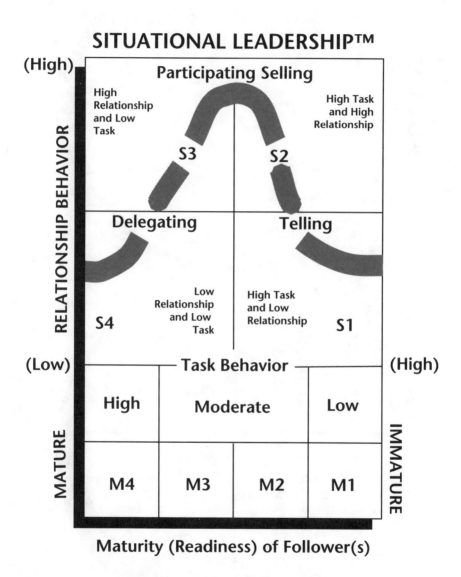

SITUATIONAL LEADERSHIP™

Reprinted by permission of the publisher.
Courtesy of Prentice-Hall, Inc., Englewood Cliffs, New Jersey.

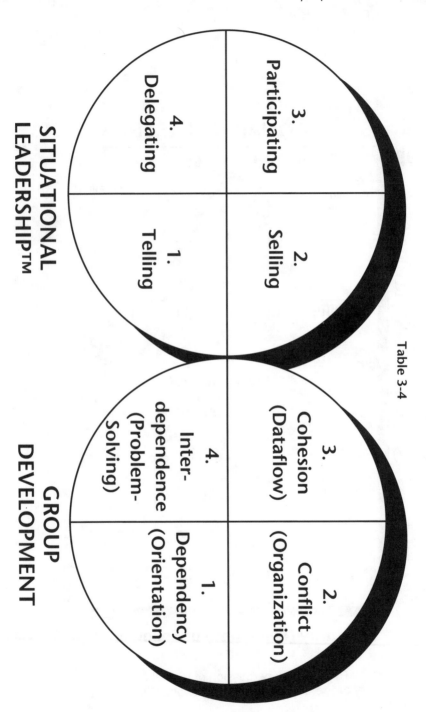

Table 3-4

SITUATIONAL LEADERSHIP™

- 3. Participating
- 4. Delegating
- 2. Selling
- 1. Telling

GROUP DEVELOPMENT

- 3. Cohesion (Dataflow)
- 4. Inter-dependence (Problem-Solving)
- 2. Conflict (Organization)
- 1. Dependency (Orientation)

responding leadership style must change also. This rapid change of situation can create an ideal learning opportunity or a difficult and demotivating experience if only a single leadership style is used. Using the two models in conjunction depicts the relevance of particular leadership styles for specific stages of group development. Table 3-4 shows both of the models.

The group might not progress further than the conflict stage. It may reach interdependence, then regress, even to dependency (if, for example, the task changes). A group may change tasks from mountaineering to kayaking, in which case followers may need to be orientated again.

Consequently, the leader must judge what stage of development the group is in or what level of maturity (readiness) in the Hersey-Blanchard model.

Until the group matures to a cohesive unit, the leadership style needs to be more leader-centered. Initially, a telling style is needed to orientate the group as they need basic information only. For example, when arriving at the roadhead they want to know how far they will be going, who is the scout, logger, etc., and when will there be rest breaks. They need only basic task information at first. Later, when using the selling style in the conflict stage, a high amount of relationship behavior is needed to create an open or supportive climate for communication. This entails being descriptive, problem control-oriented rather than person control-oriented, spontaneous, empathic, equally directed and egalitarian. Selling means that high relationship behavior is needed although the leader remains very directive.

As the group moves into the cohesive phase, the leader behavior needs to remain high relationship-wise to motivate and be supportive rather than directive. Some decision making can be shared with the leader facilitating or assisting the group in decision making as the group is cohesive and concentrating on data flow in the task function. This corresponds to Hersey and Blanchard's participating style on the leadership curve.

If the group reaches the interdependence stage of development (high maturity or readiness), the leader should delegate most decision making and keep a low profile. Followers should be willing and able to do the task. The group, however, may regress in task maturity, so the leader must be prepared to step in if necessary using one of the other styles.

The group and individual may fluctuate in either their ability or willingness, both aspects of maturity, so the leadership style must adjust by moving back and forth along the curve to the appropriate quadrant in Table 3-3. Sometimes in the outdoors and particularly on expedition-style courses there will be several fluctuations within a single day. For example, after mastering campcraft, the group may need a delegating style of leadership to eat, pack and move; a more participating style of leadership to plan a route, and, in the afternoon, a telling, style leadership to effect a rappel.

The judgment to select the appropriate style is the key to effective leadership, but this is best learned experientially. Focusing the learning by using group developmental theory and Hersey-Blanchard's Situational Leadership along with an understanding of group dynamics, will aid the process. Accepting feedback and reflecting on experiences will make it possible to learn leadership skills. An open and supportive communication climate is necessary to accomplish this.

Research in "An Assessment of a Systematic Approach to Teaching Leadership in Expedition Settings" (Phipps, 1986) found the systematic approach described above (the Group Dynamics Teaching Model and Situational Leadership) to be advantageous in the groups studied. Measurement techniques used in this research enable measurement and evaluation of the leadership styles and the group dynamics. Details of the measurement techniques are given below in Experientail Leadership Education.

Experiential Leadership Education

Experiential Leadership Education is a method of teaching and measuring aspects of the "soft" skills of leadership in a systematic way. Soft skills in leadership are the "people" skills, such as leadership styles and group dynamics, as opposed to the "hard" skills, such as logistics planning, budgeting, marketing, etc. Because of their amorphous nature the soft skills are often difficult to conceptualize. Using Experiential Leadership Education makes conceptualization easier. (It is easier to conceptualize an experience than an abstraction.)

THE EXPERIENTIAL LEADERSHIP PROFILE

The conceptualization is achieved by using an "Experiential Leadership Profile" consisting of:

1. Scores from a test instrument showing each leader their dominant and supporting, or next more frequently used style(s).

2. Scores from a test instrument showing changes in style adaptability, and effectiveness. The style adaptability score reflects the leader's flexibility with the four leadership styles. The effectiveness score reflects the correct usage of the styles.

3. Data gained from experience, i.e., actual decision making (recorded in a journal noting their own leader decisions and styles used) using a theory of leadership, for example Hersey-Blanchard's Situational Leadership.

4. Perceptions of group process from a group dynamics questionnaire given to all the group.

DECISION-MAKING JOURNALS AND CHARTS

The Experiential Leadership Profile shows results from pre- and post-course tests that illustrate changes in styles and effectiveness in hypothetical situations. But more importantly, the recording of the decision making over time using the journal decisions allows the use of charts to pinpoint incongruent use of leadership styles. Conferring with the trainee and his/her journal can enable analysis of the judgment that went into the decision making. An example of leader-style interaction is shown in Table 3-5.

The styles can be combined to illustrate leader-centered/group-centered

Table 3-5

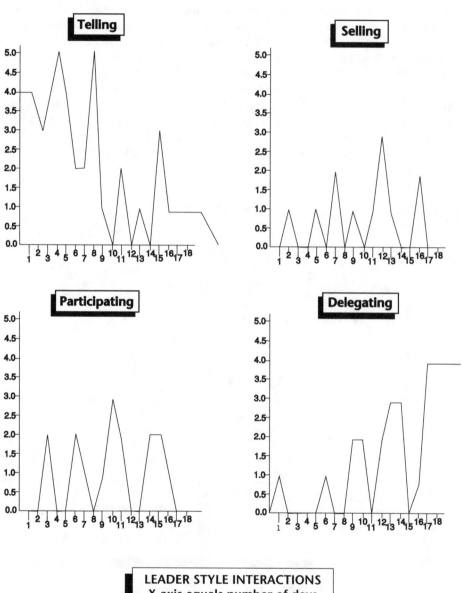

LEADER STYLE INTERACTIONS
X axis equals number of days
Y axis equals number of Decisions

decision making or high/low-relationship styles. If the decisions recorded in the journals are recorded with the "whys" (rationale), "hows" (style) and whether it was a task or relationship decision, then the leader analyst is able to more fully understand how the decisions were actually made. Charts can be made of all these trends to enable progress to be tracked. An example of a leader-centered/group-centered leader style chart is shown in Table 3-6. There are expected trends that conform to the Situational Leadership theory. For example, in most groups the frequency of leader-centered styles drops as time progresses. The chart trends can be compared to the expected trends and where incongruencies occur, the journal can be checked to see if appropriate styles were being used. This provides an effective teaching tool as the theory is put into action in a practical situation that allows detailed feedback.

Table 3-6

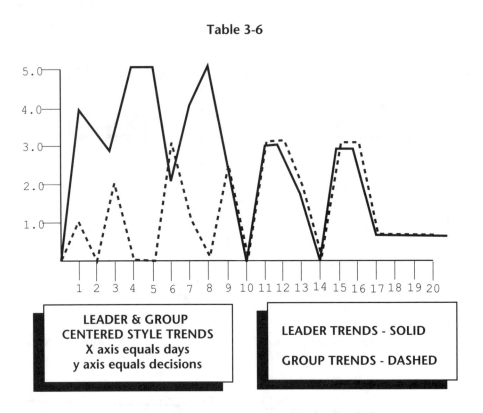

LEADER & GROUP CENTERED STYLE TRENDS
X axis equals days
y axis equals decisions

LEADER TRENDS - SOLID

GROUP TRENDS - DASHED

GROUP DYNAMICS

As the internal dynamics of a group affects its performance, this is an important aspect of leadership education. A specific teaching model is used that can be modified for different groups. It enables problem solving in the group dynamics before expected crises are reached and allows procedures for dealing with unexpected crises.

The group member perceptions are measured quantitatively and qualitatively using a Group Dynamics Questionnaire. This questionnaire establishes the components of the group process that are being dealt with positively and negatively. The Group Dynamics Questionnaire is a measure of the group climate. The qualitative statements in the instrument allow specific problems to be pinpointed; the quantitative measurements allow an assessment of what components the group needs to improve on, for instance atmosphere, cooperation, task, or some other component.

PRACTICAL APPLICATIONS

The combination of the leadership instrument scores (showing dominant style, effectiveness, etc.), with the actual decision making graphically represented and detailed in a journal, and the perceptions on the Group Dynamics Questionnaire allow a perception check for the leader. It enables the leader to visualize aspects of his/her leadership that are normally difficult to see. Often because of this amorphous nature of the soft skills, they are dealt with theoretically with very little follow-up. Teaching Experiential Leadership Profile combines the experiential and theoretical constructs of leadership using a systematic approach and allows follow-up analysis during the actual expedition. The results can be visually tracked and can also be statistically analyzed. Further details on the exact application of the measurement techniques can be gained from the original research by Phipps (1986). A workbook titled *A Systematic Approach to Learning Leadership* (Phipps, 1988) has details of the scoring techniques for the group dynamics questionnaire and leader-style tracking techniques with all the necessary tabulation forms included.

Conclusion

An understanding of the soft skills, including leadership styles and group dynamics as well as expedition behavior is essential to cope with behaviors in outdoor groups. Leadership style can affect the psychological undercurrents of an outdoor program, which can in turn affect safety. Using the appropriate leadership style and educating the group in the soft skills can prevent explosive group problems.

Equally important is the overall quality of the experience for followers. It has long been believed that outdoor experiences provide excellent avenues for personal growth. This is often why outdoor professionals are drawn into the field. For the W.E.A. leader, using the Experiential Leadership Education method enables him/her to really see the effects of his/her leadership and make changes if necessary. It is my hope that leaders will become aware of the importance of the soft skills, especially in regard to empowering followers appropriately.

REFERENCES

Hersey, Paul and Blanchard, Ken (1984). *Management of organizational behavior: utilizing human resources* (4th ed.). Englewood Cliffs, NJ: Prentice-Hall, Inc., 151-152.

Johnson, David W. and Johnson, Frank P. (1972). *Joining together* (2nd ed.). Englewood Cliffs, NJ: Prentice-Hall, Inc., 140.

Jones, John E. (1973). A Model of Group Development. In J. E. Jones and J. W. Pfeiffer (Eds.), *The annual handbook for group facilitators,* La Jolla, CA: University Associates, 129.

Macgregor-Burns, James (1979). *Leadership.* New York: Harper and Row, 37-38, 20.

Phipps, Maurice L. (1986). *An assessment of a systematic approach to teaching leadership in expedition settings.* Doctoral dissertation, University of Minnesota: St. Paul, MN.

Phipps, Maurice L. (1988). *A systematic approach to learning leadership.* San Luis Obispo, CA: El Corral Bookstore, Cal Poly.

4.

ENVIRONMENTAL ETHICS AND BACKCOUNTRY CONSERVATION PRACTICES

by David Cockrell
University of Southern Colorado

Introduction

Most of us in wilderness education believe that participants in our programs will develop an appreciation for wild places through shared adventures. We expect that appreciation of wild lands will ultimately generalize to an appreciation for all our natural resources and an awareness of the interconnectedness of life forms on the planet. We hope our participants will take action in some way to assist in the preservation and conservation of natural resources. There is some evidence that this complex of values does evolve through educational wilderness adventures (Gray, 1985), but there is also some evidence that it doesn't happen automatically (Simpson, 1985).

The specific backcountry conservation practices that we teach and model on W.E.A. courses are a microcosm for the environmentally responsible lifestyles participants might strive for continuously after the course ends. Care with water and firewood in the backcountry become the prototypes for care with fossil fuels and aluminum cans at home. For this reason alone conservation practices are one of the most important curriculum elements on any course.

The need to preserve a high level of environmental quality in our public backcountry is just as important, however, as the need to foster environmentally responsible lifestyles.

Environmental degradation in wilderness was attributed to recreational use as early as 1940 (Wagar, 1940), and mandatory certification of wilderness users continues to be a genuine possibility explicitly because of the need to reduce impact (Stankey and Baden, 1977; Shelby et al., 1982; La Page, 1984). One author has even called for a ban on organized outdoor programs from wilderness as a tactic for reducing impacts (Young, 1985). W.E.A. graduates should all be competent minimum impact campers, and our graduates must exhibit good judgment in the difficult issues of environmental ethics. If we fail in this mission, our image as an educational and certifying organization for wilderness leaders will not be credible.

The W.E.A. curriculum for backcountry conservation has been evolving for a long time. As is true with other areas of the W.E.A. curriculum, the seminal work was done by Paul Petzoldt at the National Outdoor Leadership School in the 1960s and 1970s. For this chapter, the earlier N.O.L.S. conservation practices were revised based on a review of recent research on recreational impacts on wild lands (Viles and Cockrell, 1985). In most instances, the practices recommended here are consistent with current versions of the N.O.L.S. policies (Cole, 1986; Hampton and Cole, 1988). However, the W.E.A. conservation practices are targeted specifically toward organized wilderness education programs and are separated into two sections: those designed to minimize ecological impact to the resource; and those designed to minimize psychological impact to other backcountry visitors. In several instances it will be noted that recommendations in these two sections directly contradict each other. As in other aspects of outdoor leadership, minimum impact backcountry practices require complex decisions and good judgment. In considering the recommendations presented here, remember the Paul Petzoldt axiom: "Rules are for fools!"

The most important contribution W.E.A. has made in regard to environmental ethics has not been in development or refinement of backcountry conservation practices, however, but in developing an instructional process for teaching them. Following presentation of the conservation practices in this chapter, a discussion of environmental ethics is offered. The emphasis is on maximizing the transference of learning from on the course to back home. Specific examples and strategies used in W.E.A. courses to enhance transference are presented.

Backcountry Travel

A W.E.A. course in the backcountry is often a relatively large group that is easily identifiable as an organized wilderness education program. W.E.A. courses are attracted to low-use areas and frequently travel off-trail. Given these proclivities, several basic practices can help minimize a course's impact to the soil, vegetation, wildlife and other users.

PRACTICES FOR MINIMIZING ECOLOGICAL IMPACT

1. Birds and animals need undisturbed territory. Try to stay downwind, avoid sudden motions, and never chase or charge any animal.

2. Some birds and small animals may be very friendly, but wildlife should never be fed. Even in low-impact areas, feeding wildlife can alter feeding habits, migration patterns and reproduction levels, ultimately resulting in changed species composition.

3. When following existing trails, walk on the designated path. Short-cutting a switchback or avoiding a muddy trail by walking in the vegetation causes unnecessary erosion and unsightly multiple troughs. If a trail is impassable, walk on as many hard surfaces as possible (rock or sand) and notify the managing agency responsible for that area.

4. If you travel off-trail, avoid descending steep slopes. In steep terrain, descending causes considerably more soil and vegetative impact than ascending. The soil compaction from a single hiking party can be considerable anywhere, so pass over a given route only once, travel in small groups and do not hike in single file.

Figure 4-1

PRACTICES FOR MINIMIZING SOCIAL IMPACT

1. Hike in groups of four to six people at most. Four is an optimum number, especially during off-trail travel, because in case of sickness or injury one person can stay with the victim while two people go for help.

2. Travel quietly in the backcountry, whether hiking by trail or cross country. The group will see more of the environment, including the wildlife, and other hikers will appreciate the solitude.

3. Bright colored clothes and equipment have limited advantages in the backcountry, although they may look great in a store window. Wear earth tones if possible to minimize visual impact, except when international orange must be worn for safety reasons during hunting seasons.

4. Dogs and other domestic animals chase wildlife, interrupt course activities and can disturb other visitors. They are generally not appropriate companions for a W.E.A. course.

5. If you choose a route without trails, do not blaze trees, build cairns or leave messages in the dirt. Other backcountry travelers can be confused by unanticipated markers, and in addition these signs of prior travel make their wilderness experience seem less remote.

6. Pick up any litter you can, but allow other hikers a sense of discovery by leaving rocks, plants and other objects of interest as you found them.

7. When encountering another party on the trail, a W.E.A group should be friendly but reserved so as to respect the right of the other party to remain autonomous. Offer to step aside to let the other group pass. Step to the downhill side of the trail when encountering a horse party.

Camping

Again, because W.E.A. courses can be relatively large groups and are usually attracted to pristine places, their potential for causing considerable impact is great. As Cole (1986) has pointed out, the selection of an ethical campsite is a quite complex and also important decision. W.E.A. instructors must understand the principles of ethical campsite selection and attempt to cultivate these skills in students. Fortunately, research by Cole and others in recent years (e.g., Cole and Benedict, 1983; Cole, 1982; Cole, 1981) has resulted in some broadly applicable principles that can guide the process.

Once a site has been selected, a major goal of all in-camp activities should be to leave the site with as little evidence of the group's usage as possible. Fortunately, many types of camping impacts can be avoided simply through awareness of their potentiality. Impact avoidance and amelioration can become a game. It instills pride in students to walk away from their campsite in the morning confident that no one will know they were there.

PRACTICES FOR MINIMIZING ECOLOGICAL IMPACT

1. Cole and Benedict (1983) have suggested categorizing campsites into the six classes listed below. Cole's research (Cole, 1982) has suggested that most impact comes with very light use (sometimes less than five nights per year). In order to ensure no long-lasting impact, camping on pristine sites—a practice W.E.A. commonly uses—requires good conservation skills and no repeat use. The upshot is that on pristine sites, the maximum number of nights spent should be one. If a multinight stay is desirable, then camping on moderately impacted sites is optimal. On these sites ecological impact from prolonged camping is minimized. Semipristine and lightly used campsites show rapid deterioration with increased use and should be avoided. Highly used and severely impacted sites are in need of site restoration measures and should also be avoided.

Table 4-1
Campsite Condition Classes
(Cole and Benedict, 1983)

Pristine
Never before used.

Semipristine
Use is evident but hardly recognizable.
Flattened vegetation but no bare spots.

Lightly used
Some bare spots in campsite. Still largely vegetated.

Moderately used
Little or no ground vegetation but litter and humus are still intact.

Highly used
Mineral soil exposed.
Tree roots may be exposed.

Severely used
Soil erosion and exposed tree roots are problems.
Campsites overlap.
Multiple fire rings.
Firewood is scarce.
Trees may be dead.

2. Choose a campsite well away from water sources. The choicest camping spots are often prime territory for animal forage, so take a little extra time to seek out a more camouflaged area.

3. In choosing a pristine campsite, avoid slopes to minimize soil erosion. Avoid wet sites to minimize soil compaction, erosion and vegetative impacts. Select sites with ample organic soil or sandy soil. While visual impacts may be minimized in forested areas, ecological impacts to soils and vegetation are most often less in meadows and resilient grassy areas. Forest understories are typically made up of woody plants and forbs with thick cuticles, large leaf areas and breakable stems. Fragile vegetation is under forests, not usually in lush meadows.

4. For one night, pristine campsites, cook groups of two to six should be dispersed at least 30 feet apart. For camps at moderately impacted sites, group impact should be concentrated in the areas already affected.

5. Leave the area as you found it. Avoid trenching tents, removing rocks, cutting live branches or pulling up plants or roots to make a pleasant campsite.

6. Care in breaking camp illuminates many of the successes and mistakes of conservation practices employed there. It should therefore be a distinct and important event. Pick up litter, including that which was there before you arrived if you can manage it. Rehabilitate your fire site as is described in the next section, and scatter any remaining firewood. If you cleared the sleeping area of twigs, pine cones or rocks, replace these items. Revive trampled plants at tent sites, cooking and cleaning sites, and connector trails. Scatter natural litter around the site.

Cole (1986) has also suggested that moderately impacted sites be left in a neat and attractive condition to encourage other parties to use them rather than establishing a new site.

PRACTICES FOR MINIMIZING SOCIAL IMPACT

1. Choose a site well away and out of sight of water sources, trails, and beauty spots so that others may also have access to privacy at these attractions.

2. While ecological impact is usually minimized by camping in meadows, psychological impact is most often minimized by camping in the forest understory. There is visual screening between parties there and the sounds are more muted. Many factors must be considered in weighing these competing priorities, including presence of other parties, evidence of previous use levels and impacts, vegetation and soil types, and moisture levels. Hammitt and Cole (1987) provide a valuable overview of the interplay of factors in campsite selection processes.

3. Radios and tape players interfere with the natural sounds of backcountry for other visitors and should be discouraged.

FIRES, STOVES AND COOKING PRACTICES
FOR MINIMIZING ECOLOGICAL IMPACT

1. Fires should be used primarily for cooking, if at all. Four to six people should cook at one fire to minimize the number of fires necessary. Only dead and down wood the diameter of a silver dollar or smaller should be collected. Only enough wood for a single fire should be collected at one time. If you must collect the last deadfall near the site to have firewood, don't build a fire. To conserve the valuable firewood resource, build only as big a fire as you honestly need.

2. Choose a resilient site for your fire or stove. Areas naturally free of any vegetation are most resilient (sandy areas or flat rocks). Grassy meadows are intermediate; and forested sites with woody understories are least resilient. The kitchen should be located six yards or more away from the firepit to disperse trampling impacts. Sump holes should be located either at the edge of the firepit or at the edge of camp away from other activity areas.

3. Fires should be built far from tents, trees, branches and underground root systems to avoid damage from sparks and heat.

4. Fires should never be built in litter or duff. Ignited duff below the sur-

face can smolder for weeks before actually flaming. If there is a ground cover or duff, be sure to dig through it well into the mineral soil when constructing a firepit.

5. Especially when the woods are dry, do not build fires on windy days when sparks might be dangerous.

6. Fires should not be ringed with rocks or built against reflecting rocks in order to avoid permanent blackening and unnatural exfoliating. In addition, rocks may have imbedded moisture that when heated may cause the rock to explode.

7. The preferred site for a fire is in the most prominent established fire ring in a moderately impacted site. Other fire rings in that site should be dismantled and the ashes scattered widely. If you should come across a fire ring in a lightly impacted site with new plant growth inside the ring, dismantle the ring, disguise the site and move on.

8. If a fire must be built in a pristine site, W.E.A. courses typically follow one of the following three methods developed at N.O.L.S.:

A. SURFACE METHOD:
When there is abundant mineral soil available without excavation (sandy areas, old streambeds, intertidal zones, etc.) there should be no need to disturb the topsoil by digging a firepit. Simply spread several inches of mineral soil on the ground and build a fire as usual. All wood should be burned completely to ashes before the fire goes out. Residual coals should be crushed and scattered, and mineral soil discretely replaced. Camouflage the cooking area before leaving.

B. FLAT-ROCK METHOD:
Spread mineral soil two to three inches deep on top of a flat rock over an area slightly larger than the fire will occupy, then build your fire as usual. Burn all wood completely to ashes and after the fire is out crush and scatter any residual coals. After the soil is removed and the rock rinsed, the area will be left unscarred. This method is particularly useful in areas where thick layers of rich organic soil preclude a safe firepit or surface fire.

C. FIREPIT METHOD:
Remove sod or topsoil in several large chunks from the chosen area (about 1" X 24"). Excavate the pit down to mineral soil, placing the dirt neatly in a protected pile, and pat mineral soil around the firepit perimeter to avoid drying out surrounding vegetation. The pit should be deep enough to house residual wood ash as well as the original dirt and sod, but shallow enough to ensure adequate air circulation for burning all wood down to white ash. The sod, both around the firepit and removed from it, should be kept moist. For baking, mineral soil can be spread on the sod at the edge of the firepit for a bed of coals, but be sure to replace all baking coals in the firepit to be completely burned before filling in the firepit. On breaking camp, both the bottom and sides of the firepit should be cold to the touch. Residual coals should be crushed and scattered before replacing and com-

pacting dirt and finally replacing the sod. Make sure there are no soft spots in the filled-in firepit to assure a flat, even texture of sod. Finish by landscaping the entire cooking area by scattering leaves or twigs or whatever covered the ground originally.

PRACTICES FOR MINIMIZING SOCIAL IMPACT
1. Never build a fire near a large rock, log or other natural object that may become discolored. Burn all firewood to white ash so that no half-burned logs remain as evidence of your stay.
2. Scatter all remaining firewood before leaving a camp.
3. Saws and axes should not be used as they leave unsightly scars.

Sanitation
Human waste decomposition is primarily a function of soil organism populations, which in turn are affected by soil temperature, soil moisture, soil aeration and food supply. Soil organisms are generally most prevalent in areas with organic soils (good food supply), moderate temperatures and adequate but not excessive moisture. Extremes of any of these factors can significantly inhibit organism populations and thus biological decomposition.

PRACTICES FOR MINIMIZING ECOLOGICAL IMPACT
1. Dig latrines and catholes in organic soil layers, where organism populations are higher. Waste buried below this level decomposes very slowly. Avoid wet sites.
2. In more sterile soils and harsh environments, sunlight, precipitation and temperature changes become the major breakdown agents. Here, feces should have a shallower burial or be left at the surface.
3. In all cases, feces decompose most rapidly when dispersed (i.e., cat holes). This knowledge must be tempered by the possibility of water source contamination and the likelihood of someone encountering unburied waste. Dispose of human waste at the surface or in catholes when group size is small, the area is lightly used and dispersal of impact is most appropriate.
4. In areas and seasons of abundant rainfall, waste should be buried further away from water sources than normal to minimize the possibility of contamination.
5. Latrines should be a maximum of 10 to 12 inches deep but not deeper than the organic soil and should be filled before they are two to four inches from full. Deeper burial prevents adequate decomposing bacterial action while shallower burial can foul the air and encourage animals to dig up the latrine. After each usage, feces should be covered with topsoil and compressed with a foot or shovel. Adequate decomposition can only occur when topsoil is mixed in with waste material, so a latrine containing only feces with no intermittent dirt will merely compact and hide the waste rather than decompose it.
6. Waste elimination in catholes during a hike may be encouraged as it

reduces pressure on the immediate area of a campsite. On the trail, feces should be given a shallow burial well away from the trail with proper drainage considerations. Rolling a rock to an impromptu latrine should be discouraged, especially in heavily used areas.

7. Urinate in areas with thick humus layers and drainage but try to avoid fragile vegetation because the salt contained in urine attracts plant-eating animals. Toilet paper, if used, should be completely burned, or packed out. When available, snow, leaves and other natural substitutes are preferable to toilet paper.

8. Tampons must be burned in an extremely hot fire to completely decompose; therefore in most cases they should be bagged and packed out. They should not be buried in a latrine as they decompose very slowly.

9. Bathing directly in larger water sources is acceptable when no soap is used. No soap should be used in lakes and streams. Complete soap bathing should involve jumping in the water, lathering on the shore far away from the water, and rinsing the soap off with water carried in Billy cans. This allows the biodegradable soaps to break down and filter through soil before reaching any body of water. Clothes can be adequately cleaned by thorough rinsing. Residual soap can cause skin irritation, so consider not using soap to wash clothes in the backcountry.

10. Dishes should be washed near a small sump hole dug at the edge of the firepit or the edge of camp. Natural abrasives (sand, pine cones, etc.) can be quite effective means of removing food scraps and grease, and they will help minimize the amount of soap residue you must deposit in the environment.

11. Food should be packaged in plastic bags instead of cans, glass bottles or tin foil. The bags should be carried out or burned completely.

12. Waste water (dishwater or excess cooking water) should be poured in a sump hole in the corner of the firepit or at the edge of camp to minimize the attraction of insect pests.

13. Avoid the problem of dealing with leftover food by carefully planning meals. When leftovers do occur they should be carried in plastic bags to use later or burned completely. Partial burning, which is likely to occur if an attempt is made to burn food shortly before dousing the fire, is inadequate. Remaining food odors can induce animals to dig up a buried firepit. Food particles (e.g., macaroni or noodles), which inevitably occur in some dishwashing, should be treated like bulk leftovers, either packed out or burned.

14. Fish viscera may be scattered widely away from campsites and trails. Viscera should not be returned to lakes or streams as decomposition there will be slower. If a considerable number of fish are caught at a particular campsite, the group should consider packing out viscera.

PRACTICES FOR MINIMIZING SOCIAL IMPACT
Dispose of human waste in latrines when group size is larger, the area is more heavily used, and concentration of impact is the tactic chosen to mini-

mize the likelihood of discovery by another party.

The above practices constitute the general guidelines that underlie specific decisions made by outdoor leaders in varying environments. There are many variations in the application of these practices, especially for programs conducted in the unique environments of snow, alpine vegetation, deserts and ocean coastlines. Common practices for these special settings are summarized by Hampton and Cole (1988) and by the earlier N.O.L.S. conservation practices. In each case, however, experience and observation are brought to bear on unique situations, using the decision-making process outlined in chapter 2. The goals of this process are minimizing impact to the environment while maximizing the safety and enjoyment of participants.

Teaching Strategies and the Instructional Process

It is one thing to teach someone how to climb rocks, and another to teach him/her to be an outdoor leader. Similarly, backcountry conservation, while it involves considerable judgment, is only a window opening on the expansive domain of environmental ethics. If we take up the challenge of teaching ethics, we must do more than simply encourage compliance with a few backcountry manners. We must first ask what an ethic is and how it grows. We must cultivate our own environmental ethics, and take it upon ourselves to be knowledgeable about the natural history and ecology of our instructional sites. We must set objectives and select teaching strategies explicitly to cultivate environmental values. And we must strive for strong transference from wilderness appreciation and sound backcountry conservation practices to a pervasive ethic of stewardship back home.

WHAT IS AN ENVIRONMENTAL ETHIC AND HOW DOES IT GROW?

Leopold's (1966) discussion of the land ethic in *Sand County Almanac* remains a vigorous definitional statement today for environmental ethics. For Leopold, an ethic was a voluntary restriction on individual freedoms agreed upon by members of a society for the good of the community. The land ethic simply broadens the notion of community to include the land and other life forms. The land ethic proclaims that "a thing is right when it tends to preserve the integrity, stability and beauty of the biotic community. It is wrong when it tends to do otherwise" (Leopold, 1966, p. 222).

Social psychologists treat ethics as socially derived psychological states or orientations similar to broad, fundamental values. In a recent comprehensive effort to understand the processes of instilling an environmental ethic, Gray (1985, p. 193) discussed the environmental ethic by saying:

> If the ethic has a strong objective and cognitive basis as well as substantial drive strength issuing out of affective processes, and if all this is deeply internalized, the prospects of solving the social aspects of environmental problems will be bright indeed.

Following Rokeach, Gray (1985) suggested that specific informational programs, like classes on backcountry conservation practices, must be supplemented if deep values and ethics are to be cultivated. Informational strategies should be designed to address self-cognitions (self-efficacy, self-esteem), terminal values (freedom, equality, a world of beauty) and higher level cognitive processes. Suggested behavior change strategies include "shared coping" and the "direct nature" experience. Finally, Gray suggests that the enhanced awareness and positive feelings that grow from an outdoor experience should transfer to future environmental contacts because of "stimulus generalization."

Stimulus generalization, or transference, from the wilderness course is a key outcome if environmental ethics are to be enhanced. Simpson (1985) has already pointed out that a love for wilderness may not transfer very far into other environmental issues. Gass (1985) described three types of transference that can occur in wilderness courses: specific, nonspecific and metaphoric. In specific transfer, specific skills and knowledge learned in a program become useful in a subsequent situation. In nonspecific transfer, the learner generalizes basic principles from one learning situation to another. In metaphoric transfer, principles are also generalized to a subsequent situation. The principles being transferred, however, are not equivalent, but rather analogous or metaphorical to those learned in the initial experience.

For example, students in W.E.A. courses learn the principles of ethical disposal of wastes: urine and feces, liquid and solid food wastes, fish viscera, and dirty or soapy wash water. Techniques espoused strive to minimize visibility to other backcountry users, ensure rapid decomposition, and minimize effects on other life forms. If a specific transference is successful, the student will continue to use these practices on subsequent trips to similar environments, and this is valuable. If a nonspecific transference occurs, the student may seek other ways to minimize his personal impact on other life forms, perhaps in a variety of outdoor settings. This is a more value-laden change, and perhaps more profound. If a metaphoric transfer occurs, the student may come to see the unified collection of minimum-impact camping practices as symbolic of a lifestyle to be actualized every day. Thus, the influence might extend to personal recycling and sewage disposal decisions, automobile use, or even voting patterns. This level of transference can begin to build an environmental ethic.

STRATEGIES

The problem, of course, is what instructors can do to maximize appreciation and conservation from on the course to the everyday environment back home. What follows is a summary of nine different strategies from a variety of sources that have proved useful in maximizing transference on W.E.A. programs.

1. DESIGN CONDITIONS FOR TRANSFER BEFORE THE COURSE ACTIVITIES BEGIN.
Tight objectives should be developed about the kinds of skills students will demonstrate on the course, the kinds of attitudes and intentions that will be expressed concerning future courses and trips, and the lessons to be learned about lifestyles. These, as a minimum, should address backcountry travel, campsite selection and organization, fires, stoves and cooking, sanitation and ethical issues in special environments. Instructors' decisions concerning itineraries, routes, instructional sites, rations and equipment should all take into consideration these environmental ethics objectives.

2. CAREFUL PLANNING CAN ENHANCE TRANSFER OF ENVIRONMENTAL ETHICS.
A major goal of the course should be learning to live comfortably for the long term, in harmony with the wilderness. Careful selection of gear, clothing and food for comfort can therefore enhance the "classical conditioning" of positive associations with wilderness discussed by Gray (1985). Also, avoiding survival situations is one of the best ways to lessen impact. Desperation can encourage the selection of an unethical campsite, the construction of an unethical fire, the abandonment of gear, etc. Time, energy and climate control plans are, therefore, also conservation plans.

Another aspect of planning includes the acquisition and preparation of information by the instructor. Instructors should know the basic conservation practices in the previous section of this chapter. They should also know how and when they will modify these practices through judgment. And, they should have ideas about how these practices can serve as metaphors for environmental ethics in everyday life. Instructors should also be conversant about the geology, ecology, weather and natural history of the course site. They should have reliable knowledge about edible plants, fish and wildlife, and many trees and flowers of the area. They should prepare information packets for students on these topics before the course begins, and be prepared to share the information through direct instruction. State departments of conservation/fish and game or local university biology departments often have brochures or flyers on local flora and fauna that can be used for this purpose.

3. INSTRUCTORS SHOULD ROLE MODEL ENVIRONMENTAL VALUES.
Many of our deepest values are acquired through observation of the value-laden behaviors of respected others. Instructors should practice on a continuous basis the conservation practices they preach. They should also explain when a particular backcountry conservation practice has influenced their own overall lifestyle. Examples might include the use of biodegradable soaps in the home, or maintenance of a vegetable protein-based diet in the home rather than a meat-based diet so as to maximize the efficiency of societal food production. When an authoritarian decision by the instructor is appropriate on a conservation issue (say, campsite selection on the shakedown), he/she should explain the ethical judgments that went into the de-

cision as fully as possible. It is important, however, not to appear more idealist or "purist" than one really is. Honesty is the basis of credibility.

4. BACKCOUNTRY CONSERVATION INVOLVES INTENSE USE OF THE DECISION-MAKING PROCESS AND IS A PRIME OPPORTUNITY FOR ENVIRONMENTAL VALUES EDUCATION.

Ecologically, it generally causes less impact to camp in meadows rather than forest understories. However, this maximizes the psychological "presence" of a large group for others. Human wastes always decompose more quickly when they are dispersed (suggesting the use of catholes), but concentrating the impact lessens the chance for discovery by another party (suggesting latrines). There are many such contradictory principles involved in backcountry conservation. The decision-making process requires good outdoor leaders to be able to recognize a problem that needs resolution, collect relevant information and compare it to generalized concepts, select and carry out a course of action, and evaluate the outcomes. The process of teaching good decision making is described in detail in chapter 2 and is critical for the application of conservation practices to specific situations.

The process of teaching good judgment relative to environmental ethics is quite similar to the process of environmental values education (E.V.E.) espoused by several environmental educators. Caduto (1983) and Harshman (1979) suggest values clarification, values analysis and values change as three distinct steps in E.V.E. Thus students might be asked to take a public position on some issue (say, situations in which building a campfire is ethically sound). In the second stage, each position is examined through group discussion to assess its logic, and the desirability of its consequences. Thus, the logic of using campfires as a heat source can be questioned because of the time it takes to get a fire large enough, the inefficiency of heat transfer, and the large amount of fuel wood consumed. Opportunities for position changes are offered, and students might be asked to verbalize personal intentions either for the next day or for later trips. Knapp (1983) suggests that through E.V.E., students should (1) evaluate certain actions taken relative to the environment as either desirable or undesirable; (2) make rational decisions in resolving or alleviating environmental issues; and (3) function as members of a group in reaching a consensus on moral behavior and practice.

5. DIDACTIC COMMUNICATION OF INFORMATION THROUGH CLASSES AND BOOKS HAS A PLACE.

There is often a kind of philosophical uneasiness among instructors to engage in a didactic transfer of knowledge from teacher to learner as a valid educational strategy. While it would be foolish to think an environmental ethic (or any ethic) could be force-fed through lectures, the provision of directly relevant information not readily accessible through an immediate experience can have a place in building environmental ethics. Among the "classes" that should be considered are: a basic class in conservation practices on the shakedown; basic ecology, or the ecology of a special environment to be visited like a forest or cave; local geology; local weather; tree, wildflower, bird or other wildlife identification; resource planning and management; and environmental advocacy. We have gone so far as to take a day in the middle of a W.E.A. course to drive to Washington, D.C. and visit the Wilderness Society!

As many educators have pointed out over the years, the timing of information is critical. Interest, curiosity and motivation must be developed through direct experience before the provision of information can have maximal effect. Also, if the information is presented too late, commitments to certain values may have already crystallized and will have to be reexamined.

6. OPPORTUNITY TEACHING IS MORE CONCRETE AND SHOULD BE THE PRIMARY VEHICLE FOR BRINGING CONCEPTS TOGETHER WITH REALITIES.

Each time a campsite is selected, whether by an instructor's decision, the leader of the day's decision, or by consensus decision, the principles of campsite selection should be reviewed in relation to that site. The practice of walking straight down a deep, muddy trail in a meadow is best justified while standing in a meadow with 20 parallel trails crossing it. The nocturnal adaptations of a screech owl are best understood after one has been seen or heard.

The principle used in opportunity teaching is the same as in timing classes. When curiosity and motivation are strong, information has a better chance to be integrated into cognitive structure and associated with positive feelings. Thus, opportunity teaching is critical in building environmental ethics.

7. THOROUGH PROCESSING ENHANCES TRANSFER OF VALUES.

"Processing is an activity which is employed for the purpose of encouraging the learner to reflect, describe, analyze and communicate in some way that which was recently experienced" (Quinsland and Van Ginkel, 1984). The nonspecific and metaphoric transference of backcountry conservation practices to larger environmental ethics depends to a large degree upon reflection about the meaning of the principles and their application on the course. Processing should occur through "morning meetings," campsite "inspection" conducted by peer review, individual student-instructor interviews (perhaps at midcourse and final evaluations), personal reflection and journal writing.

Quinsland and Van Ginkel (1984) suggest that instructors begin the facilitation of a processing session low on Bloom's (1956) taxonomy of cognitive processing (like remembering the details of an experience), and try to move to cognitively complex questions (like evaluation). Bloom's taxonomy includes the following levels:

1. **Knowledge:**
   Remembering information by recognition or recall.

2. Comprehension:
Interpreting or explaining knowledge in a descriptive literal way.

3. Application:
Correct use of knowledge.

4. Analysis:
Breaking down knowledge in component parts and detecting relationships between them.

5. Synthesis:
Putting together pieces to form a whole.

6. Evaluation:
Making judgments about the value of ideas, solutions, events.

Clearly, processing environmental ethics involves dealing with specific practices at each of these levels. For example, the debriefing of an unethical campsite selection made at dusk in a storm might begin with a simple narrative of what exactly happened. As students begin to examine the reasons why certain decisions were made throughout the day, they may begin to get a bigger picture of why they were "trapped" into that site. Then they are in a position to reevaluate what should have occurred. We have found that the debriefing of lessons early in a course is best focused on lower levels of thinking, and can progressively be moved through analytical states. Late course debriefings are sometimes exclusively focused on the application of newly acquired knowledge to complex future leadership roles.

8. WHEN STUDENTS ACHIEVE A FEELING OF ONENESS WITH THE ENVIRON-MENT THROUGH A "PEAK" EXPERIENCE, THERE IS A GREAT POTENTIAL FOR EN-ERGIZING ENVIRONMENTAL VALUES.
Borden's (1985) work characterizing the personality dimensions of ecologically committed persons has pointed to peak experiences as powerful catalysts in the development of an environmental ethic. Among highly ecologically concerned persons, the energy source seems to be from within. Pleasure is derived from experiencing nature as it is and expressing abilities through demanding but intrinsically motivated activities. Borden reports that the values shift sometimes comes as a catastrophic realization with feelings of being renewed or being "at one with" the environment. Such peak experiences do happen on courses. When they occur, their potential for energizing profound changes in environmental values should not be overlooked. Again, careful progressive processing and explicit transference are critical.

9. FOLLOW-UP ACTIVITIES SPECIFIC TO ENVIRONMENTAL ETHICS SHOULD BE CONSIDERED AFTER THE COURSE ENDS.

There were many influences on a student's environmental values before his/her W.E.A. course, and there will be many after the course. Some continuous link with the values developed on the course will help the transference remain strong. Reunion trips are one alternative. They can have an environmental focus for example, wild river clean-up trips, or service projects in national forests. We have had some success with a newsletter reporting news about environmental issues and new backcountry conservation information, among other things.

In sum, the cultivation of environmental ethics in prospective outdoor leaders is an important goal for W.E.A. courses. Backcountry conservation is the primary vehicle for accomplishment of this goal, but instruction in natural history, resource management and environmental advocacy can also play roles. Careful planning and decision making, instructor modeling, formal classes, opportunity teaching, thorough debriefing and follow-up are all important techniques for maximizing the transference of wilderness lessons to future lives.

REFERENCES

Borden, R. J. (1985). Personality and ecological concern. In D. B. Gray (Ed.). *Ecological beliefs and behaviors*. Westport, CT: Greenwood Press.

Caduto, M. (1983). A review of environmental values education. *Journal of Environmental Education,* 14 (3), 13-21.

Cole, D. N. (1986). *The N.O.L.S. Backcountry Conservation Practices*. Lander, WY: National Outdoor Leadership School.

Cole, D. N. (1982). Wilderness campsite impacts: Effect of amount of use. U.S.D.A. Forest Service Intermountain Forest and Range Experiment Station Research Paper INT-284. Ogden, UT.

Cole, D. N. (1981). Managing ecological impacts at wilderness campsites: An evaluation of techniques. *Journal of Forestry,* 79 (2), 86-89.

Cole, D. N. and Benedict, J. (1983). Wilderness campsite selection. *Park Science,* 3 (4) 5-7

Gass, M. A. (1985). Programming the transfer of learning in adventure education. *Journal of Experiential Education,* 8 (3), 18-24.

Gray, D. B. (1985). *Ecological beliefs and behaviors*. Westport, CT: Greenwood Press.

Hammitt, W. E. and Cole, D. N. (1987). *Wildland recreation: Ecology and management*. New York: Wiley.

Hampton, B. and Cole, D. N. (1988). *Soft paths*. Lander, WY: National Outdoor Leadership School.

Harshman, R. (1979). Values education processes for an environmental education program. *Journal of Environmental Education,* 10, 30-34.

Knapp, C. E. (1983). A curriculum model for environmental values education. *Journal of Environmental Education*, 14 (3), 30-34.

La page, W. (1984). Financing the wilderness with user taxes or "When will the dinosaur die?" Paper presented at the conference on fees for Outdoor Recreation on Lands Open to the Public. Durham, NH

Leopold, A. (1966). *A Sand County almanac, with other essays from Round River*. New York: Oxford University Press.

Quinsland, L. K. and Van Ginkel, A. (1984). How to process experience. *Journal of Experiential Education*, 7-2), 8-13.

Shelby, B., Danley, M. S., Gibbs, K. C. and Peterson, M. E. (1982). Preferences of backpackers and river runners for allocation techniques. *Journal of Forestry*, 80, 416-419 .

Simpson, S. (1985). Short-term wilderness experiences and environmental ethics. *Journal of Experiential Education*, 8 (3), 25- 28 .

Stankey, G. H. and Baden, J. (1977). Rationing wilderness use: methods, problems and guidelines. Research paper INT-192. Ogden, UT: U.S.D.A. Forest Service, Intermountain Forest and Range Experiment Station.

Viles, C. and Cockrell, D. (1985). The National Outdoor Leadership School Conservation Practices: Suggested Revisions Based on a Review of Literature on Environmental Impacts from Outdoor Recreation. Virginia Tech Division of Health, Physical Education and Recreation, Blacksburg, VA.

Wagar, J. V. K. (1940). Certified outdoorsmen. *American Forests*, 46, 490-492.

Young, A. B. (1985). Leave wilderness alone. *Camping Magazine*, 57 (6), 14-15, 35.

5.
BASIC WILDERNESS SKILLS

by Jack Drury
and Bruce Bonney
North Country Community College
and David Cockrell
University of Southern Colorado

W.E.A. courses have appealed to people with a broad range of outdoor skills. Some students arrive for their course bringing years of outdoor leadership experience, seeking simply to fine tune their teaching skills. Others have never lifted a pack. The basic wilderness skills curriculum quickly becomes a common denominator for several reasons. First, before a student can legitimately consider assuming leadership responsibilities for others, he must be confident in his own ability to take care of himself in the wilderness environment. Thus, these skills are practiced to mastery by everyone on a course. Basic wilderness living and travel involve knowledge of certain principles that are taught explicitly as part of the course curriculum, but it also involves judgment decisions based on these principles. Clothing selection, navigation and campsite selection therefore serve as forums for examining the quality of decision processes. Finally, because some students have already mastered certain basic skills, this area of the curriculum provides opportunities for peer instruction and feedback on teaching techniques. Wilderness skills taught on a national standard course can be grouped into three general areas:

1. Clothing and equipment selection

2. Backcountry travel
   Backpacking
   Trail techniques
   Navigation

3. Basic camping skills
   Campsite selection
   Health and sanitation

Most of the basic skills summarized in this chapter were not developed by W.E.A. and have been explained in detail in a number of other works. References that we have found particularly useful include Colin Fletcher's (1974) *The New Complete Walker*, Manning's (1975) *Backpacking: One Step at a Time*, and Peters's (1982) *Mountaineering: The Freedom of the Hills*. Of course, Petzoldt (1984) and Simer and Sullivan (1983) are also important sources. All of these works devote several chapters to basic wilderness skills and are regarded as prerequisite reading for W.E.A. instructors. As always, W.E.A.'s most important contribution and the focus of this chapter is on the whys behind the various practices and the strategies for teaching them.

Clothing Selection and Use

CLOTHING FUNCTIONS

Outdoor clothing must perform several essential functions. Foremost, it assists the body in retaining heat when external temperatures are cool and the body is inactive, but it must also permit heat to be dissipated when there is an excess. Clothing must also allow water vapor produced by the body to evaporate into the atmosphere without unnecessary or prolonged evaporative cooling. Finally, clothing must protect the wearer from skin injuries in the backcountry such as sunburn, abrasion, insect bites, poisonous plants, briars, etc.

Several principles can be formulated that guide the clothing selection process for an outdoor experience and maximize the effectiveness with which clothing performs its essential functions. First, some of the clothing selected must keep the wearer warm. As is summarized in Table 5-1, heat is lost from the body in five ways. It is radiated from the body in the form of infrared radiation. It is lost through convection as the air immediately adjacent to the body is warmed and then disturbed by wind. It is similarly lost through respiration as cool air is taken into the lungs, warmed and then exhaled. Heat loss also occurs by conduction when the body comes in direct contact with some cooler surface, such as the ground, cold pots, snow, rocks, etc. And finally, heat is lost when moisture on the body's surface evaporates —an exothermic chemical reaction. Because an active hiker or climber can sweat four to six liters of perspiration in a day, evaporative heat loss has special implications for clothing selection.

In order to prevent radiation and conduction, some clothing articles must be capable of providing the wearer with "insulation": a thermal barrier of trapped dead air space that conducts heat away from the body as slowly as possible. Because the body, and sometimes the sky, are continuously exposing insulating clothing to moisture, it is a valuable asset for clothing to insulate even when it is wet.

A second fundamental principle is to select clothing that keeps the wearer dry. Clothes should allow the wearer to ventilate excess body moisture during periods of vigorous muscular activity so as to avoid saturation by sweat. Garments should have plentiful and easily accessible zippers, buttons or velcro tabs to facilitate ventilation. Inner layers should be of materials that absorb minimal amounts of moisture, but rather "wick" the moisture away from the skin. Middle insulating layers should "breathe" easily, allowing for the passage of body moisture. Protective layers of outer clothing should repel precipitation so that it does not soak through to the inner layers of insulation. They must also stop the wind to protect the wearer from convection heat loss, and allow ventilation to minimize evaporative heat loss. Finally, all layers of clothing should dry rapidly, preferably from body heat alone.

Table 5-1
Mechanisms for Body Heat Loss and Its Prevention

Types of Heat Loss	Methods of Prevention
Radiation	Insulation: Hats, coats, sweaters
Convection	Wind gear
Respiration	Moderate pace, balaclavas, coats with large hoods
Conduction	Insulation: Gloves, mittens, foam sleeping pads
Evaporation	Moderate pace, ventilation

Outdoor clothing should facilitate the activities the wearer performs. Clothes should allow complete freedom of movement and must not hinder blood circulation. Inner garments should be easy to launder. Outer garments should have large pockets, conveniently located that can be securely fastened. Clothing should not have extra decorations or attachments that may break or tear, compromising the function of the garment.

Finally, clothing selected should be dependable and versatile. Stitching, zippers and buttons must be strong. External layers should be of heavy-weight fabric with reinforcements in high wear areas such as knees, elbows and seat. Garments should most often be selected so that they can be "layered" with others to meet the demands of varying situations most efficiently. Each item should also be capable of multiple uses (shorts doubling as swim suit or long john top as a nightshirt). And, of course, clothing should be light weight and compressible to minimize space occupied in the pack.

CLOTHING MATERIALS AND THEIR CHARACTERISTICS

There are several fabrics that are widely recognized as effective in meeting the demands of outdoor clothing. These are discussed in detail elsewhere (e.g., Simer and Sullivan, 1983) and will only be summarized and updated here. Wool is traditionally the most common insulating material found in the backcountry. The wool fiber itself contains lanolin and absorbs relatively little water. Wool fibers are rough and uneven and therefore also trap dead air space for insulation nicely. Body heat will tend to push moisture through the wool in a gaseous state where it either escapes (from a thin garment) or condenses in the outer layers (on a heavy garment). Thus wool only loses about half its insulating ability when it is wet (Forgey, 1986). Moreover, it is often inexpensive and can be reasonably tough and wind resistant when it is tightly woven. Its disadvantages are its itchiness to tender skin as an inner layer and its weight as a thick insulator. It is our opinion that wool still competes well for medium-weight pants, sweaters and shirts, and for hats, gloves and mittens.

For lightweight inner layers, the synthetic fiber polypropylene has competed favorably with wool since the late 1970s. It absorbs even less water in the fiber than wool, wicks the water away more effectively because the fibers are more uniform, and does not irritate the skin. However, polypro tends to shrink and "pill" when it is laundered (fibers separate and form balls on the fabric surface). Also, the fabric holds body odors tenaciously. As of this writing (1991), the current crop of polyester fabrics, such as Thermax and Capilene, appear more durable and washable without sacrificing the advantages of polypropylene.

For heavier insulating layers, polyester piles also have some advantages over wool. The primary one is weight. Pile fabrics offer the same insulation value for half the weight of wool (Simer and Sullivan, 1983). As with wool, water is wicked along the outsides of the fibers to the outer layers, and the garment retains much of its insulating value even when wet. There are currently a variety of weights (Polarpile, Polarplus, Polarlite, etc.), and one company has experimented with laminating a 20 ounces composite pile to a Capilene liner for added comfort and warmth. One problem with pile has been its susceptibility to abrasion damage, although most applications now include nylon reinforcements in critical places. Expense continues to be an ongoing disadvantage for all the synthetic insulators, especially in outfitting organized outdoor programs like W.E.A. courses.

Cotton plays a role in outdoor clothing because of its comfort and durability. Cotton fibers absorb and hold water for long periods of time, however, so its use is limited to lightweight fabrics in warm-weather climates.

The choices for fills in heavy-weight insulators at the time of this writing include down, Celanese Corporation's Polarguard, Dupont's Hollofil and Quallofil, and 3M's Thinsulate. Down's light weight and compressibility have always made it a tempting choice, but it provides no insulation when it is wet. The cost of down is again a factor in outfitting programs. Down should probably be avoided any time cold, wet weather is anticipated.

Nylon is the primary fabric used in outer layers to protect the insulation from wind and moisture. As with other synthetics, it is available in a number of different forms: taffeta; lycra for stretchability; ripstop for tear-resistance with light weight; and cordura for abrasion resistance. A 60% to 40% (or 65/35) blend of cotton or polyester and nylon has been popular for years as wind and light rain gear. This blend provides good wind protection, and it is durable. However, it should not be regarded as rain gear under any circumstances, and it can stay wet or frozen for long periods after a soaking.

A primary decision in the selection of foul-weather gear is the choice of a coated waterproof material or a breathable/waterproof material such as Goretex. Goretex, the most popular of the breathable/waterproof fabrics, consists of a porous Teflon-like film laminated between inner and outer layers of nylon. The pores are large enough to permit water vapor molecules to pass, thus permitting perspiration to escape, but too small for water droplets to enter. Goretex has been a clear advance in addressing the dilemma of breathability versus rain protection, and most high-quality backcountry storm parkas are now made with Goretex. The choice of Goretex storm gear eliminates the need for separate wind and rain gear. It does, however, have some drawbacks. Soiling of the Goretex layer will reduce its breathability, but special care must also be taken in laundering. The Goretex layer itself is quite thin and fragile. Its durability is dependent on quality lamination, construction and care. It has been our experience that the garment will not remain waterproof as long as a coated garment. As a result of the care needed in construction, Goretex gear also tends to be quite expensive. Because of these drawbacks, several state-of-the-art manufacturers have recently gone back to producing coated, waterproof storm gear with a renewed emphasis on imaginative ventilation systems.

Table 5-2 summarizes items typically listed in a W.E.A. course clothing list for spring, summer, or fall in temperate climates. Judgment must dictate modifications necessary for specific climates and terrains, of course.

Table 5-2:
Typical W.E.A. Course Clothing List

1.   One pair cotton-polyester boxer shorts—light weight, abrasion, re-sistant easy to launder, prevent chafing between legs.

2.   One polypropylene, Capilene or thermax long underwear top serves as pajama top, cool-weather inner insulation layer.

3.   One or two long-sleeve cotton-polyester light-weave dress shirt—dry fast, protect against insects, warm-weather garment, should have button breast pockets.

4.   One long underwear bottom; Capilene, thermax or polypro-wool blend—optional for people who sleep or hike cold.

5.   One pair wool trousers—100% wool or poly-wool blend military trousers. Should have smooth finish. Fit slightly large in the waist for freedom of movement and tucking in wool sweaters or shirts.

6.   One gym nylon shorts—loose fit for comfort while walking. Nylon shorts can double as swim trunks and underwear.

7.   One heavy C.P.O.-type wool or pile shirt—should be long in torso. Ideally should not have cotton neck or wrist lining. Should ideally have breast pockets. Button or snap full-front closures.

8.   One to two sweaters—wool, pile or bunting

9.   One rain parka or cagoule—Goretex or coated nylon. Should extend to crotch and have ample ventilation. Hooded parkas are a matter of choice since hoods can restrict visibility and hearing.

10.   One nylon wind parka—shirt should be light weight and roomy enough to wear sweaters underneath; pockets are convenient. Good for warm, "buggy" weather. Goretex parka good for both wind and rain.

11.   One pair breathable nylon wind pants—protects legs from wind chill and insects. Can be layered over wool pants or worn over undershorts in warm weather. Drawstring closure at waist makes for easy access. Zippers at bottom of legs helpful for putting on over boots. Pockets are very useful.

12.   One wool watch cap or balaclava—insulates head; must cover ears and back of neck.

13.   One wool liner gloves—keep hands warm while working.

14.   One wool mittens—layer over gloves in cold weather.

15.   One cotton work gloves—use around fire to protect hands from drying heat; also use as pot holders.

16.   One wide-brim felt hat or baseball cap—wide brim keeps rain out of eyes and off neck; keeps sun out of eyes.

17.   Bandannas—several extra large cotton-polyester handkerchiefs; multitude of uses.

18.   One belt—should be made of thin material, preferably nylon webbing. Leather and cotton webbing will absorb sweat and mildew. Material should be thin so as not to chafe hips when worn under padded hip belt of pack.

19.   One pair of sunglasses with effective infrared and ultraviolet filters —essential for withstanding glare off sand, water, or ice.
20.   Four to five pairs socks—should be medium-heavy wool rag type socks. Socks should extend well above boot top to area of calf. Two pairs of socks should normally be worn with boots to minimize blisters.
Should always have an extra set of dry socks along on trail or day hikes.
21.   Sneakers—lightweight, nylon fabric sneaker good for camp alternative to wearing boots all day; must fit with heavy wool socks.

FOOT WEAR
Several principles concerning foot wear are important to mention. Multiple layers of socks help to minimize friction, and two pairs worn at once usually maximize this benefit without constricting circulation. Medium-heavy rag wool or wool-blend socks provide relatively soft fibers and maximize warmth. A popular current combination is one pair of rag wool socks worn over a lightweight polypropylene liner.

Boot selection is often a major issue for W.E.A. students, and the progression of advance in boot construction technology makes the issue an ever-changing one. In general, the weight of boot selected should depend on the ruggedness of terrain traveled and the weight of the pack. Easy trails and light packs call for lighter-weight boots. Big packs and rough trails require boots of sturdier construction. Boots must support the ankle and protect the sole of the foot. Heavy, full leather boots with several midsoles will clearly maximize ankle and foot support in rugged terrain. However, there are currently many boot/running shoe hybrids that provide considerable support at a fraction of the weight. These "new generation" boots mix leather reinforcements with cordura or Goretex uppers, and layer closed-cell foam midsoles of varying stiffness to cushion and support the sole.

Boot selection is largely a matter of personal comfort, but the boots should fit the packer's feet comfortably when wearing two pairs of hiking socks, even allowing for foot expansion late in the day under heavy loads. Toes should always have enough room to wiggle and should not touch the front of the boot when it is scuffed against a solid object. A little heel lift is normal, but the hiker should not feel like he/she is stepping out of the boot.

INSTRUCTIONAL PROCESS
For a W.E.A. course, much of the clothing selection information must be communicated to students before the course begins. Some affiliate universities teach this material in the classroom prior to the National Standard Course. Others communicate through detailed, annotated equipment lists or precourse orientations. Careful communications of the concepts are a highlight of the first day of the course as gear is being issued. This can occur through a formal class and through individual tutorials. Subsequent classes in the field on clothing and equipment selection can serve to recapitulate the principles after their usefulness has become clear. These classes can be

taught as demonstrations or open seminars, often coordinated by knowledgeable students. Thus, they also serve as forums for demonstrations of imaginative teaching styles and for giving and receiving feedback on teaching techniques.

Equipment Selection and Use

The environments in which W.E.A. courses have been taught are quite varied: from Alaska to the Gila Wilderness of New Mexico; from Newfoundland to North Carolina. Travel modes vary as widely. It would not be consistent with this book's objectives to detail the technical specifications and debates about the innumerable items of outdoor equipment potentially applicable to courses. Only packs, sleeping bags and stoves will be addressed here, as they seem common denominators for all courses. Cook gear is addressed in some detail in the following chapter. It is assumed that W.E.A. instructors would supplement this curriculum area with information from various guides and manufacturer's specifications for equipment specific to their courses.

PACKS AND PACKING

Perhaps the most prominent issue that faces any wilderness traveler concerning packs is the choice of an internal versus an external frame pack. The "frame" of an internal frame pack usually consists of two flat malleable aluminum stays inserted into sewn sleeves in the packsack itself. External frames are rigid welded aluminum, magnesium alloy or plastic frames with separate packsacks attached to them by clevis pins. There are, of course, many different designs and styles of each. See any of the references mentioned at the beginning of this chapter for more complete descriptions.

There are advantages and disadvantages to each style. Internal frame packs almost always provide a more sensitive mechanism for securing the pack's weight close to the body. By design, they flex and move as the packer moves. These features provide a more natural balance, especially important for skiing, climbing, traversing talus slopes or other difficult terrain. Internal frame packs often are more adjustable and can therefore be fitted quite well to any size and shape of the packer.

A rigid external frame, on the other hand, can be an excellent crutch for huge punishing loads (greater than, say, 60 pounds). The rigid frame seems to help stabilize the heavy load and can allow greater control in distributing it between shoulders and hips. Also, while internal and external frame packs are available in equivalent volume capacities, external frame packs tend to be easier to pack in a balanced way. They are also more convenient for modular packing: strapping on tents, food sacks and sleeping bags externally. Finally, some packers who sweat profusely find they can ventilate better and stay cooler with an external frame pack. As usual, the selection of a pack, either for an individual or a program, is a matter of judgment: applying general principles in a specific application to maximize efficiency.

To teach pack packing on a W.E.A. course, we have coined the term "conveniently balanced system" (C.B.S.) This acronym can be used to remind students of the basic considerations in efficient pack packing. A pack that is conveniently organized so as to permit access to its contents as needed greatly enhances the efficient use of time and energy for its wearer. The itinerary for the day should be considered when packing a pack, and the arrangement of equipment in the pack should reflect the probability of equipment use during the day. External pockets should hold items that are predicted to be most frequently needed because of terrain, weather, etc. Items that may be needed quickly for safety or other reasons should be packed in known areas of easy access. Such items might include the first aid kit, repair kit, water purification system, rain fly, etc. Items of gear such as sleeping bags, eyeglasses or cameras, requiring protection should be packed in special waterproof bags.

A pack that is well balanced with proper distribution of weight throughout the pack adds to the comfort and safety of the wearer. Heavy loads are most comfortably carried when the weight is placed directly in line with the largest and strongest bones and muscles of the body: the pelvic girdle, the upper thigh bones, and the muscles of the thighs and buttocks. Thus the heaviest part of the pack should usually be centered as close to the body and as near to the top of the spinal column as possible. Heavy loads are most comfortable when they are balanced left to right, top to bottom, and front to back.

The terrain over which the hiker will pass during the day should also influence the way weight is distributed in the pack. For flat, easily traveled terrain, the pack may be packed for maximum comfort with the center of gravity near the shoulders and close to the body. However, for rough terrain, steep inclines, talus hopping, river crossing, etc., the center of gravity should be lower to improve balance.

A pack that is organized according to an efficient and consistently maintained system speeds the process of daily packing and makes it easier to find things. Individual items of equipment should be grouped together and packed in a series of stuff sacks. For example, one might have a toilet kit, clothes bag, food bag, personal repair kit, "night" bag, etc. Packers should strive to keep their packs streamlined and neat. All items of equipment should be placed inside the pack bag and its pockets securely lashed to the pack frame to avoid annoying losses on the trail. No odds and ends should be tied on or protrude from the pack sack. Tent poles, ice axes or other long items should be lashed along the vertical line of the pack to prevent their becoming impediments to progress through narrow passages.

SLEEPING BAGS

The debates concerning expeditionary sleeping bags reach their truly feverish pitch only in extremes of cold, wet conditions. For any long trip, however, a sleeping bag should be chosen with the attention to the basic issues of warmth, weight, comfort and expense. The "three-season" bag is a middle- weight bag often appropriate for W.E.A. courses and will be the focus of attention here. Three-season bags are often "rated" to temperature levels of 0°-20° Fahrenheit. with an average "loft" (the thickness of the top layer of the bag) of four to six inches. The accuracy of sleeping-bag temperature ratings varies widely across individuals, however, and should be used as a comparative measure only.

As always, there are trade-offs. The four popular insulators at the time of this writing are goose down, Polarguard, Hollofil and Quallofill. Down is light in weight (625 to 700 cubic inches of excellent trapped, dead air space per ounce), highly compressible, expensive and worthless when wet. Some state-of-the-art three-season down bags currently have an outer shell of Goretex which significantly ameliorates the problem of loft reduction from moisture. Unfortunately, Goretex further increases the expense. The Goretex shell also only protects the down from outside moisture. Some of the water vapor given off by a person sleeping in the bag will pass through the Goretex, but not all of it. A vapor barrier liner should be used inside the bag to be truly effective. During periods of extended rain, snow, or high humidity on a long trip, the bag will eventually become somewhat wet. With care, this problem is usually not fatal, but it is a disadvantage.

The synthetic insulators are comparatively heavy and bulky, relatively inexpensive, and reasonably warm and comfortable when wet. A three-season Polarguard or Hollofil bag now weighs 3-1/2 to 4-1/2 pounds., while a comparably rated down bag weighs a full pound less. More importantly, the down bag will stuff 25% to 30% smaller than the synthetic bag. Quallofill is a bit lighter and more compressible than the other synthetics but is still no match for down. One must weigh each of the above factors in selecting a personal bag for a specific application. In our experience, price, durability, ease of washing and utility in wet weather usually outweigh the disadvantages of weight and bulk in purchasing bags for an outdoor program like W.E.A.

STOVE SELECTION AND OPERATION

The issues in stove selection are heat output (measured in B.T.U.s or minutes required to boil a quart of water), burn time for the supplied or integral fuel tank, reliability in cold weather or at elevation, durability, weight and convenience. In our experience, stoves fueled with propane or butane are not a good choice for long programs like W.E.A. They do not function well in cold weather, and the fuel canisters are awkward to pack both before and after they are used.

For multifuel or white-gas stoves used on expeditions, we believe the stove should have a boil time of four and one half to five minutes or better, a burn time of at least an hour and weigh no more than about two pounds. Further, the stove should have a broad, stable base, a pump to maintain fuel pressure, and a minimum of working parts.

Operating the stove is probably the second most dangerous activity on a W.E.A. course (next to driving to the trailhead), and a few basic precautions about stove operation are an important part of the curriculum. First, stoves should be regarded as the primary heat source for cooking, rather than a backup for campfires. In most locations, impact to and number of campsites, firewood scarcity, or slow tree growth will preclude the use of a campfire. If there is any doubt about the severity of impact associated with a campfire, a stove should be used.

The stove site selected should be level, stable and protected from wind or highly flammable vegetation. Cooking in tents is not advisable unless there is truly no other option, and a stove should never be started inside a tent. The stove should be filled with fuel away from the cook site. Lids to both the fuel bottle and the stove fuel tank should be thought of as precision tools. They play critical roles and only require a little care to perform well.

The stove should be started and operated according to manufacturer's instructions. There should be some forethought to the possibility of a malfunction and flare-up. An empty billy can is a handy tool for smothering a flare-up. Water will only spread the flame. When the stove is turned off, it should be cooled before packing, and the pressure released from the fuel tank. Stoves should be packed upright to minimize the possibility of leakage, and they should be separated from food. A stove stuff sack is convenient for protecting the stove and containing leaks.

INSTRUCTIONAL PROCESS

Pack selection and packing should be taught very early in a course, preferably before the first full day on the trail. The lesson may be taught as a lecture/demonstration in which the instructor displays all his/her own gear, describes his/her system and proceeds to pack his/her pack explaining the reasons for what he/she is doing. An experienced student might assist or even teach this session.

Sleeping bags, tents, and specialized items of equipment are often addressed later in a course, using a seminar format. This session makes a good rainy-day activity.

Stove selection, operation and maintenance are usually taught the first morning in the field before breakfast. Students bring stoves and fuel bottles to the class. This class may be taught in conjunction with the first cooking class so students can immediately put their knowledge into practice.

Teaching Trail Techniques

W.E.A. trail techniques closely follow the approach developed by Paul Petzoldt at N.O.L.S. They are now widely recognized and will only be summarized here with an emphasis on teaching strategies.

The concept of energy conservation underlies many of Petzoldt's trail techniques. A task should be accomplished quickly and efficiently expending as little as possible. This is important to minimize changes in body temperature and heart rate so as to maximize the chances of accomplishing an objective without exhaustion and frustration. Key components in the philosophy of energy conservation include rhythmic breathing, setting a pace, using the rest step and following a time-control plan.

Rhythmic breathing is the synchronization of a person's step and breathing. As the terrain gets steeper, the load heavier or the oxygen thinner, the hiker shortens his step length and increases the number of breaths between steps. Pace is one of the most difficult things for a leader or scout to master. The tendency is to hike too fast, tiring oneself or one's weaker party members. Exhibiting patience and the ability to hike at a pace appropriate for the whole group is a sign of a good leader. The rest step is the practice of resting one's skeletal structure with a locked knee in between steps. Every step should attempt to minimize muscle exertion.

Time-control plans have as their objective resting to prevent exhaustion rather than because of exhaustion. Depending on such factors as the group's physical condition, trip objectives and the hiking terrain, hiking times and resting times range from hiking 20 minutes and resting 10 (20/10) to hiking an hour and resting five minutes (60/5). It is important to agree to a plan at the beginning of a hike and attempt to stick to it. The plan then gives weaker members of the group a goal to work toward and something to look forward to. One person (the logger) may be designated to keep time and select the location and time of the break. Flexibility is important in keeping the hike enjoyable, but structure is too. Weak hikers will often suffer rather than slow the group down unless there is a structured mechanism for their needs to be considered.

There are, of course, many important little tips for increasing efficiency and enjoyment on the trail. Many of these are summarized in Drury's lesson plans, which accompany this book. Hiking group organization is one important consideration. So as not to excessively intrude on the wilderness experience of others, hiking groups should be four to six people at most (see chapter 4). Four is a minimum number for safe wilderness travel, especially in winter.

A useful way to organize this small hiking party is to assign members the roles of scout, smoother, logger and sweep. The scout sets the pace, hikes in the front and determines the route to be taken. In off-trail travel, the smoother hikes second in line and attempts to improve on the route selected by the scout. In off-trial orienteering the scout and smoother may flip flop roles as one becomes a sighting point for the compass bearer while the other forges ahead.

The logger keeps track of the time-control plan and coordinates the breaks. The logger should keep a (written) log of the day's activities and give an account of the trip at the day's debriefing. The sweep is the last person in line. He/she is responsible for making sure the pace is appropriate, no one is suffering, and the group is not becoming too spread out. To be effective, the sweep will need to be in communication with the scout. A course instructor or hiking group leader may hike anywhere in the group. This person has overall decision-making authority and may coordinate such activities as campsite selection, monitoring individual progress, or any other function most appropriately centralized in the leader.

INSTRUCTIONAL STRATEGIES

The time-control plan should be an actual estimation of how long it will take to reach the planned destination given the planned hiking/resting times. It is recommended that students write individual time-control plans on a regular basis and submit them to the leader of the day. At the next debriefing the time-control plans can be compared to the logger's report. This activity allows students to start creating an experience base by which they can estimate how long a given trip will take. The activity can actually be turned into a game, with a prize awarded to the individual with the most accurate time-control plan.

A supplementary exercise is to assign one student the responsibility each morning of counting the contour lines on a topographic map (both up and down) that will be traversed on the day's route. This activity has two values. It develops map-reading skills, and it stresses the role elevation change has in the time it takes to get to the group's destination.

Teaching Navigation

Navigation with map and compass in a wilderness environment is another set of skills that W.E.A. instructors are presumed to have. The concepts and skills are addressed by Kjellstrom (1976) and are regarded as prerequisite to this discussion. Teaching navigation is another skill entirely, however, and W.E.A. instructors have developed a fairly standard sequence that may make a confusing curriculum area a bit more manageable. There are four essential components to be addressed: reading and using topographic maps; reading and using compasses; combining the map and compass to select and follow a route; and combining the map and compass to locate one's current position.

Basic map skills addressed in the introductory component should include the following:

Background and sources of topographic maps

Map margin information

Scales and series

Cultural symbols

Water symbols

Map directions, including declination

Contour lines

Benchmarks

Map folding

Early map skills can be developed along the trail and during breaks. One standard U.S. Geological Survey topographic map or its equivalent should be provided for every two students at the least. Calling attention to prominent topographic features and then locating them on the map arouses student interest, introduces map terminology, and encourages students to become more aware of their natural surroundings. Asking students to predict upcoming terrain features encourages them to continue map use on the trail. Asking students to measure distance traveled encourages awareness of map scale and builds a base of experience for later time-control plan development.

Formalized map class may be a combination of lecture and discussion depending upon the extent of student knowledge. In general, the class should focus on a general overview of all map features and their identification on sample maps. Instructors may ask students to conduct a theoretical journey across the map and describe the identifiable map features, obstacles, or land forms that they will encounter on the way.

More advanced map skills are best developed in practice on a bushwack (off-trail hike), where students must concentrate on observing terrain features in order to follow their progress on their maps. Treeless mountain tops make excellent classroom sites for understanding contouring, distance and terrain changes over time. Ask students to orient their maps without the use of their compass—use opportunity to identify prominent land features.

Basic compass skills should include the following:

Concepts of "direction" and degrees

Parts of the orienteering compass

The function of a compass

Taking and following a field bearing.

Introduction to the compass can start while on the trail by simple exercises to establish the general direction of travel along trail, the location of north, etc. Compass parts terminology may also be introduced during breaks.

Early formal classes on the compass should combine lecture demonstration with an immediate opportunity for practice. Following instruction in the technique of establishing field bearings, students should immediately apply this knowledge in the surrounding environment by taking bearings on various easily visible landmarks. Once students have gained confidence in taking bearings, a short compass course or simple bushwack may be in order to allow students to practice following a bearing in the field. Special care should be taken to ensure that the bushwack or compass course area is completely "safe" in the sense that disoriented students cannot get lost. Students should be teamed up so that route determination is a group effort. This allows for mutual teaching, reinforcement, and confidence.

Once an individual has gained experience with maps and compasses separately, the two skills can be combined to maximize their potential. It is im-

Figure 5-1

portant to stress the danger of over-reliance on one or the other. A person shouldn't blindly follow a bearing that takes him/her through swamps and up cliffs when an easier route is nearby. Neither should the traveler follow an easy trail that doesn't take him/her where he/she wants to go. Skills involving combination of the map and compass include:

Taking a map bearing

Incorporating the angle of declination into a map bearing

Orienting a map with the compass

Route finding

The teaching of the concept of declination should inspire especially creative efforts on the part of the instructors. Since this concept is difficult for some students to grasp, instructors should be prepared to use a number of approaches to illustrate the same idea. Visual aids (diagrams) and props (colored shoe strings representing true north, magnetic north, and line of travel) may be employed to help students visualize the concept in different ways. Mnemonic devices may be used to help students remember how to convert map bearings to field bearings.

As confidence builds, students should be encouraged to plan and execute progressively more difficult off-trail hikes. Planning sessions for the trips should include instruction and discussion of each of the following:

(a) Terrain considerations in route planning

(b) Identification of potential "hand rails,"

i.e., natural features that help guide hikers
    (c) Altitude loss or gain—counting contour lines
    (d) Distance estimations
    (e) Development of time-control plan

Students might be asked to submit written estimates/predictions for each area of concern. These can then be compared to the experience on the trail at debriefing to help build a basis of knowledge.

The final lesson in this curriculum sequence is triangulation, the process of locating an unknown point by the use of intersecting bearings taken on three known points. This is an advanced map and compass technique and should be taught after participants have some degree of familiarity with both map and compass. Triangulation is best taught on treeless mountain tops or at least in areas of open visibility where clearly distinguishable land marks can be seen. Students might well triangulate an already known (present) location for practice. Then, bearings provided by an instructor may be used to identify a hypothetical "unknown" location on the map. Students should attempt to locate their approximate position at some convenient time on a bushwack using triangulation.

Basic Camping Skills

There are numerous skills associated with safe, comfortable camping in the wilderness environment. Among those that the W.E.A. instructor should expect to know and teach are the following:

    Campsite selection
    Tentsite selection
    Tent and fly pitching
    Breaking camp
    Water purification
    Personal hygiene
    Food waste disposal
    Latrine construction
    Firepit construction and restoration
    Fire building
    Knots
    Food protection
    Weather prediction in the field.

These skills are described by the references listed at the beginning of this chapter, and lesson plans are provided by Drury (1991). Environmental issues pertaining to camping practices are addressed in chapter 4. A few more technical points are offered here on water purification and fire building that might enrich the teaching of these issues in the field.

WATER PURIFICATION

The need and techniques for backcountry water treatment are a growing concern. The issues are technical, but there is fortunately a fairly simple, reliable procedure for assuring safety. Waterborne diseases to which one is exposed in North American backcountry include salmonella infections, amoebic dysentery, giardiasis and infectious hepatitis, among others.

Much concern has been raised in recent years about backcountry exposures to intestinal parasites of the genus *Giardia*, *G. lamblia* in particular. In a study of humans, domestic animals and wildlife as vectors (carriers) of *Giardia*, Suk, Riggs and Nelson (1986) studied 60 stream sites over a 220-mile area in the California Sierras. *Giardia* cysts (the dormant stage of *Giardia*'s life cycle, which can survive for years in the environment) were found in 27 of 78 backcountry water samples. Forty-five percent of the streams receiving heavy human use were contaminated, while only 17% of the lightly used streams were contaminated. *Giardia* was detected in 8.4% of the 309 cattle stool samples collected, and in 10.8% of 731 wild mammal stool samples. Mammalian species identified as vectors included coyotes and a variety of rodents. *Giardia* is transmitted through contact with contaminated feces or when contaminated feces enter into water sources. Unfortunately, current research is indicating that fecal matter, including *Giardia* cysts, decompose much more slowly than originally thought. Thus, feces deposited anywhere near a lake or stream are likely to become contaminants eventually. Watersheds receiving appreciable use by humans, domestic animals or wide-ranging canine species or rodents should be considered suspect.

There are three primary techniques for killing amoebic cysts and enteroviruses, the most resistant pathogenic microorganisms in water. First, you can boil it. Temperatures of 100 degrees Celsius will kill *Giardia* (Suk, n.d.). At elevations higher than 10,000 feet water should be boiled at least two or three minutes to be certain that it reaches this temperature.

Second, you can pass the water through a filter. Unfortunately, the pore sizes of a filter effective against *Giardia* must be so small that a pump is required to force the water through. There are a number of effective filters commercially available, but they continue to be fairly expensive.

Probably the most convenient method of purifying water is to treat it with a chlorine-based chemical (Halizone) or iodine. The effectiveness of Halizone is tenuous. If the pH of the water is seven or lower, chlorine combines with oxygen in the water to produce hypochlorous acid, an effective germicide. However, if the pH is higher than seven, the chlorine hydrolizes to hypochlorite, which is much less effective. If there is considerable organic material or pollution in the water, hypochlorous acid is quickly converted to the relatively ineffective monochloramine (Kahn and Visscher, 1977). Thus, depending on Halizone can be much like playing Russian roulette.

The method recommended by Kahn and Visscher seems the most reliable and simple. They suggest carrying four to eight grams of crystalline iodine in a one ounce clear glass bottle with a 2.5 cc leak-proof cap. To disinfect water, the bottle is first filled itself, recapped and shaken vigorously for one minute. This produces a near-saturated iodine solution that is then added to the drinking water to achieve a final concentration of four parts per million iodine. The crystals are not used directly. The amount of saturated iodine solution needed varies with the temperature according to the guidelines in Table 5-3, below, reproduced from Kahn and Visscher (1977). These quantities assume a contact time of 15 minutes before drinking. If the wilderness traveler is willing to wait 40 minutes before drinking, the quantities added may be reduced by 500%, greatly enhancing palatability. Thus, water temperature and wait time are the critical variables. The same iodine crystals may be reused 1000 times for this process, and they have an unlimited shelf life. Effectiveness is not affected by pH level or organic content in the water. The bottle and iodine crystals are now available commercially from a number of outfitters, as are measured iodine tablets for direct application to water.

Table 5-3
Volume of Near-saturated Iodine Solution Needed to Yield a 4 ppm Concentration in 1 Liter of Water at Various Temperatures

Temperature	Volume Needed	ppm at Near Saturation	Capfuls to Add
3C (37F)	20.0 cc	200	8
20C (68F)	13.0 cc	300	5+
25C (77F)	12.5 cc	320	5
40C (104F)	10.0 cc	400	4

FIRE BUILDING
As with the other skills addressed in this chapter, there are a few little technical concepts about building a campfire that can greatly enhance one's effectiveness and understanding. Petzoldt always explained these concepts on courses as a part of fire-building classes. Explaining the reason behind every action is the essence of teaching judgment and quality decisions in the field. In an early draft chapter on judgment written in 1981 for the *New Wilderness Handbook*, Petzoldt outlined the principles of successful fire building. We close this chapter on basic wilderness skills with a selection from that essay, both to share Petzoldt's teachings and to remind the reader that quality judgment and decision making permit the successful use of basic skills in the wilderness environment.

The Quality Judgment Method

Tell (explain) and demonstrate how to gather small, dry, burnable material, how to lay the fire, how to light the fire, etc., etc., etc., etc.

In addition to the above, the instructor is explaining and demonstrating the reason for each action, each decision and how those actions and decisions promote the accomplishment of the desired goals of the educational program.

Let us give an example of one way the above could be accomplished.

GATHERING SMALL MATERIAL TO START A FIRE.

Why is small material necessary? Most students will answer because "it starts easier." Be sure they know why "it starts easier." The flame of the match does not start the fire. The heat from the flame starts the fire. The burnable material must reach a certain temperature before it will ignite. If the piece of burnable material is too large (has too much volume in relation to its surface), the cool interior of the material keeps absorbing the heat from the match so the surface of the material cannot reach the combustible temperature. Even if the surface starts to burn while the match flame is active the fire may go out as soon as the match flame goes out because the cool interior cools the exterior below the combustible temperature. In small, dry burnable material the surface area is large in comparison to the volume of the interior of the material. This surface can then reach the combustible or igniting temperature before the match is used up. The above can be illustrated.

Now the student has judgment as to why small burnable material is necessary—or large surfaces compared to volume such as twigs, paper, grass, etc., etc., etc.

USING DRY MATERIAL TO START A FIRE

In our (previous) memorization and demonstration methods we said the material needed to be small and dry. Why dry? Of course, the answer is that "it starts easier." Why does it start easier?

Material will not burn when it is wet because the water in the material cannot be heated beyond the boiling temperature (212 degrees Fahrenheit at sea level). This is below the combustible temperature of our material. However, when the water in the material reaches the boiling temperature it turns to steam and evaporates and the material will become dry enough to ignite or dry enough to reach the combustible temperature.

Now the student has some judgment why the fire starting material needs to be small and dry. The student has the judgment after understanding and experiencing the above to draw further valuable conclusions, decisions and judgments but the instructor will need to teach how to draw further judgments such as the following:

It is easier to start a fire on a hot day (90 degrees F.) than on a cold day (minus 40 degrees F.).

Since the burnable material gathered outside will probably be the same temperature as the air, the match will need to raise the temperature of the cold day material 130 degrees F. before it reaches the starting temperature of the warm day.

It is easier to start a fire on a dry day (when the humidity is 80 percent).

Since the burnable material gathered from outside will probably be as damp as the air the material gathered on a day of high humidity will contain more water which will take more heat to evaporate so the material can reach the combustible temperature.

It is easier to start a fire on top of a base of burnable material than on the bare ground or rock.

The ground or rock near the starting flame will transfer cold to the burnable material or take heat from the burnable material helping to keep the material from reaching the combustible temperature. If for example a base of wood is used under the starting fire the wood has insulating power (contains air pockets) and it will prevent cold being transferred from the ground or rock to the combustible material.

Since warm air dries we light a fire by putting the match under the small dry starting material so all the heat from the match and the first material to light will flow upward through the other material to start heating it to the igniting stage of temperature. The heat is being more efficiently used to start the fire than lighting the upper material of the pile which will waste the rising heat.

Through using quality judgment and being taught how to make quality judgment decisions by the instructor the student has now the experience and information to make a judgment decision why adding too much new burnable material to a fire might put it out.

Of course, how easy, the cold new material will transfer its cold to the burnable material and that material's temperature will be lowered to below its combustible temperature and go out.

The above examples show how any instructor can teach judgment. The same method is workable in most or part of most outdoor teaching.

REFERENCES

Drury, J. K. (In press). Wilderness Education Association Instructor's Lesson Plans. Saranac Lake, NY: Wilderness Education Association.

Fletcher, C. (1974). *The New Complete Walker*. Englewood Cliffs, NJ: Prentice-Hall.

Forgey, W. W. (1987). *Wilderness Medicine*. Merrillville, IN: ICS Books.

Kahn, F. H. and Visscher, B. R. (1977). Water disinfection in the wilderness: A simple method of iodination. *Summit.* April-May, 11-14.

Kjellstrom, B. (1976) *Be expert with map and compass.* New York: Charles Scribner and Sons.

Manning, H. (1975). *Backpacking: One step at a time.* New York: Vintage Books.

Peters, E. (Ed.). (1982), *Mountaineering: The freedom of the hills. (4th Ed.)* Seattle: The Mountaineers.

Petzoldt, P. (1984) *The New Wilderness Handbook.* NY: Norton

Simer, P. and Sullivan, J. (1983). *National Outdoor Leadership School's Wilderness Guide.* New York: Simon and Schuster.

Suk, T. (n.d.). *Eat, drink and be wary.* Davis, CA: California Wilderness Coalition reprint.

Suk, T., Riggs, J. L. and Nelson, B. C. (1986). Water contamination with Giardia in backcountry areas. In R. C. Lucas (Ed.) Proceedings—*National Wilderness Research Conference: Current Research.* U.S.D.A. Forest Service Intermountain Research Station Gen. Tech. Rep. INT-212.

6.

RATIONS PLANNING AND FOOD PREPARATION

by Jack K. Drury
and Bruce L. Bonney
North Country Community College
and David Cockrell
University of Southern Colorado

Planning, preparing and eating food are major events on W.E.A. courses. (Some have even made mention of the Wilderness Eating Association!) During the logistics day at the beginning of a course, instructors build suspicious visions of deep-dish pizzas in the backcountry, luscious lasagnas, blueberry cobblers, sweet 'n sour rice, salads of edible greens and extravagant Mexican casseroles. Incredulous students become even more angry at these seemingly cruel lies when they are handed a complex rations list replete with such items as bulgar, millet, soy flour, spinach noodles and tomato flakes. Just the idea of a class in something like food identification smacks of a compulsory reorientation to life for 33 days. For some it is a major reorientation. But alas, the instructors' visions do come to pass. And potluck dinners later in a course become vital opportunities for creative personal expression and occasionally even fierce competition.

The W.E.A. method for planning, packing and preparing food was developed and refined at the National Outdoor Leadership School during the years when W.E.A. was just coming into existence. Both W.E.A. and N.O.L.S. are continually fine-tuning the rationing process, of course, but the major principles that guide the process are tried and true. These principles are well summarized by Simer and Sullivan (1983) and Petzoldt (1984). The *New N.O.L.S. Cookery* (Richards, Orr and Lindholm, 1988) is also an excellent reference for recipes using standard N.O.L.S./W.E.A. rations. What W.E.A. instructors have added to the process that is perhaps noteworthy is a system for teaching rationing that remains relatively constant across courses. The system yields an identifiable knowledge base in students that is adaptable to their subsequent leadership responsibilities in diverse other settings. This chapter describes the W.E.A. rationing process and the rationale behind it in some detail. A few keystone recipes are summarized. The chapter closes with a discussion of the W.E.A. process for teaching rationing on a course.

Nutrition and Ration Planning

There are several good reasons why cooking and eating are such a major component of a W.E.A. course. Being well nourished plays an important role in fighting illness and disease, a battle that is at least as important in the wilderness as elsewhere. Food, especially protein, enables the building and repairing of body tissues. Food provides the energy that allows us to take part in physical activity and keep warm. Without good nutrition, disposition and attitude deteriorate rapidly, as do decision-making ability and other cognitive processes.

Perhaps the most important issue in expeditionary rations planning is the provision of sufficient energy to accomplish the objectives of the expedition. As most of us know, human energy expenditure is measured in kilocalories, which are units of heat sufficient to raise one gram of water one degree Celsius. Individual daily caloric needs range from approximately 1,800 calories per day for a sedentary individual to over 6,500 for an expeditioneer in severe weather. In general, individual daily caloric needs for campers range from 2,800 to 4,000 in summer, and from 3,800 to 6,000 in winter.

However, as Simer and Sullivan (1983) point out, no one wants to ingest 3,500 calories by eating a one-pound block of butter and a half pound of cheese. Fortunately, the variety we want is often the variety we need. Calories for energy are contained in three types of foods: carbohydrates, fats and proteins. Carbohydrates are the simplest combinations of carbon, hydrogen and oxygen and the most easily accessible form of energy. Pure carbohydrates provide four calories/gram (Lappe, 1975). The simplest carbohydrates, sugars, become accessible to the body within a few minutes of eating. These, of course, make good trail foods. Examples include dried fruits, sweetened fruits, sugar, syrup, candy, jam, honey and fruit drinks. More complex carbohydrates, such as starches, require longer digestion time but are still relatively quick energy foods. These might be an emphasis at breakfast and include breads and cereals, potatoes, corn, pasta, pudding and cocoa. Because of the need for easily prepared, accessible energy in the outdoors, carbohydrates are the primary fuel. This becomes even more important for a course at elevation (above 7,000 feet) because of the increased difficulty of aerobic metabolism of fat and the lower boiling point making cooking more difficult.

Fats are also important because they supply a much larger amount of energy in a small amount of food, nine calories per gram. Fats also provide "essential fatty acids," which aid in skin health and they carry the fat-soluble vitamins A, D, E, and K (Leverton, 1971). These carbon compounds are more complex and so require from several hours to overnight to digest. When fats are incorporated into dinner, the wilderness traveler receives a more lasting form of energy for sleeping warmly and getting going in the morning. Examples include margarine, cooking oil and shortening, cheese, nuts and fatty meats. Approximately 25% of an outdoor diet should be composed of fats, with a higher percentage in winter (Simer and Sullivan, 1983).

So, why couldn't a hiker get by on carbohydrates and fats alone? While all three energy sources contain carbon, oxygen and hydrogen, protein alone also contains the essential substances nitrogen, sulfur and phosphorus. Protein is needed to rebuild the tissues continuously being broken down in the skin, nails, hair, cartilage and tendons, muscles and the organic portion of bones. It also makes up the substance of hormones, enzymes and hemoglobin, the oxygen-carrying molecule of the blood. Blood proteins regulate pH level and water balance, and new protein synthesis is needed to create antibodies to fight infections (Lappe, 1975).

Not only is protein a critical element of the diet, but the body's requirements for the form in which it receives proteins are fairly rigid. First, while most nutrients are depleted from the body fairly slowly, our protein reserves are drained in a few hours, necessitating a continuous replenishment. Proteins are made up of various combinations of 22 different amino acids. Eight of these cannot be synthesized within the body and must come from outside sources. Unfortunately, the body must receive each of these eight essential amino acids at more or less the same time (same meal) in order to achieve protein synthesis. Also unfortunately, we need differing amounts of each essential amino acid, so that they must all be present in basically a fixed proportion.

Now, contrary to popular belief, most food proteins do contain all eight essential amino acids, but the proportions vary widely and always differ to some extent from that one required pattern. The body will accept a divergent proportional combination and begin to synthesize and use proteins, but it quits as soon as it runs out of one of the essential amino acids. From that point on, the remaining food protein is simply burned as carbohydrate fuel and the body's protein needs go unfulfilled (Lappe, 1975).

The key, then, is to try to combine protein foods so that an amino acid shortage in one is complemented by a strength in another to maximize net protein utilization (N.P.U.). Individually, the percentage of protein in a food that can actually be used as protein ranges from a low of about 40% to a high of 94%. At the top end of the range are eggs, milk, fish and cheese, all foods that can be eaten on a wilderness course (eggs and milk as powders). Meat (usually described as a complete protein) is in the middle of the range. Sources of vegetable protein, which include nuts and seeds, legumes (beans) and grains, are slightly lower.

When combined, however, individual protein sources can increase their N.P.U. as much as 50% above the average of the sources if they were eaten separately. For example, white bread and cheese would yield an average N.P.U. of about 64% if they were eaten separately, but a cheese sandwich has an N.P.U. of 76%. Maybe there was method in the Earl of Sandwich's Madness! Figure 6-1 summarizes the complementary relationships between the four basic nonmeat food groups and gives examples of particularly effective combinations. It can be seen that combinations of grains and milk products, grains and legumes, and legumes and seeds most often yield the highest N.P.U.s.

A final issue in regard to protein used for bodily repair is "How much is enough?" The base level recommended by the National Academy of Sciences Recommended Dietary Allowances, Food and Nutrition Board in 1974 was .213 gram per pound of body weight of usable protein. Lappe (1975) translates this for an average-sized American male (154 lbs.) to nine ounces of meat, 10 oz. of fish, six cups of milk, seven eggs, 15 1/3 oz. dry beans or 14 1/3 oz. nuts, eaten in isolation. Of course, when proteins are combined complementarily, less is required. Lappe summarizes the factors that increase protein needs as increased heat, heavy work, stress, inadequate supply of energy foods and infection.

It is generally thought that essential vitamins and minerals are either adequately provided in wilderness rations, or the body has a sufficient reservoir to provide for a 35 day W.E.A. course. This is probably accurate but would make an interesting and valuable research topic. Vitamin A is normally found in butter, dairy products and some fresh vegetables, and it is essential in maintenance of the skin, mucous membranes and eyes. B-complex vitamins are found in meat, fish, dairy products, beans, grains and potatoes. They play central roles in digestion and nervous system functioning. Vitamin D is found in milk, butter and sunshine and is important in calcium digestion and bone building.

Three essential nutrients perhaps worthy of conscious concern are iron and vitamins C and E. Iron is normally obtained through liver, meat, eggs and green leafy vegetables, items not common in W.E.A. rations. Raisins and dried apricots are good sources of iron, however, and might be taken specifically for this reason. Vitamins C and E, both water-soluble, are typically obtained from some fresh fruits and vegetables not taken in wilderness rations. Vitamin C plays the important roles of helping to resist infection and fatigue, and helping to heal wounds. Among other things, vitamin E helps the body to retain vitamin C. Regular doses of powdered fruit drinks supplemented with vitamin C are a convenient way to address this issue. Also, many wild greens and berries are rich in vitamin C, such as lamb's quarters,

Figure 6-1

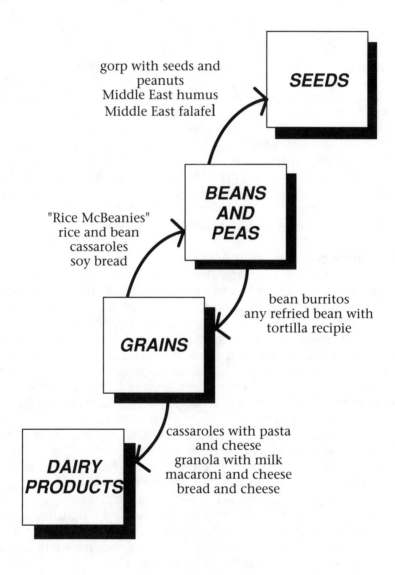

gorp with seeds and
peanuts
Middle East humus
Middle East falafel

SEEDS

"Rice McBeanies"
rice and bean
cassaroles
soy bread

**BEANS
AND
PEAS**

bean burritos
any refried bean with
tortilla recipie

GRAINS

cassaroles with pasta
and cheese
granola with milk
macaroni and cheese
bread and cheese

**DAIRY
PRODUCTS**

wild strawberry (leaves and berries), elderberries, and sumac stalks (Pringle, 1978).

Salt depletion and replacement has been a controversial subject over the years. The most noticeable effect of salt depletion is cramping in the voluntary muscles such as calf muscles. The problem is that cramping can also be symptomatic of depletions in calcium, potassium, magnesium or vitamin B, or electrolyte imbalance (Fixx, 1977). Further, when salt is lost through sweating, considerable amounts of water are also lost. A fixation on salt replacement to the neglect of water replacement can lead to further dehydration, compounding the problem (Forgey, 1987).

Forgey (1987) reports that a nonheat-acclimated person working under heat stress for an eight-hour period sweats four to six liters with a salt content of 18 to 30 grams. The average American diet contains 10 to 15 grams/day of salt, meaning the unacclimatized worker could suffer a 3 to 20 gram salt deficit. The average American diet emphasizes prepackaged foods and sauces that provide most of us with rather large and uncontrolled portions of salt. W.E.A. rations, on the other hand, emphasize whole foods and cooking from scratch. It is probably prudent, therefore, to pack and use salt in cooking. The use of concentrated doses of salt such as salt tablets is not advised, especially in treatment of heat stress under conditions of potential dehydration. For a more complete treatment of this topic, see Forgey (1987).

The Rations-planning Process

There are a number of criteria that must be taken into consideration in selecting foods for a backcountry experience. The length of a trip and its objectives are perhaps the foundation to build upon. Thus, food for river trips can be slightly heavier (and can sometimes be acquired en route), foods for long trips in summer must resist spoilage, foods for high elevation must be easier to cook because water boils at a lower temperature, etc. The energy requirements and nutritional balance considerations discussed above become the next overlay to consider. There must be complementary proteins, a mix of easily accessible and not so accessible carbohydrates, palatable fats and adequate vitamins and minerals.

There are then a series of factors to evaluate. Caloric content must be considered in relation to both weight and bulk (e.g., Grape Nuts versus Puffed Wheat). Expense is always an important factor, especially for organized outdoor programs (e.g., freeze dried versus cooking from scratch). Availability can become a problem as well. Ease of packaging and handling are issues (e.g., sugar versus honey), as are ease and length of preparation time (e.g., lentils versus kidney beans). The longer the trip the more important food variety becomes as a consideration. Also, the more variety, the better the chances of appealing to everyone's tastes.

Although there are variations between programs, spoilage almost always becomes a limiting factor of some kind. For almost any kind of summer ration, fresh meats must be excluded, and this is one reason protein complementarity is an important knowledge base for leaders. Some prepared meats such as pepperoni and summer sausage do quite well, but on programs the length of a W.E.A. course meats are really reduced to the role of flavoring agents.

Most fresh vegetables and fruits must also be left in town, both because of their spoilage potential and because their high water content makes them too heavy for their caloric value. Fortunately, in most communities there are now reliable, inexpensive sources of dried fruits and vegetables. While their water-soluble vitamins have been removed, dried vegetables provide an important source of flavor and color in many dishes. Dried fruits are one of the most important sources of easily accessible carbohydrates eaten as a trail food.

Dairy products are also subject to spoilage, and powdered milk is the usual strategy for providing dairy protein. Powdered whole milk has more calories and vitamins than instant nonfat dry milk, but it is more difficult to dissolve. Fortunately, cheese is much more resistant to spoilage than most people think. After it has been in a warm environment for a while the oils will separate, and a mold may develop on the surface. This may be cut off, however, and the cheese will remain edible for quite some time. Firmer cheeses such as cheddar and Swiss tend to do better than softer cheeses such as Muenster and mozzarella.

Another strategy for surmounting the spoilage problem is to supplement rations with wild foods. There are a number of easily identifiable edible wild greens, tubers, and fruits, and W.E.A. instructors often go through a frenzied period of learning to identify edible plants. Knowledge of what will be in season locally is important precourse information. Salads of spring beauties, sheep sorrel and watercress, berry pies, and sumac tea can greatly enhance spirits after a tough day. In many locations fishing can also be a valuable way to augment rations, although one should never count on catching fish. Hunting would also provide supplementary protein, but the complexities of equipment and time needed, safety, and environmental concern essentially make it prohibitive for a program like W.E.A. In factoring wild foods into the rationing decisions, the instructor must ask himself/herself several questions: Are they available? Can they be harvested legally? Can participants be taught to identify them adequately to prevent accidental poisoning? Can they be harvested without adverse impact to the environment?

Given all the complexities of planning expeditionary rations, W.E.A. has found it useful to employ a comprehensive planning process that some instructors describe as "total food planning." This process is based on determining caloric needs and making sure the group has enough food, in a nutritionally balanced distribution, to meet caloric needs within weight and budget constraints. Typical parameters of the model are:

1. During summer months between 3,200 and 3,750 calories are
    planned per person per day depending on activity level and weather.
2. Approximately two pounds of food per person per day are required
    during warm weather.

3. Nutritious meals can be provided for between $2.00 and $4.00 per person per day.

Let us examine the rations plan for a typical course, taught for 33 days during summer months in a mountainous environment. We will say there are a total of 12 people on the course. The total number of calories needed would be 12 (people) X 33 (days) X 3,500 (calories) = 1,386,000 total calories. The total weight of these rations would be 12 (people) X 33 (days) X 2 (pounds/person/day) = 792 total pounds of food. The cost would be 12 (people) X 33 (days) X $3.25 (person/day) = $1,287 total cost. With these total parameters and the planning considerations discussed above, a food list can be generated that meets the necessary criteria.

Such a list and the selections made by our hypothetical course are summarized in Table 6-1. Normally, instructors will develop a generic list like this one that reflects the most commonly used foods available from the program or the local whole-foods co-op. The generic list will contain information about calories per pound and cost per pound but will not specify pounds ordered. This list is then used as a work sheet for students as they plan rations. There are several advantages to the total food planning approach. A large variety of foods can be selected, providing for an endless variety of available meals. The process provides for a spontaneous and creative type of cooking and eating, and does away with the need to plan specific meals. Students can eat what they want when they want, and there should be sufficient food for the course.

If it seems to you as though Table 6-1 were generated by a computer program, you are entirely correct! Jack Drury has used a spreadsheet software program called Lotus 1,2,3 to do rations planning with a microcomputer (Drury, 1986). Given number of pounds, calories per pound and cost per pound as input commands for each food item, the computer will perform the computations necessary to calculate total calories and total pounds. Perhaps more importantly, this same program is capable of performing a nutritional analysis. Given input information on the percentages of each food that is used by the body as protein, fat and carbohydrates, the program will calculate total percentages and total amounts of the overall ration available in each food group.

The potential of this computerized approach as an instructional device is enormous. Students can vary portions of specific foods to optimize the nutritional balance within given budgetary and weight constraints. They can see what is gained by adding an extra dollar per person per day, or by subtracting a half pound per person per day. By planning rations for a variety of types and lengths of trips on the computer, students begin to acquire the judgment necessary for expedition planning in a convenient, expeditious way.

Table 6-1

1 Wilderness Recreation Leadership Program

2 North Country Community College

3 20 Winona Ave.

4 Saranac Lake, NY 12983

	A	B	C	D	E	F
5						
6	Names: 1. Sample	Total	12 Total		33	
7	2.	People	Days			
8	3					
9		Pounds	Calories	Total	Cost	Total
10		Ordered	per Lb.	Calories	per Lb.	Cost
11						
12	Apples-dried,	8.59	1600	13737	$1.41	$12.11
13	Apricots-dried,	13.9	1200	16741	$2.07	$28.88
14	Bacon-pieces,	0.00	3750	0	$1.99	$0.00
15	Baking Powder,	3.22	500	1610	$0.90	$2.90
16	Bagels,	0.00	1800	0	$1.24	$0.00
17	Beef Base,	3.22	1800	5795	$2.32	$7.47
18	Bread,	0.00	1100	0	$1.05	$0.00
19	Brownie Mix,	7.51	1850	13898	$1.33	$9.99
20	Bulgar,	3.22	1275	4105	$0.32	$1.03
21	Candy-hard,	8.59	1700	14595	$1.76	$15.11
22	Cashews,	0.00	2500	0	$1.77	$0.00
23	Cheese Cake Mix,	4.29	3500	15024	$2.23	$9.57
24	Cheese-chedder,	22.54	1800	40566	$1.88	$42.37
25	Mozzarella,	21.46	1800	38634	$1.78	$38.20
26	Muenster,	40.78	1800	73405	$1.75	$71.37
27	Colby,	33.27	1800	59883	$1.83	$60.88
28	Chicken Base,	2.15	1800	3863	$2.32	$4.98
29	Chili Base,	1.07	1450	1556	$2.55	$2.74
30	Chocolate Bars,	0.00	1650	0	$3.38	$0.00
31	Cocoa w/milk,	25.76	1650	42498	$1.99	$51.25
32	Coconut,	2.15	3000	6439	$0.93	$2.00
33	Corn Meal,	0.00	1600	0	$0.22	$0.00
34	Crackers,	0.00	1800	0	$2.35	$0.00
35	Cream of wheat,	0.00	1750	0	$1.12	$0.00
36	Dates,	6.44	1200	7727	$1.34	$8.63
37	Eggs-freeze dried-					
37a	1 lb=32 eggs	0.00	2760	0	$6.83	$0.00

37a	A	B	C	D	E	F
37b Names: 1. Sample		Total	12 Total		33	
37c	2.		People	Days		
37d	3					
37e		Pounds	Calories	Total	Cost	Total
37f		Ordered	per Lb.	Calories	per Lb.	Cost
37g						
38 Egg Noodles,		8.59	1700	14595	$0.59	$5.07
39 Fruit drink - Orange,		51.51	1950	100449	$0.99	$51.00
40 Lemon,		0.00	1950	0	$0.99	$0.00
41 Fruit,		0.00	1950	0	$0.99	$0.00
42 Tang,		0.00	1950	0	$1.65	$0.00
43 Flour-unbleached,		0.00	1650	0	$0.22	$0.00
44 Whole Wheat,		0.00	1500	0	$0.27	$0.00
45 Gingerbread mix,		11.80	1950	23020	$1.47	$17.35
46 Granola,		0.00	2000	0	$1.19	$0.00
47 Ham-cooked,		0.00	1800	0	$3.00	$0.00
48 Honey,		18.24	1400	25541	$0.78	$14.23
49 Hot Cereal (Wheatina),		5.37	1750	9390	$0.96	$5.15
50 Jello,		4.29	1700	7298	$1.84	$7.90
51 Macaroni,		18.24	1700	31015	$0.55	$10.03
52 Margarine,		39.71	3300	131034	$0.57	$22.63
53 M & M's,		8.59	2100	18029	$2.39	$20.52
54 Mighty Mush,		5.37	1750	9390	$0.80	$4.29
55 Milk-powdered,		22.54	1650	37185	$1.47	$33.13
56 Mushroom soup base,		2.15	1700	3649	$3.44	$7.38
57 Nuts-mixed,		3.22	2500	8049	$2.11	$6.79
58 Oatmeal,		28.98	1750	50707	$0.26	$7.53
59 Onions-dried,		3.22	1800	5151	$2.56	$8.24
60 Pancake mix,		19.32	1850	3737	$0.70	$13.52
61 Pancake syrup,		4.29	1600	6868	$0.79	$3.39
62 Peanut butter,		20.39	2600	53015	$1.12	$22.84
63 Peanuts,		13.95	2650	36971	$0.88	$12.28
64 Pepperoni,		12.88	2000	25756	$4.40	$56.66
65 Peppers-dried,		1.07	1000	13	$17.80	$19.10
66 Popcorn,		2.15	1650	3541	$0.28	$0.60
67 Potatoes, sliced,		4.29	1650	7083	$2.56	$10.99
68 powder,		3.22	1650	5312	$1.15	$3.70
69 Prunes,		6.44	1550	9980	$0.84	$5.41

70 Pudding-chocolate,	3.22	1650	5312	$2.05	$6.60
71 vanilla,	2.15	1650	3541	$2.05	$4.40
72 Raisins, regular,	24.68	1300	32088	$.73	$18.02
73 golden,	0.00	1300	0	$0.75	$0.00
74 Rice,	11.80	1650	19478	$0.42	$4.96
75 Salami,	0.00	1500	0	$4.40	$0.00
76 Salt,	0.00	0	0	$0.16	$0.00
77 Sloppy Joe Base,	1.07	1400	1502	$2.22	$2.38
78 Soup Blend-					
78a Dried Vegies,	7.51	1600	12020	$5.12	$38.46
79 Sour Cream,	2.15	1600	3434	$5.09	$10.92
80 Soy Nuts,	7.51	1800	13522	$0.76	$5.71
81 Spaghetti,	17.17	1700	29190	$0.56	$9.44
82 Sugar-Brown,	17.17	1700	29190	$0.70	$12.02
83 White,	7.51	1700	12771	$0.36	$2.70
84 Sunflower seeds,	8.59	2550	21893	$0.82	$7.04
85 Tea (Bags) reg-$/bag,	0.00	0	0	$0.01	$0.00
86 spice-$/bag,	0.00	0	0	$0.05	$0.00
87 Tomato Base,	8.59	1350	11590	$6.58	$56.49
88 Trail Mix,	10.73	2000	21463	$1.70	$18.24
89 T V P - Beef,	4.29	1500	6439	$2.96	$12.71
90 Chicken,	4.29	1500	6439	$2.96	$12.71
91 Ham,	4.29	1500	6439	$96	$12.71
92 Vanilla,	0.00	0	0	$14.16	$0.00
93 Vegetable Oil,	12.88	4000	51512	$0.87	$11.20
94 Vinegar,	0.00	54	0	$0.49	$0.00
95 Walnuts,	5.37	2950	15829	$1.98	$10.62
96 Yeast,	0.00	1250	0	$1.16	$0.00
97					
98 Total Total	689	Total	1,323,568	Total	$996.57
99 People -12					
100 Total		Total			
101 Total Pounds		Calories		Total	
102 Days - 33 Needed		Needed		Budget	
103 Summer	792	Total	1,386,000	Total	$1,287.00
104					

Food Packaging and Identification

After the whirlwind of rations planning and packing are over, and a course is in the field, students are commonly asked to bring their rations bags to an introductory cook class right away. "What are all these white powders? How come everything is in plastic bags? Isn't that ecologically unsound?" These timeless questions ring from the hills and must be answered.

The most common packaging for most rations is a plastic bag approximately 8 inches X 14 inches X 1.75 mil in thickness (at least). There are several brands of freezer bags like this commercially available, and they are available in bulk through most food co-ops and buying clubs. These bags are used for several reasons: They are lightweight compared to glass, cans, and aluminum foil; they do not create the safety hazard that glass does; they are easy to pack out once the contents are used and are therefore less likely to become litter. Bags are usually sealed with a simple, loose overhand knot. This closure is truly watertight and can be repeated conveniently over and over if the knot is not tied too tightly. Twist ties are discouraged because of their potential for puncturing holes in other bags and becoming litter. Ziplock style bags tend to become unworkable as the zipper tracks clog with food after multiple uses. Some food items that leak easily or can puncture bags (e.g., flour or spaghetti) may need to be double-bagged.

A few foods need a different approach. Gooey foods to which daily access is desirable (e.g., margarine, honey) are better off in wide-mouth plastic jars with tight-fitting screw-on lids. Most spices and liquids requiring only a small quantity (e.g., soy sauce or vinegar) pack well in 35 mm film cans or small plastic screw-top bottles. In hot and humid weather it is sometimes advisable to wrap cheese in plastic before packing it in a plastic bag. The plastic absorbs some of the oils and leaves the cheese easier to handle.

Plastic food bags and containers are then grouped together into zippered nylon rations bags. Foods should be organized by type of meal, alphabetically or according to any preferred method. It is important to maintain this order throughout a trip, however, so that mealtimes don't become scavenger hunts.

Food identification is largely a matter of experience and is quickly learned, especially when students select their own rations before a course departs. However, a short class focusing especially on the confusing white powders can be helpful. Table 6-2 summarizes some of the distinguishing characteristics we have found useful on the most confusing foods.

Table 6-2
Confusing Foods and Their Distinguishing Features

Pearl Barley
Roundish, white with brown specks; larger than Cream of Wheat, grits or millet

Millet
Smaller than barley, larger than grits

Quick Grits
Coarser and whiter than Cream of Wheat

Cream of Wheat
Finer than grits with brown specks; coarser than wheat flour

Whole Wheat Flour
Soft and fine with brown specks

White Flour
Soft and fine; more yellow than baking powder

Baking Powder
White; heavy; crunchy; very fine

Powdered Milk
Yellowish; light weight; crunchy

Rye flour
Whiter than wheat flour; darker brown specks

Corn Flour
Soft and fine; yellowish

Corn Meal
Coarser than corn flour; more yellow than grits or Cream of Wheat

Wheat Germ
Coarse, lightweight flakes; brownish

Chicken Base
Grayish but with many colors; fine and heavy

Potato Flakes
White; lightweight flakes

White Sugar
Very white; coarse but regular granules

Lemon Drink Mix
Easy to confuse with white sugar; distinctive odor

Cooking Tools, Organization and Safety

There are several somewhat unique tools and procedures that have been developed through the N.O.L.S./W.E.A. approach to cooking. All have as objectives the enhancement of safety, conservation and convenience. Brief descriptions of the most standard cook tools are provided in Table 6-3. However, there is considerable variation across programs in the tools used. As with most aspects of outdoor cooking, exploration and imagination should lead the way. Again, the W.E.A. way is only ONE way. Typically, a cook group of two or three people on a course will be issued a stove, a billy can, a teflon-coated pot with a lid for baking and a frying pan (or a tote oven), one or two serving spoons, pot grips and spatulas, a set of cotton gloves and stuff sacks, and water bottles and personal eating gear for each person.

Table 6-3
Standard W.E.A. Cook Tools

Billy can
#10 can, used for all boiling, carrying water, washing clothes and body, and smothering flames on a leaking stove. Toxic inner lining of corrosion resistance must be scorched off in fire before using

Pot grips
Cast aluminum plier-type grips, used for handling hot pots

Fry pan / tote oven
Large, shallow pot and a high lid with a welded oven ring for containing hot coals on the lid. Used for frying and baking.

Stove-top oven (ring pan) and stabilizing tin
Aluminum ring pan and lid assembly, capable of oven forcing heat down onto dough from the lid.

Serving spoons
Wooden or hard plastic spoons

Spatulas
Metal or plastic (depending on surfaces of pots/pans)

Collapsible
One- to two-and-a-half gallon water jug

Personal eating gear
Lexan or soft plastic bowl (to avoid breaking), cup (insulated plastic recommended), spoon; must be submersible in boiling water for sterilization.

Wide-mouth plastic bottle
One liter size. Holds water for the trail; used to soak beans and rice; used in cooking.

Cotton gloves
Protects hands from excessive drying and burning when working with the fire; function as pot-holders.

Stuff sacks
Nylon or polyester, sufficiently large for pots; helps in protecting pack contents from soot-covered pots.

The organization of tools and rations in the cooking area can make the difference between a frustrating wrestling match and an efficient gourmet meal. First, the area for preparation of food should be separate and distinct from the cooking area. There are two reasons for this. The cook needs safe, uncluttered access to the stove or fire with a minimum of uncontrollable interference. Also, fires tend to attract a lot of attention and traffic, which means concentrated vegetative damage and soil compaction. Preparing food away from the fire can help disperse some of the impact.

All utensils, pots and pans required for cooking the meal should be organized and laid out in an orderly fashion in the cooking area. Ensolite pads, jackets, or stuff sacks spread on the ground can function as tablecloths and can help keep utensils clean and organized. Cooks should be encouraged to put all utensils back in place on the cloth after each use. This helps avoid confusion while cooking and prevents the loss of equipment, particularly pot grips and serving spoons.

All ingredients required for preparing the meal should be organized in the "kitchen" area. Foods to be used in the meal preparation should be removed from the rations bag and arranged on the tablecloth. All knots closing food bags to be used should be opened to allow quick access during preparation. Some cooks like to arrange ingredients in the order of their use, replacing each item back into the food bag after it has been used. This maintains order and helps prevent double dosing of ingredients into the pot. All preparations for a meal should be completed before lighting the stove, if possible, to save fuel.

Cooking is the second most dangerous activity on a course (next to driving to the trailhead), because of the potential for burns, cuts and explosions. Safety in the kitchen must be an explicit part of learning to cook. The kitchen and cooking areas should be located well away from tents, packs, sleeping bags, or other combustible nylon items so that sparks from the cook fire do not ignite or damage equipment. Several policies are typical for the three to five-foot "safe" zone surrounding the stove or cook fire. No one walks through, reaches over, or horseplays in the safe zone. Only cooks immediately involved in food preparation should work in the safe zone. This area should be as free as possible from natural hazards that may trip, poke, or otherwise hinder the cook's freedom to work safely around the cooking area. Stoves should be filled with fuel elsewhere, and no open fuel bottles should be in the safe zone.

Sterilization of serving and eating utensils before eating is an important safety policy. One of this chapter's authors once had an epidemic of viral pneumonia on a course that was clearly spread by lax sanitation practices. While nursing five students with 103° degree fevers in the backcountry was an interesting experience in group dynamics and decision making, it certainly reflected poor judgment, and was avoidable. If the group is cooking on stoves, one or two cook groups can easily be designated as sterilization stations. They simply boil a large billy can of water into which utensils are dipped. When fires are used, each firepit should have a sterilization pot. It should be noted that it is relatively useless to sterilize utensils after a meal, as they will be contaminated when packed away.

There are a number of other small safety precautions that an instructor should point out. Most are common-sense issues, but simply pointing them out can enhance safety awareness.

1. Use gloves and/or pot grips when handling hot items.

2. Pour hot liquids or grease away from the pourer. Never pour into a hand-held cup.

3. Billy cans containing hot ingredients should be removed from the fire or stove for stirring.

4. Remove pots from the fire before adding food items to prevent plastic bags from burning.

5. Do not pass hot items over another person. Take special care with ankles and feet.

6. Keep a billy can filled with water near the cook fire to douse uncontrolled flames. Keep an empty billy can near a stove to smother a flare-up.

7. Watch loose clothing (e.g., wind pants, long parkas) and long hair around the fire.

8. Be careful with knives. Cut on a hard surface (rather than on your leg);

and cut away from you, not toward you.

Figure 6-2

Introductory Cooking and Baking

Beginning cooks can have as pleasurable a time experimenting as a gourmet chef. We saw a beginning cook start out to make a light vegetable soup one time with a beef base. He added "a little flour" to give the soup "substance" and was shortly faced with something about the consistency of pancake batter. The chef then elected to add chopped pepperoni, additional spices and bulgar to give this new stew "body." As the bulgar cooked and absorbed liquid, the mix thickened further, of course, yielding a heavy dough. Not being one to go against the flow, our cook simply added baking powder mixed with water and some grated cheddar and baked a quite unusual and aromatic bread!

Once again, let us say that exploration and imagination are the hallmarks of the W.E.A. style of cooking. From the rations described in this chapter dishes are possible from something as simple as pasta in a garlic, parsley and butter sauce to complex casseroles and baked goods. Simer and Sullivan (1983), Petzoldt (1984) and *The New N.O.L.S. Cookery* (Richards, Orr and Lindholm, 1988) provide wonderful examples of the recipes that are possible. Here we wish to provide only a few simple suggestions and two foundational recipes.

Simer and Sullivan (1983) point out four basic problems encountered by beginning cooks, and all of them are preventable with a little practice. Burned food probably heads the list. Beginners should be encouraged to keep the heat lower than they believe is necessary, and to keep stirring. It is also important to keep adding water to many recipes. Keeping pots clean can also help prevent food from sticking to the bottom. Bland versus overspiced food is also always an issue. The cook should taste the dish before spicing: It may truly need nothing! Spices (including salt) should be added one at a time. If four spices are mixed in and the meal tastes terrible, it is difficult to tell what the culprit is. For similar reasons, it is usually advisable to pour the spice from the container into your hand before it goes into the pot to guarantee quantity control. Spicing may also become an expedition behavior issue when cook partners have different tastes. Overdone food can be prevented by timing the meal properly. Add dehydrated items first. Let them rehydrate for 10-15 minutes; then add pastas. Add thickeners last. Lumpy food can usually be avoided by mixing powders in a cup thoroughly, sometimes adding cold water next, and then adding the mixture to the pot.

Granola is really a good beginner's recipe that forces the cook to make choices in basically a no-lose environment. A number of W.E.A. courses teach this recipe during the first cook class.

GOOD EARTH GRANOLA
INGREDIENTS:
Rolled oats (oatmeal)
Dried fruit of choice: raisins, chopped dates, chopped apricots, etc.
Nuts and seeds of choice: almonds, peanuts, sunflower seeds,
    cashews, etc.
Sweeteners of choice: honey, brown sugar, etc.
Margarine
Salt
Peanut butter (optional)
M & Ms
Dried milk and water (if eaten as a cold cereal)

PROCEDURES:
Assemble all ingredients and cooking utensils in the kitchen area. Start the stove, boil water and sterilize the utensils. Melt 3-4 T. margarine in the frying pan. Add oatmeal, stir and brown. Add a pinch of salt. Add nuts of choice and cook until brown. Add sweeteners of choice to taste. Simmer and stir until sugars have melted and mixed with other ingredients.. Add fruit of choice, chopped into bite-sized morsels. Continue to fry until mixture is browned to preference. Serve warm with milk as a cereal, or allow to cool, bag, and use as a trail snack.

The preparation of nutritious, good-tasting baked goods can directly contribute to the success of any backcountry expedition. Baked goods add variety to the common back country menu, and they can frequently add courses to a meal that would otherwise be absent: appetizers, desserts, etc. Baking also allows individuals within a group to demonstrate skills and creativity in a noncompetitive way. Baking for the group and sharing can serve as a means of showing affection and caring for others. "Nothin' says lovin' like somethin' from the oven," so to speak. In short, baking in small groups provides an opportunity for group members to share a relaxing, productive, social occasion that fosters communication, mutual cooperation, and understanding.

Again, a few simple suggestions provide a foundation to build upon. If a campfire is to be used for baking, try to select hardwoods that will produce hot, long-lasting-coals. Maple, oak, and apple are all good baking woods. Try to acquire an ample supply of firewood before the project begins. If the dish is to be baked in the firepit itself, one corner of the pit should be enlarged to accommodate the tote oven or baking pot and any handles it might have. Typically, the baking corner of the firepit is a very shallow area so that reaching down into a hot, deep fire to check progress is not required. Baking over a fire is usually most efficient if performed by two people: one to start and maintain the fire, and one to prepare the baked goods. Many cooks prefer not to bake directly in the same fire where other cooking is done. They mound up a low platform of mineral soil adjacent to the firepit which serves as a baking area. A small depression in the top of the platform is hollowed out, coals are placed in the depression and the oven is placed directly on top.

Whether baking in the fire pit or on a platform, the temperature of baking coals should be regulated to maintain as even a temperature as possible. Coals beneath the oven should feel hot but not searing to a hand placed six inches above them. They may only need to be changed once or twice every half hour during the baking time. Coals on top of the oven should be maintained at a higher temperature and therefore changed more frequently. At no time should baked goods be exposed to open flames, as this virtually guarantees burning.

Baking on a stove is generally easier and quicker than using a campfire, although many experienced outdoorspeople find it less aesthetically satisfying. Baking can be accomplished by using the tote oven on the stove over a very low flame. For a heat source on top of the oven, a small hot "twiggy" fire must be built in the lid. If a ring pan is used instead of the tote oven, it is important that the tall ring-pan assembly is completely level.

The basic baking-powder bread recipe used by W.E.A. has come to be called "bannock," after the breads carried by early Native American wilderness travelers. Virtually all other doughs and breads that are baked with baking powder start from this recipe or one very similar in composition.

BASIC BANNOCK
INGREDIENTS (ALL MEASUREMENTS ARE APPROXIMATE):
3-4 cups white flour (up to 1/2 of this amount may
be substituted by other types of flour, e.g., whole wheat, corn, rye, soy)
1/2-1 cup powdered milk
1/2-1 T. baking powder

pinch of salt
1 cup cold water

PROCEDURES:
In a large frying pan or billy can, combine 3/4 of the total amount of flour to be used with salt, powdered milk and baking powder. Mix these dry ingredients thoroughly. Add small amounts of water to the dry mix and stir until thoroughly mixed. Continue this process until the dough thickens to the point where stirring is impossible.

Thoroughly dust hands with flour and sprinkle about a handful of flour on the mix. Using fingers, fists, and knuckles, knead the dough so that fresh flour becomes thoroughly mixed in the dough. Continue the process of adding flour and kneading until dough can be picked up and manipulated by hand without sticking to the fingers. Form the dough into the desired shape for baking or frying: ball, loaf, flat bread, etc. Grease the inside of the baking pot well. With most cooking pots not coated with Teflon, it is advisable to coat the pot with flour after it has been coated with shortening or oil.

As indicated in the recipe, this dough can be formed into a variety of shapes and fried as well as baked. Yeast breads also provide an interesting if slightly more advanced variation in the backcountry bakery.

Teaching Strategies / The Instructional Process

The instructional process for teaching rations planning and food preparation is really one of the more involved process modules in the curriculum. The goals are ambitious: To have students be able to plan food rations for wilderness expeditions and outings varying in length, setting, season and clientele groups with an understanding of the nutritional requirements involved. Further, they should have the knowledge and skill to prepare a variety of palatable and nutritionally balanced meals using the planned rations and be able to teach these skills to others. There are a number of steps in the instructional process, and they vary slightly among affiliates and instructors. The usual sequence includes most of the following steps:

Nutrition and rations-planning class
Food purchasing and packing exercise
Food-identification class
Basic cooking I, stove starting, and fire-building classes
Basic cooking II class
Switch cook partners and reration exercise
Potluck dinners with recipes
Food-pooling exercise
Expedition-planning exercise

NUTRITION AND RATIONS-PLANNING CLASS

Most W.E.A. courses have students plan their own food as part of the shakedown exercise, in which case this class is taught the first day. The class begins as a lecture, and information is provided on caloric requirements, energy sources, protein complementarity, vitamins, minerals and water requirements. The planning considerations for expeditionary rations are described, and the total food-planning process is introduced. In a few programs, the use of the computer in rations planning is brought in at this point. The rations list work sheet is almost always distributed at this time. The class requires approximately two hours.

FOOD PURCHASING AND PACKING EXERCISE

Almost immediately following the rations-planning class, students choose a cook partner for the shakedown and plan their first ration. There are inevitably many questions, and most of the instruction that takes place is on an individual tutorial format. After instructors have checked work sheets for total calories, weight and cost, students go to the rations warehouse or food co-op and pack rations. It is important that each cook group keep careful records and actually weigh their total ration so that later reevaluation can occur.

FOOD-IDENTIFICATION CLASS

A basic food-identification class usually occurs during the first two days in the field. At North Country Community College, granola preparation is taught the first morning out, and food identification is addressed the second or third day. At UNC-Wilmington, food identification is taught in conjunction with stove starting before the first day's dinner. Either foods of similar texture and color are passed around the circle for examination, or students find their own foods as the instructor identifies them.

BASIC COOKING, STOVE STARTING AND FIRE BUILDING

These are usually divided into two classes, as there is really too much material for one sitting. The format is essentially lecture/demonstration with questions. The fire-building class can be quite involved, as was described in chapter 5, and trying to get very much cooked in a simultaneous demonstration is difficult. Good candidates for recipes to prepare in these classes are soups, cobblers, pasta dishes, rice pudding, granola, peanut brittle, etc.

INTRODUCTION TO BAKING CLASS

This lecture demonstration class should be taught as soon after the basic cooking classes as is convenient, but certainly before the end of the shakedown. The basic bannock bread recipe is demonstrated from start to finish. While the bannock is baking (either on the fire or the stove) another application can be demonstrated. Good candidates would be pizza, rolled cinnamon buns, or any variety of fry breads. All cook classes are best timed to end just before a meal so that students can be encouraged to put their new-found knowledge to use. Having a copy of *N.O.L.S. Cookery* (Richards, Orr and Lindholm, 1988) available is also a good strategy.

SWITCH COOK PARTNERS AND RERATION

One of the primary purposes of coming out of the field after the shakedown is to give students the experience of correcting their previous mistakes in rationing. The day before the rerationing, shakedown cook partners should be allocated time to sit with their remaining rations and previous rations lists and identify mistakes. What did they bring that they didn't use? What did they need that wasn't there? How did their total weight and caloric supplies compare with what was actually needed?

At the completion of this exercise, new cook partners come together and compare their lists of lessons from the shakedown. They then proceed to plan rations for the remainder of the course (which is typically two more identical rations).

POTLUCK DINNERS

Potluck dinners are wonderful social experiences that provide an opportunity for skills demonstrations, creativity, and expressions of caring for the group. These can begin any time after the first baking class. The potluck should be debriefed either during the meal or the next morning, and everyone should be encouraged to write recipes in their journals. Potential problems to watch for include making sure that each cook group prepares only enough for itself. If each group prepares enough for the entire course, there will be way too much. Also, competition can emerge in potlucks, and it can be healthy. It can also be destructive and must be monitored. Finally, the leader of the day must aggressively coordinate the timing of the meal so that groups do not begin eating early, and all the dishes are present.

FOOD POOLING

An interesting exercise that can illustrate the efficiency of the total food planning process is to pool all the food on the course about one or two days before the end of a ration period. Then, using some egalitarian process, each cook group takes what it wants from what remains. It is rewarding to see how satisfied everyone is with the redistribution, as they reclaim a treasured morsel, unwanted in someone else's ration but long since depleted in their own.

EXPEDITION-PLANNING EXERCISE

A good final exercise to integrate all the rations-planning experience acquired on the course and redirect the knowledge base toward future judgment decisions is to ask students to develop a rations plan for a hypothetical trip quite different from the course in setting, season, objectives or clientele. This exercise can be carried out in the journal and submitted as a part of the final course evaluation process.

Conclusion

There are many good reasons for eating well in the backcountry, not the least of which is that it is fun. Fun and enjoyment are explicit program objectives on W.E.A. courses. Fun is not to be taken lightly (so to speak)! There are strong ties between the concepts of wilderness and leisure (Leopold, 1966) and wilderness education is in some respects leisure education.

Aristotle defined leisure as "freedom from the necessity of being occupied" (DeGrazia, 1963). In fact, no "occupation" is admissable in leisure for Aristotle, not even recreation, which is necessary as restoration for work. Music and contemplation are the exemplary classical leisure experiences. Csikszentmihalyi's (1975) "flow" experiences emphasize similar psychological dimensions: a contraction of the perceptual field, a heightened concentration on the task at hand, a feeling of control leading to elation and finally to a transcendent loss of self-awareness.

Gourmet outdoor cooking can be this type of deep play. It is not entirely necessary; the rewards are mostly intrinsic. It is extremely involving and pleasurable. At completion of the entire process, the only "product" you have to show is a stack of dirty dishes. What a natural activity on a wilderness trip! Long live the Wilderness Eating Association.

REFERENCES

Csikszentmihalyi, M. (1975). *Beyond boredom and anxiety.* San Francisco: Jossey-Bass.

DeGrazia, S. (1963). *Of Time, Work and Leisure.* New York: Anchor Books.

Drury, J. K. (1986). Wilderness Food Planning in the Computer Age. *The Journal of Experiential Education, 18,* 36-40.

Fixx, J. F. (1977). *The Complete Book of Running.* New York: Random House.

Forgey, W. (1987). *Wilderness Medicine.* Merrillville, IN: ICS Books.

Lappe, F. M. (1975). *Diet for a Small Planet.* New York: Ballantine Books.

Leopold. A. (1966). *A Sand County Almanac.* New York: Ballantine Books.

Leverton, R. M. (1971). *A Girl and Her Figure.* Chicago: National Dairy Council.

Petzoldt, P. (1984). *The New Wilderness Handbook.* New York: Norton.

Pringle, L. (1978). *Wild Foods.* New York: Four Winds Press.

Richard, S., Orr, D. and Lindholm, C. (1988). *The N.O.L.S. Cookery.* Lander, WY: National Outdoor Leadership School.

Simer, P. and Sullivan, J. (1983). *National Outdoor Leadership School's Wilderness Guide.* New York: Simon and Schuster.

7.

ADVENTURE SKILLS AND TRAVEL MODES

by Jerry Cinnamon and Edward Raiola Unity College, Maine

Outdoor educators and leaders need to give considerable effort to planning for traveling with a group in the wild out-of-doors well before the adventure begins. Planning should take into consideration factors that allow for safe, efficient, comfortable travel as well as factors that lead to learning and minimizing impact on the environment. Instructors and participants also need to establish a framework of safety. Within this framework is the understanding that accidents are the result of dangerous interactions between the dynamic natural environment and personal factors that people bring to the out-of-doors. Environmental knowledge, leadership skills, and judgment play a major role in preventing these potentially dangerous interactions. This chapter examines the knowledge and skills needed to move safely with a group through the wild out-of-doors. Near the chapter's end general safety policies are presented and guidelines for risk management are examined. Safety policies and guidelines for risk management form a foundation for decision making as the instructor encounters specific environments and situations. Most importantly, this chapter assumes that judgment can be taught and learned and that the instructor can learn to make decisions that are consistent with the purpose and goals of outdoor adventure education.

Purpose and Goals of Outdoor Adventure Activities

Becoming familiar with the purpose and goals of outdoor adventure activities is the first step in helping adventure educators and outdoor leaders become more effective and efficient in their work. A starting point is to remember that W.E.A. provides both educational and recreational experiences for participants while minimizing impact on the natural environment.

The term "adventure activities" is applied to those activities that relate directly to a particular outdoor environment—hills, mountains, rocks, woods, rivers, lakes, oceans, ice, snow or caves. Most outdoor adventure activities are limited to nonmechanical, individual or group activities involving a certain amount of risk, exploration and travel.

Outdoor adventure activities usually center on cooperation between humans and interaction with the natural environment. One of the most important themes in adventure activities is that the participants should be provided with the necessary skills, both mental and physical, to enable them to experience success in using and preserving the outdoors. The emphasis is not on winning or losing, but rather on facing the challenges of the activity. Some of the generally accepted goals are personal growth, skill development, excitement and stimulation, challenge, group participation and cooperation and understanding of one's relationship to the natural environment.

Two key words, intention and attention, come to mind when discussing leadership and the goals of outdoor adventure activities. Intention refers to a design or plan of action: what one hopes to achieve or attain. It signifies a course of action or a purpose to follow. In terms of being a W.E.A. instructor, your goal or course of action is crucial to the success and safety of your course. In order to be successful and manage risk associated with adventure activities, you must develop goals that will guide your action. You have to develop a clear picture of what you hope to achieve or attain.

Attention implies a close, careful observing or listening. It is your ability or power to concentrate mentally. In your pretrip planning as well as during the field experiences, concentration and observation are important to providing an enjoyable and safe experience for your participants.

Before you begin any course ask yourself:
What are your intentions?
Can you maintain your attention?

General Principles Transferable to a Variety of Settings

Most professionals (Buell, 1983; Cousineau, 1977; Green, 1981; Priest, 1988; Raiola, 1988; Swiderski, 1981) agree that leading people in outdoor adventure activities requires competence in three distinct areas of responsibility: knowledge of specific outdoor skills, knowledge of the environment and knowledge of human needs. There has been much debate about which is most important, the technical skills, people skills, or the knowledge related to the environment. From our position all are essential for the wilderness educator. It should be noted that the three knowledge areas (human needs, technical skills and the environment) are transferable to a variety of settings and activities, and are the foundation of any adventure-based program. The following is a discussion of general principles for leading or instructing adventure activities.

PARTICIPANT NEEDS

The wilderness educator is first and foremost a leader who happens to be working with people in an outdoor setting. He/she must be comfortable working with small and large groups of people. One of the most common mistakes that occurs with novice leaders is that they become so excited about being outdoors doing a specific activity that the needs of the group become secondary to personal involvement in the activity. Results of this attitude can range from frustration for the leader, and a lowering of the quality of the experience for the participant, to someone being injured.

The leader must be aware of the basic needs of each group member. In order to begin to accomplish this a leader should be aware of the common physiological and psychological needs of the participants.

PHYSIOLOGICAL NEEDS

The comfort and safety of both leaders and participants depend on understanding the basic physiological needs and how to obtain them in the outdoors. All of us need air, water, food, shelter and adequate rest and sleep to allow us to maintain our body temperature and function properly. Moving out into the wild outdoors and asking our bodies to perform sometimes in harsh weather or in stressful conditions puts a greater demand on our systems. For the most part, participants are individuals who have not paid much prior attention to meeting those physiological needs that will allow them to operate successfully at the levels of efficiency required on an extended wilderness outing.

We are asking our participants to leave behind their warm and secure homes, to perform at great efficiency, sustained by whatever food and shelter that can be carried, and by obtaining water from natural water sources. These all may be new or altered realities to participants.

Air

Most of the problems associated with air intake are related to working with groups in higher-altitude environments. You need to become aware of the problems associated with high elevations (Hachett, 1978). Generally as elevation increases, especially above 5,000 feet, the body is stressed by the decreasing concentrations of oxygen in the air. Become aware of the effects of hypoxia such as AMS (acute mountain sickness), HAPE (high altitude pulmonary edema), and CE (cerebral edema). Anyone who plans to travel above 6,000 to 8,000 feet should become aware of the signs and care for these and other altitude-related medical problems. See chapter 8 for more specifics.

Water

There are two important aspects associated with water. The first is to ensure that the water supply is safe to drink, and the second is to ensure that each participant has access to drinking water at all times. There are many potential pollutants in backcountry water supplies, ranging from detergents, bacteria, and flagellates like *Giardia lambia*. The only way to ensure safe water supplies is to purify it yourself using methods such as boiling, halogen, iodine crystals, halizone, common bleach or filtration. See chapter 5 for more discussion on specific techniques.

The amount of drinking water needed varies with each individual and with varying environmental conditions and activities. The thing to remember is that impure water or inadequate water intake leads to serious physiological problems that may require evacuation and hospitalization.

Food

Food serves two purposes: It is a source of energy for our bodies and it plays an important role in maintaining the spirit of the group. When planning for the course, one should understand the relationship between nutrition, good-tasting food, and ease of preparation and weight. See chapter 6 for specifics.

Shelter

Shelter, at its most basic, is related to maintaining our body's core temperature. The spirit of a group is affected by proper or improper shelter. Without adequate protection from the elements, which includes appropriate clothing, we run the risk of serious physiological problems such as hypothermia, hyperthermia, or skin and eye damage. See chapter 8 for specifics.

PSYCHOLOGICAL NEEDS

In addition to insuring that basic physiological needs are being met, the challenge to the wilderness educator is to understand the uniqueness of each participant. This role requires that the wilderness educator be more than just a leader of activities. Instead, he or she is a leader of people, all of whom are different. The educator must provide support and direction to each participant leading to a feeling of security, belonging, and respect for self and others. Further, participants need to succeed and be creative within the context of group acceptance and the outdoor environment so that this new wilderness experience can be seen as a stable way of making sense of the world. As leader, your chief job is to create a learning environment that will help participants grow toward their own capabilities, potential, and talents in a physically and psychologically safe framework.

INSTRUCTOR NEEDS

In addition to selecting the right equipment, choosing and sequencing appropriate activities, etc., a key ingredient to the success of any wilderness program is the instructor. As a wilderness educator, you are responsible for the care and safety of yourself as well as your participants. A common mistake that novice leaders make is that they neglect to address their own physiological and psychological care. In order to take care of your group, you must be sure that you are meeting all of your own basic needs. You don't have to carry the heaviest pack, or ignore small injuries, or be the first up and the last to go to sleep each night. You can create opportunities for small breaks of 10 to 15 minutes away from your group. You can allow some of your group members the chance to be in a responsible leadership role and let them be the last person to secure the campsite before going to bed or the first person up in the morning. Building in small breaks, late mornings or slow days during a course, not only helps your group in terms of rest and relaxation, but it also gives you a chance to relax and recharge your personal energy supply. Finally, you must be sure to eat and drink properly, stay warm and get enough rest. The responsibility of ensuring the safety, care and enjoyment of your group begins with your own self-care.

A careful leader recognizes the importance of being alert and in top physical and mental condition to succeed. Lack of sleep is accompanied by reduced muscle energy and mental agility. The leader must be sure that he/she gets good rest before a strenuous trip and that all participants do also. Out in the field, midafternoon naps, late mornings, or an occasional long rest will help you and the group recover from fatigue.

TRAVEL ORGANIZATION FOR GROUPS

How do you organize your group for movement be it backpacking, canoeing, day hiking or cross-country skiing? No matter what the activity that you will be leading there are some basic guidelines to follow in preparing to travel with a group. These guidelines include traveling as a unit, as well as control plans for movement that use time to your best advantage and minimizes both energy expenditure and climate variations.

TRAVELING AS A UNIT

The wilderness leader is responsible for the overall supervision and safety of the group. When moving as a group the leader must develop a system that will allow him/her to travel anywhere that is desired within the group. For example, one may want to be at the rear of the group at the start of a hike and then work your way up to the front. In order to do this W.E.A. uses a system that includes a guide, a smoother, a logger and a sweep. This system was originally developed for trail movement, but can easily be adapted to water or even vehicle travel with minor modifications.

CONTROL PLANS FOR MOVEMENT

In the *Wilderness Handbook*, Paul Petzoldt (1984) described three concepts that are essential principles related to movement with groups. They
are: time control, energy control and climate control. It is important to realize that attention to these control plans, particularly time control and climate control can also be considered impact control plans as well as movement plans. By faithfully following proper time control and climate control
plans you will minimize the risk of being placed in extreme conditions that
may endanger your group. You will also not be placed in a position that
might require tree cutting for fires or shelters, or otherwise disturb the natural environment in a nonrepairable manner.

Time-control Plan

Time control is simply a schedule or plan of where you and your group
are going to be at a given point in a given day. It is something that has to be
both realistic and flexible. It needs to be formulated for the specific group
and situation and requires frequent checks. In order to formulate a schedule
you need to know the terrain in which you will be working, the group's abilities and the weather conditions. You need to consider such things as rest
breaks, bathroom stops, equipment adjustments, and realize that a group of
six to 12 people will move much more slowly than one or two individuals.
Plans should be checked frequently and if you find that your estimated goals
are not being reached, you must re-evaluate and come up with a new plan.

Energy-control Plan

Energy control is a systematic approach to ensuring that we conserve our
body's energy. The purpose is to minimize and even out the efforts of physical demands. In this way we can maintain reserves for further effort. While
on the trail, the plan is a combination of good nutrition, trail techniques
such as rhythmic breathing, and controlled pace. The plan can also include
the development of a pretrip fitness program.

Climate-control Plan

Weather can be one of the most benign or severe influences affecting
group movement. If the weather is mild, most people do not pay much attention to it; however, if you get extreme changes in wind, precipitation, or
temperature you will notice the effects immediately.

To formulate your plan you should find out the proposed five-day fore-
cast, the average day and nighttime temperatures, the coldest and warmest

temperatures ever recorded, wind velocity, and precipitation patterns. With this information you plan for the right kind of equipment and gear to take along and what types of activities and routes that will be appropriate for the conditions that you will probably encounter.

As you can see, the time control, energy control, and climate control plans are all interwoven into a systematic effort to ensure that you have a safe and successful trip. They are essential ingredients to the planning of any adventure activity and greatly help to minimize the risks associated with the program.

A Framework of Safety

TRANSPORTATION—GETTING TO THE ROADHEAD

One of the most unsafe aspects of outdoor recreation involves getting to the trailhead from base camp. Transportation is usually done by van or personal automobiles. In general, transportation has an accident rate exceeding rates associated with moving water, alpine mountaineering expeditions, ropes courses, and rock climbing which are all viewed as "high-risk" activities (Meyer, 1979). Transportation risk can be minimized by pretrip testing of drivers to cover the following points:

1. Vehicle checks for safety include a check to ensure that the tires not only meet legal tread depth but are capable of dealing with the heavy loads associated with groups using the out-of-doors for recreation. A trailer, with properly installed light connections, will help to minimize overloading of the vehicles related to carrying backpacks and heavy gear, etc., in addition to passengers. Similarly, safety checks and needed repairs of brakes, cooling system checks, steering, brakelights, headlights and turn signals will help prevent accidents. A battery check will possibly prevent stranded groups, resulting in irritation and missed itineraries. Vehicles should be equipped with first aid kits and emergency accessories such as chains, tools, fire extinguishers, and flares and/or reflectors.

2. Pretrip testing of drivers should go beyond a license check for insurance purposes and include a road test in the vehicle to be used on the trip.

3. Group policy and legal needs should be reviewed as to requiring passengers to buckle seat belts, avoiding passenger transport on top of a truck-

load, and avoiding transport in open vehicles except under well-controlled conditions. On longer trips policy for scheduling driving shifts should be decided upon in advance.

4. Pretrip coordination among drivers as to routes, speeds and stops will help minimize driving hazards related to uncertainty in the minds of the drivers.

THE INTERACTION OF ENVIRONMENTAL FACTORS AND PERSONAL FACTORS AS A MODEL FOR SAFETY MANAGEMENT

Many accidents evolve from common roots. The environment, on one hand, with its steep slopes, avalanches, loose rock, gravity, storms, lightning, and other recurring natural events, exists in an ongoing dynamic interaction. When we enter the wilderness, we bring personal factors such as knowledge and skill, personal and group goals, peer pressure and group dynamics, differing levels of physical conditioning, and a limited human perception of the time scale and processes involved in recurring natural events. These normal environmental and personal factors will occasionally come together in a dangerous way, usually a dangerous act, unless we glean all of the information that we can from our own experiences and the experiences of others. Then, based on reflection, we can internalize a reasonable set of guidelines for operating in the out-of-doors and for coping with the unexpected situations that are normal as we travel through the wilderness. This, of course, is the process of developing good judgment discussed in chapter 2.

NATURAL HAZARDS

Natural hazards are commonplace in the outdoors and need to be viewed from the perspective of potential accidents involving a group or individuals. Accidents occur when a participant or instructor misjudges this accident potential. For example, crossing a spot that requires an individual with a heavy pack to jump can lead to twisted ankles or knees, necessitating a lengthy evacuation. This type of accident can occur in a group when the first person of a group makes a conscious, but unwise,decision to act based on an estimation of his/her own ability to complete the act. If this lead person succeeds, those behind will be less likely to question their own ability to act. They may be less capable of acting successfully, and may fail.

A second concern involves understanding the mechanisms by which well-studied natural hazards such as lightning strikes or avalanches work. For example, a survey of hikers and climbers on Mt. Hood, a snow-covered and avalanche-prone mountain, revealed that 92 percent of these recreationalists did not have enough simple knowledge about avalanches to take the most basic precautions to safeguard themselves (Couche, 1977). Reasons for this gap between known mechanisms of natural hazards and personal knowledge appear to be related to lack of education.

There are two things that you can do to safeguard yourself with regards to natural hazards. First, many natural hazards, like avalanches, are well understood as to their mechanisms of formation and ways to test for their probable occurrence. A W.E.A. instructor should be aware of what hazards have been studied and take advantage of opportunities to learn about these. For example, the National Ski Patrol, among others, presents both classroom and field experiences to educate the public about avalanches. Second, specific natural hazards, for example avalanche paths, recur in a given area, and pre-trip discussions with individuals who know the local area can give you specific information about sites to avoid or to be especially aware of if you must travel through these areas.

THE LEADER'S PERSONAL ACTIVITY SKILLS
Leadership implies self-knowledge and an acceptance of your own personal limitations. Activities that are fun and exciting for two skilled friends who are pushing their limits can be dangerous for groups where skill level, knowledge, aspirations and group dynamics vary widely. A leader needs advanced knowledge in an activity in order to anticipate what might go wrong in that activity with individuals of differing skill levels. An example, a rappel failure occurring in a beginning rock-climbing class from a university's education department (Williamson and Rosenbaum, 1983):

> The class was practicing rappelling. The victim of this accident was making his second descent. Each member of the class had made one descent on the rope which was anchored around a rock. Witnesses described the victim as moving down three meters, then "fidgeting" with the rope, as if there was a problem. The rope "popped" off the anchor rock. The victim fell about 20 meters and died instantly.

The analysis of this accident seems straightforward as to its immediate cause: If the rappel station had more than one independent anchor, as is common practice, a backup would have prevented total anchor failure. Also, inexperienced rappelers are commonly belayed with the belayer secured by a separate anchor. We can infer that the leader in this situation was unaware of these two safety procedures and from this we might conclude that this leader was relatively inexperienced to lead this type of activity. This accident might have been anticipated by a leader with greater personal experience than required for the specific activity as well as experience in working with groups of beginners in this type of setting.

PROBLEMS OF GOAL ORIENTATION AND PEER PRESSURE
Goal orientation can be a problem for both large and small groups. Many outdoor people seek achievement such as that found in gaining a summit or traversing a wilderness basin. One of the amazing aspects of experience in the outdoors is the extent to which individuals and groups sometimes invest

in these goals and carry on in the face of extreme difficulties to achieve the goal. In the face of difficulty and danger, peer pressure can sway the group into continuing when individuals have self-doubts about the safety of attempting the goal. Unspoken peer pressure can keep a group moving through the critical moments of a trip and turn out to have a positive effect. This is true when a member of a group is filled with self-doubts that are a normal part of attempting new and difficult goals. Peer pressure, however, is not always positive and can lead an individual or group to attempt to reach goals that they are neither experienced enough nor equipped to attempt. As outdoor leaders, we should understand that peer pressure, whether positive or negative, is an ever-present factor in our outings with others and be prepared to both discuss and act on that knowledge to our own and the group's best interests.

Since goal orientation seems such a prominent part of group behavior in the outdoors it might also successfully be dealt with openly. This can be done verbally by openly talking about goal orientation before group members invest in a particular goal. On a winter trip that we were leading, the group's first thought of a goal was to climb New Hampshire's Mt. Washington in order to stand on the top of New England in winter. On previous trips we had been able to do this. However, on any given day winds can be above 100 MPH and avalanches can be part of the experience. So as to avoid the pressure of achieving what might be an unrealistic goal, as a group we discussed two goals. The second goal was a two-day ski cross country through a tree-covered wilderness area. When the final expedition came, avalanche conditions and winds up high forced us to give up the climb of Mt. Washington. The cross-country ski was fun, and challenging in its own way. Most importantly, in achieving or even taking on this goal it became the primary experience. Possibilities of climbing Mt. Washington were tucked into the back of memory along the way. A group on a time budget might pick at least two worthwhile potential goals, one of which is achievable in almost any weather conditions. It is important that both of these goals be presented to the group as equal without implying that one is a "lesser" goal.

RISK-MANAGEMENT PRINCIPLES

Managing risk to a large degree involves managing human errors related to natural environmental hazards. This implies gaining knowledge through both personal experience and through the experience of others. Experience, skills and knowledge can be gained through a teaching progression accompanied by an increasing awareness of the environment and how it works. The teaching progression of instruction should match the physical and psychological needs of the participants. A common teaching progression in beginning climbing classes follows the sequence of (1) bouldering near the ground where the participant learns about body movement sequences and safety considerations such as spotting and helmets; (2) learning about equipment including ropes and their construction, how to tie knots and harnesses; (3) conducting a "ground school" that duplicates the cliff site, but on flat ground. During this time participants learn about the belay chain with discussions of anchors, body stances, rope manipulation requirements, back-up systems, communication codes and their significance, and procedures to be followed at the top of a climb; (4) on the cliff climb participants put into practice the skills studied earlier and discover gaps of knowledge, come to truly understand the utility of the belay chain, gain confidence, and come to trust both the system, their fellow students and the knowledge of the instructor; (5) following top-roped climbing the sequence can continue with multipitch climbing in which participants learn about clipping into anchors on stances, rope restacking, and the removal of rock protection, among other skills.

Principles of safe outdoor experiences can be gained by a participant through direct experience, in a structured program, and by learning from the experiences of others through case studies. A partial list of sources of written case studies is given below. The guidelines that arise from these studies do not form the sole basis of decision making but are useful direction indicators to help form a decision based on all of the data available in any particular situation. A partial list of guidelines for risk management is presented near the end of this chapter.

Table 7-1
Sources of Case Studies of Accidents and Guidelines

Williamson, J. and S. Rosenbaum (Ed.) (1983) *Accidents in North American Mountaineering*, Published by the American Alpine Club & The Alpine Club of Canada, AAC 113 East 90th Street, New York, New York 10028 or AAC, P.O. Box 1026, Banff, Alberta TOLOCO. This is one specific issue of an annual publication that has been published jointly by the American Alpine Club and the Alpine Club of Canada under different editors since 1951.

Williamson, J. A., Harvard, P. Lev, Bangs, C. and Shaw B. (1986) *The BaseCamp Program and the Mount Hood Accident Reports of the BaseCamp Inquiry Committee to the Board of Trustees of Oregon Episcopal School*, published by The Oregonian publishing Co. Vol. 136 - No. 44.821 Friday, July 25.

Walbridge, C. C. (Ed.) (1986) *River Safety Reports*, American Canoe Association, River Safety Task Force, 7217 Lockport Place, P.O. Box 248, Lorton, Virginia 22079. This is one specific issue of publication.

Snyder, J. (1985) "*A 'Collection of Accidents and Incidents to Learn From' Gleaned from the Records of the North Carolina Outward*

Bound School." An unpublished M.S. thesis in Experiential Education from Mankato State University, Mankato, Minnesota.

Williams, Knox (1975) *The Snowy Torrents: Avalanche Accidents in the United States 1967-71*, U.S.D.A. Forest Service, General Technical Report RM-8.

Johanson, K. M. (Ed.) (1987) *Common Practices in Adventure Programming*, The Association for Experiental Education, Safety Committee, Box 249, University of Colorado, Boulder 80309.

Skill Training for Particular Adventure Activities

CERTIFICATION PROGRAMS AND LEADERSHIP PROGRAMS

Certification programs provide specific skill training that attempts to establish a standard within the field of outdoor education. The prototype of these programs might be considered the American Red Cross Basic and Advanced First Aid Programs that establishes minimum standards on a national basis for these skills. Outdoor education programs, W.E.A., N.O.L.S. and Outward Bound attempt to establish minimum skills in low-impact camping and safe movement in the wild out-of-doors as part of their programs. These outdoor education programs also run instructor training programs to familiarize participants with the methods of teaching used within the particular program. Outward Bound has established the National Training Institute to present short courses on a wide variety of topics and skills such as group counseling, first aid, and skill management.

The main thrust of W.E.A. courses is to develop sound judgment and leadership skills. As such, W.E.A. teaches skills such as climbing and first aid in support of judgment and leadership development. W.E.A. encourages its graduates to develop advanced skills in working with people by participating as members or leaders of all kinds of community, college, or national groups, and by acquiring counseling skills through organizations that offer this type of training as well as through personal mentoring.

GUIDELINES FOR SELECTING A TRAINING PROGRAM IN
ACTIVITY SKILLS AND/OR A MENTOR

Selecting a training program in skill activities and/or a mentor can be full of uncertainty. However, there appear to be a few guidelines that make sense. A learner should seek someone truly interested in the process of teaching/learning. This person will have good communication skills and show a personal interest that will enable the learner to relax and trust his/ her instructor in the face of uncertainty or fear that is normal to beginning a new activity. A good instructor, for example in kayaking, will probably exhibit skills that the learner may feel that he/she is not capable of achieving. The learner should understand that a high level of skill is acquired over many years of participation in the specific recreational activity at hand and was acquired slowly by the instructor. These skills should be exhibited in such a way that they are a natural part of the process of teaching and not done to show off. If the instructor does not have a high level of skill and a personal concern for the student then the student should look elsewhere for instruction.

A second aspect of the process of finding an instructor involves looking for an organization that has been in existence for a period of years. Established outdoor-education schools such as W.E.A., N.O.L.S., or Outward Bound have a track record of many years and have demonstrated a continuing concern for safety of participants. These organizations have worked with many hundreds of thousands of individuals with an excellent safety record based on institutional concern for safety that extends from the boards of trustees down to the field instructors. Procedures are constantly reviewed for safety concerns at all levels. Established commercial guide schools or professional organizations for guides such as the American Professional Mountain Guides Association, and institutions such as the American Canoe Association, are also safety conscious and have excellent safety records. W.E.A. graduates are encouraged to take advantage of the training that they make available.

Organizing a High-adventure Outdoor-pursuits Activity

High-adventure outdoor activities often use a specific site for top rope rock climbing or rope courses, as well as broader area sites where the group moves through potentially hazardous terrain, such as in mountain snow travel or whitewater canoeing. These differing activities have in common specialized skills and knowledge that can only be gained by long apprenticeship. For this reason, these activities are most safely conducted under the guidance of instructors who have extensive knowledge, personal experience, and experience working with groups in settings similar to those that will be used for a specific activity. In addition, if the specialist is familiar with the specific cliff site, ropes course, mountain slopes, or river to be used on a trip, then site-specific hazards and group interaction with these can be anticipated.

To run a wilderness trip the organizer needs to be concerned with factors such as trip organization, securing necessary permits from the responsible agencies, knowledge of potential rescue agencies, basic safety standards, practices and equipment to be used. Instructor/student ratios vary for differing activities as instructor qualifications. General safety practices, which apply to all program levels and to all activities, are listed below. These are modified from Johanson (1987).

1. Safety policies established by a program apply regardless of the skill level of the participants. For example, accomplished technical climbers may

believe that they will find beginning climbs within their ability to climb un-roped. They should not do so even if it is true that there is little danger for them. This establishes both an absolute safety standard for the group and a model of expected group behavior. As a result, less skilled climbers will not be lured into what for them is a dangerous activity and the focus of the pro-gram remains on learning.

2. Written policies provide a basic foundation for judgment; conditions may warrant more restrictive practices.

3. Any departure from specific safety policies must only be in emergency situations to significantly enhance safety, and involve a carefully developed, rational and defensible plan. Good written policies develop from previous instructor experiences and should continuously be reviewed to keep them up-to-date. However, no set of policies can cover all possible field condi-tions, particularly emergency situations. When policies are modified by an individual instructor in the field the modifications must be well thought out, and be defensible to the extent that other instructors might follow the same course of action in a similar situation.

4. Illegal drugs and alcohol: Unless prescribed by a physician, drugs are incompatible with adventure programming. The use of drugs while on a field experience potentially jeopardizes the safety of both participants and staff members. Therefore, staff or participants should not possess or use illegal drugs or alcohol on any field experience. Participants who refuse to refrain from using illegal drugs or alcohol while taking part in a program activity should be removed from the activity.

5. The instructor immediately responsible for participants should be fa-miliar with the environment to be used for an activity and trained to con-duct the activity during the seasons of scheduled operation. For example, an instructor familiar with traveling through the Teton Range in midsummer with a group would require advanced knowledge, experience and training before working with a group during the late fall, early spring, or winter in the same area.

6. A safety briefing that sets the tone should be part of every potentially dangerous activity. Participants should understand the risks inherent in the activity before it begins and be aware of any program rules that may apply. This briefing is best if it is ongoing throughout the course exploring new conditions and reminding participants of previous situations.

7. Minimum staff/participant ratios should be established for all field ac-tivities. For example, for basic hiking/camping there should generally be two instructors for each group of 10 to 12 participants; however the ratio may

vary according to the type of participants, terrain and activity.

8. No participant should be placed in a position of responsibility for the safety of others without having received specific instructions and demonstrated to the supervisor(s) the ability to perform satisfactorily.

9. Participants should not be permitted to participate alone (i.e., on their own, away from the group or instructor) in an unplanned manner in most adventure-program activities. Programs should be aware of the legal implications of permitting unplanned solo activities. In addition, each specific activity such as backpacking, expeditions, desert hiking, caving, rock-climbing, etc. needs to have a specific written list of qualifications for instructors and practices for activities.

10. Final expeditions are a normal part of a W.E.A. course. The expedition is used as a culminating activity that provides an opportunity for unaccompanied participants to demonstrate acquired skills and to make situational decisions. This is normally done at the end of a course after participants have acquired the skills necessary to succeed. Plans for these expeditions should be made by participants in consultation with the instructor. Plans should be in keeping with terrain, participant and group abilities, equipment available, known hazards and expected weather. Instructors should be familiar with the routes that groups follow and should explain safety restrictions and emergency procedures to participants. When there is more than one group, each group should know the proposed route of the instructors, the proposed route of the other groups and the location of base-camp. Checkpoints, group and instructor contacts and the manner in which the instructor will monitor the progress of the group should be decided and discussed by both parties before the final expedition.

A PARTIAL LIST OF GUIDELINES TO RISK MANAGEMENT IN THE WILD OUT-OF-DOORS

These guidelines have been developed from the examination of specific case studies of accidents and near misses, personal experiences, and educational opportunities (Cinnamon, 1989) and have been generalized. Knowing which guideline to apply in a particular situation is, of course, a decision making process that requires judgment. Judgment can be learned and the instructor on the spot is the person who can best adapt written guidelines or policies to special situations.

LEADERS AND PARTICIPANTS:

1. Leaders of an outdoor activity should have more experience, knowl-

edge or skill than required for the activity at hand. This additional experience gives the leader a cushion of knowledge, and skill to handle the experience at hand if anything should go wrong. Importantly, advanced knowledge and experience allows the leader to anticipate what might go wrong in the situation and to take steps to prevent the accident. This reserve of experience and skill is one component of what we call good judgment. Good judgment is based on experience and analysis of each specific situation, rather than written rules to be followed to the letter. This is a cornerstone of safe outdoor experiences.

2. Besides exceeding our abilities we need to understand the dangers of approaching our abilities in the environmental setting at hand. This is especially true when we are entrusted with the lives of others. As an example, adventurers need to lower their goals and maintain a much larger margin of safety when operating in very cold temperatures where a minor accident, a sprained ankle, can quickly become life threatening.

3. A novice learning an adventure activity needs to work with a skilled mentor concerned with the novice's well-being. Leaders, instructors and mentors need to have technical skills, people skills, and knowledge related to the environment. The mentor needs to be safety conscious within the context of the activity engaged in, whether that activity is mountaineering or another high-adventure outdoor activity. Leadership style may have a direct impact upon group safety.

GROUPS:
1. Objectives need to fit the physical fitness and abilities of the group whether it is an organized group or an informal group joined together for a common adventure. Groups may be oriented toward goal attainment such as hiking a particular trail, or place primary emphasis on education. Participants in both types of groups should be physically trained for conditions expected in attempting a particular goal to avoid fatigue that may affect motor control and decision making. Illness and hypothermia lead to an inability to make safe decisions.

2. Safety does not lie in numbers but rather in personal competence and good planning.

GOALS AND DECISIONS:
1. Goal orientation is a normal function of groups and may be positive or negative in its effects. Since goal orientation seems a prominent part of group behavior in the outdoors, it might successfully be dealt with openly.
2. Peer pressure, whether positive or negative, is an ever-present factor in our outings with others. Leaders need to be prepared to act on that knowledge to function in the group's best interest.

3. Groups on a time budget are advised to pick at least two worthwhile potential goals, one of which is achievable in almost any weather conditions by all members of the group. If the group does split up, each group should be under competent leadership and contain enough internal strength to reach its goal safely.

4. High-adventure activities, where there is not much room for error, should always be based on personal aspirations and ability and not re-quirements. Examples include expeditions above tree-line where shelter from cold or storm is difficult, winter camping, whitewater canoeing, etc.

5. In informal groups of adventures-in-common, or the small groups typical of a final expedition that is part of an educational wilderness course, group members will benefit by discussing decision-making questions and procedures before heading out. This will establish that a consultation process is expected when important decisions are to be made.

MOVEMENT:
1. A basic rule of safety in backcountry travel is that members of the par-ty not lose sight of one another.

2. Traditional practices can be a potential cause of accidents. Individuals or groups often have initial doubts about an activity. However, if the first trip or event succeeds without incident, subsequent doubts are partially dis-missed on the basis of past success. This produces a cyclic-reasoning process that allows the activity to continue on the basis of its traditional usage even though it is known to be potentially unsafe. Breaking this cycle of tradi-tional but potentially unsafe practice appears to be difficult once it becomes established. One way to break this cycle might be to listen carefully to new voices that question any traditional practices whether the new voices are those of novices or seasoned practitioners. Safety review committees can also attempt to break this cycle. Examples of such traditional practices that proved to be unsafe include a bridge crossing (Synder, 1985) and climbing into a severe recurring storm (Cinnamon, 1989).

A MODEL OF ACCIDENTS:
The two factors that are common to accidents are environmental factors and human factors (Hale, 1984). The role of guidelines in preventing ac-cidents is to establish a barrier between these environmental hazards and un-wise human actions that stem from the human factors. This may be summed up as the environment, on one hand, with its steep slopes, avalanches, loose rock, gravity, storms, lightning and other recurring natural hazards, exist in an ongoing dynamic interaction. On the other hand, what we bring into the wilderness are personal factors such as knowledge and skill, personal and

group goal orientation, peer pressure and group dynamics, physical conditioning or fatigue, and a limited human perception of the time scale and processes involved in recurring natural events. Accidents occur when human and environmental hazards come together in a dangerous manner. The role of guidelines, judgment, and experience is to prevent this interaction.

Learning to Adventure and to Lead Adventures

It should be understood that learning to adventure in the wild out-of-doors in a safe, enjoyable, and educational manner can best be thought of as a process. It is an ongoing process that takes time, effort, many experiences and reflection on those experiences. Experience can be gained in many different ways including being a participant in a group, assisting or leading an adventure-based educational group, and working with a more experienced mentor as well as professional guides. Knowledge can also be gained through analyzing case studies. Each of these modes of learning can reinforce the other and will ultimately help the novice become a better leader.

In order to move safely through the wilderness the novice needs to learn to initiate planning before the trip begins, to develop an understanding of risk management principles while gaining environmental knowledge and leadership skills, and to develop the judgment necessary to adapt this planning and knowledge to specific situations as they happen. In the process of gaining this, the novice leader begins at a level where he/she is unaware of the skills, knowledge and experience associated with effective leadership. Through stages he/she learns to operate at higher levels of skill and abilities when traveling through the wild out-of-doors. At all times, leaders need to keep in focus principles of moving through the wilderness and taking care of both themselves and members of their groups that are discussed throughout this text.

REFERENCE

Buell, L. (1983). *Outdoor Leadership Competency: A Manual of Self-Assessment and Staff Evaluation*. Environmental Awareness Publisher, P.O. Box 990, Greenfield, MA.

Cinnamon, C. G. (1989). Risk Management in High Adventure Outdoor Pursuits. In J. Gilbert and E. Brunner (Eds.) Proceedings of the 1988 National Conference on Outdoor Recreation. Available from Jim Gilbert, Ed.D., Department of Health, Physical Education and Recreation, the University of Mississippi, University, MI38677.

Couche, S. (1977). *Avalanche Awareness Survey*. In J. Throop, (Ed.), *Mazama Journal*, 909 N.W. Nineteenth Ave., Portland, OR: Mazamas.

Cousineau, C. (1977). A Delphi Consensus on a Set of Principles for the Development of a Certification System for Educators in Outdoor Adventure Programs. Unpublished doctoral dissertation. University of Northern Colorado: Greeley, CO.

Green, P. J. (1981). The Content of a College-Level Outdoor Leadership

Course for Land-Based Outdoor Pursuits in the Pacific Northwest: A Delphi Consensus. Unpublished doctoral dissertation, University of Washington, Seattle.

Hachett, P. (1978). *Nepal: Mountain Sickness: Prevention, Recognition & Treatment.* Mountain Travel, Inc.: Albany, CA.

Hale, A. (1984). Safety Management for Outdoor Program Leaders: A Workshop Presented by National Safety Network, Bellefontaine, OH 43311.

Johanson, K. (Ed.) (1987). *Common Practices in Adventure Programing, 3rd Ed.* Boulder, CO: The Association for Experimental Education.

Meyer, D. (1979). The Management of Risk. *The Journal for Experiential Education,* 2 (2), 9-14.

Petzoldt, P. (1984). *The New Wilderness Handbook.* New York: W.W. Norton & Co.

Priest, S. (1988). Outdoor Leadership Training in Higher Education. *Journal of Experiential Education,* 11 (1).

Raiola, E. O. (1988). Outdoor Wilderness Education: A Leadership Curriculum. *Journal of Parks and Recreation Administration* 6(2).

Swiderski, M. J. (1981). Outdoor Leadership Competencies Identified by Outdoor Leaders in Five Western Regions. Unpublished doctoral dissertation, University of Washington, Seattle.

Synder, J. (1985). "'A Collection of Accidents and Incidents to Learn From,' Gleaned From the Records of the North Carolina Outward Bound School." Unpublished M.S. thesis, Mankato State University, Mankato, MN.

Williamson J. and S. Rosenbaum, (1983). Rappel Failure, Inadequate Protection, Utah, Diamond Fork. In Accidents in North American Mountaineering. New York: American Alpine Club.

8.

WILDERNESS EMERGENCY PROCEDURES AND TREATMENT

by William W. Forgey, M.D.
Indiana University Northwest

Introduction

Wilderness emergencies are precipitated by environmental, traumatic, or infectious causes. Prevention must be given emphasis. Evacuation or assistance networking must be identified. Medical-legal aspects of wilderness first aid must be understood.

The Wilderness Education Association's curriculum does not attempt to duplicate the important emergency procedures taught in Red Cross Advanced First Aid courses or in the Department of Transportation's Wilderness First Responder or Emergency Medical Technician's Curricula. Rather, the W.E.A. curriculum emphasizes emergencies unique to the expeditionary environment and emergency management considerations specific to expeditions. This chapter is, therefore, not intended as a comprehensive overview of wilderness first aid and medicine.

Because environmental injuries are a primary source of emergencies specific to expeditions, they are addressed in some detail here. An effort is made to address physiological processes, symptomatology, and treatment of each. Brief discussions of traumatic and infectious injuries then follow, and the chapter closes with a description of wilderness medical kits.

The assumption here is that W.E.A. instructors have competence equivalent to Red Cross Advanced First Aid or DOT First Responder. This chapter is an attempt to enrich that understanding with more thorough explanations and updated information for a few specific issues.

Environmental Injuries

The most potentially dangerous risk to an outdoor traveler comes from environmental exposure. Proper prevention, recognition, and methods of field treatment are essential skills for W.E.A. instructors. Of primary concern are injuries relating to hypothermia, hyperthermia, the various high-altitude illnesses, and lightning injury.

An important aspect of prevention of the heat-stress injuries is proper hydration, nutrition, clothing, and equipment. These topics are addressed in the chapters on basic wilderness skills and rations planning.

HYPOTHERMIA

The term "hypothermia" refers to the lowering of the body's core temperature to 95 degrees Fahrenheit; "profound hypothermia" is a core temperature lower than 90 degrees Fahrenheit. The term "hypothermia" applies to two distinctly different disorders. One is "chronic hypothermia," the slow-onset hypothermia of the outdoor traveler exposed to conditions too cold for his equipment to adequately protect him. The other is "acute," or "immersion hypothermia," the rapid-onset hypothermia of a person immersed in cold water (Auerbach, 1986; Nelson, 1985; Forgey, 1985; Wilkerson, 1986).

The W.E.A. instructor must understand the distinction between chronic hypothermia and acute hypothermia. These injuries are dissimilar in that the body's response to each is quite different. Ideal treatment is also quite different in the hospital setting, but in the field we sometimes must rely on the old-fashioned cuddle technique for both types of victims (Forgey, 1985).

PREVENTION IS THE HALLMARK OF SURVIVAL

Hypothermia is the most likely of the environmental injuries that will be encountered in the outdoors. As in other elements of the W.E.A. philosophy, prevention is the hallmark of survival. The factors that protect trip members from hypothermia must be understood by all W.E.A. instructors. These factors include:

PROPER PRETRIP PHYSICAL CONDITIONING—The ability to perform work is obviously directly related to the level of an individual's physical condition. All work that is performed, such as hiking, skiing, shivering, or jumping in place, converts to metabolic heat. Persons in poor physical condition are unable to continue work, or shiver in response to cold, for as long a period of time as other, more fit individuals. Thus, for a W.E.A. course, precourse travel plans must account for the ability of the weakest student.

ADEQUATE NUTRITION—Loss of energy stores will negate adequate physical condition. Proper nutrition will include the adequate ingestion of calories with an adequate time interval to allow the body to absorb and metabolically process this food into the molecules used as fuel sources. These molecules cells as an energy source. It takes at least 45 minutes to begin adequate substrate regeneration, with two hours being required to replace 85% of substrate substance. Snacking on the run is an acceptable method of providing low levels of nutrients and helping with a psychological uplift, but it will not adequately resupply nutrients to a depleted individual.

PHYSICAL EXHAUSTION—Exhaustion reflects, among other things, the depletion of the high energy stores mentioned above. An exhausted person will require rest as well as adequate nutritional replacement. Physical exhaustion is the most important warning that exists of impending hypothermia! If a trip member becomes fatigued, and weather conditions are adverse, hypothermia will soon develop in that individual. Your golden opportunity to make a decision as a W.E.A. instructor for that individual's protection is at that moment. Either adequate additional clothing or shelter for rest must be provided, or an attempt to end the trip soon will have to be made.

PREVENTION OF DEHYDRATION—A 10% dehydration results in significant loss of thermal control, including increased risk of frost bite. As humans do not feel thirst until they are at least 5% dehydrated, ensure that all trip members drink adequate replacement fluid volume. Trip members should receive 13 to 20 ounces of water before an activity and 16 ounces of water hourly.

The extent of dehydration can be followed by noting the color of urine. If the color deepens beyond a pale yellow, that individual requires additional fluid.

ADEQUATE CLOTHING—Most chronic exposure hypothermia deaths occur at temperatures of 30 degrees to 50 degrees F. A day that starts out at a balmy 75 degrees can easily drop into that range with a sudden cloud cover or loss of sun behind a mountain or the horizon. Preparing for sudden wind, rain, and temperature drop is critical. Chapter 5 discusses proper clothing selection in depth. In case of loss, damage, or wetting, even modern synthetic fabrics lose enough of their insulation ability to become inadequate. Ensure adequate wind and rain garments are carried, and that a replacement set of clothing is available. Extra gloves or mittens and dry foot wear must be carried during cold-weather trips.

CHRONIC HYPOTHERMIA

Chronic hypothermia is the lowering of the body's core temperature over a period of greater than six hours. The essential aspects of surviving the chronic hypothermia situation are: being prepared to prevent it, recognizing it if it occurs and knowing how to treat it. Dampness and wind are the most devastating factors to be considered. Dampness enhances hypothermia potential by reducing the effective insulation of clothing and causing evaporative heat loss. Wind augments this potential as the increased convection heat loss can readily strip away body energy, the so-called wind-chill effect.

DIAGNOSING HYPOTHERMIA IN THE FIELD:

Detection of hypothermia is generally made by two observations. The first is to watch for exhaustion. An exhausted person is not necessarily hypothermic yet, but he/she will be unless he/she can obtain adequate rest and clothing. The second is loss of coordination. A person who cannot walk a straight line of 30 feet length is hypothermic. This same test was formerly used by the police to detect inebriation, which also causes loss of coordination. Both impair mental processes. For that reason, when hypothermia is detected in a person, his judgment must be suspect. More than not trusting his decisions, instructors must help such people. They must be treated for hypothermia. Additional clues for the detection of hypothermia can be found by referring to the adjacent chart of hypothermia signs and symptoms.

TREATMENT OF CHRONIC HYPOTHERMIA IN THE FIELD:

The treatment for hypothermia has essentially seven components.

1. PREVENT FURTHER HEAT LOSS. Never rub the person with snow or allow further exposure to the cold. Wet clothing must be removed and replaced with dry clothing. At the very least, it must be covered with rain jacket and pants—and this in turn covered with more insulation. It is probably best to avoid undressing the person exposed to the environment—do this in a sleeping bag or other sheltered area if at all possible. A "thermal wrap" of multiple layers of insulation, which can prevent virtually any further additional heat loss, is an essential technique in preparing the profoundly hypothermic victim for litter evacuation. Try to warm water before giving the patient a drink, if possible.

2. TREAT DEHYDRATION. Chronic hypothermia causes vasoconstriction, which in effect shrinks the fluid volume of the victim. The low relative humidity of cold air also increases fluid loss through respiration. All chronic hypothermic people are, indeed, very dehydrated. This volume needs replacement.

3. TREAT THE VICTIM GENTLY. Very cold people can suffer cardiac rhythm problems if they are jarred around. If they are being carried during an evacuation, avoid bumping them along the ground or dropping them from a stretcher.

4. ADD HEAT. Campfires, in general, are not to be relied upon to prevent hypothermia for they are an ineffective source of heat. A very large (and ecologically unsound) roaring fire can, however, replace a massive number of calories. Practically speaking, if a patient can stand on his own by the fire, he/she is not so profoundly hypothermic that you would have to worry

Table 8-1

SIGNS AND SYMPTOMS OF HYPOTHERMIA

CORE TEMP.	SIGNS AND SYMPTOMS
99° to 97°F (37° to 36°C)	Normal temperature range Shivering may begin
97° to 95°F (36° to 35°C)	Cold sensation, goose bumps, unable to perform complex tasks with hands, shivering can be mild to severe, skin numb
95° to 93°F (35° to 34°C)	Shivering intense, muscle incoordination becomes apparent, movements slow and labored, stumbling pace, mild confusion, may appear alert, unable to walk 30 ft. line properly — BEST FIELD TEST FOR EARLY HYPOTHERMIA
93° to 90°F (34° to 32°C)	Violent shivering persists, difficulty speaking, sluggish thinking, amnesia starts to appear and may be retrograde, gross muscle movements sluggish, unable to use hands, stumbles frequently, difficulty speaking, signs of depression
90° to 86°F 32° to 30°C)	Shivering stops in chronic hypothermia, exposed skin blue or puffy, muscle coordination very poor with inability to walk, confusion, incoherent, irrational behavior, BUT MAY BE ABLE TO MAINTAIN POSTURE AND THE APPEARANCE OF PSYCHOLOGICAL CONTACT
86° to 82°F (30° to 27.7°C)	Muscles severely rigid, semiconscious, stupor, loss of psychological contact, pulse and respirations slow, pupils can dilate
82° to 78°F (27 to 25.5°C)	Unconsciousness, heart beat and respiration erratic, pulse and heart beat may be inapparent, muscle tendon reflexes cease
78° to 75°F (25° to 24°C)	Pulmonary edema, failure of cardiac and respiratory centers, probable death, DEATH MAY OCCUR BEFORE THIS LEVEL
64°F (17.7°C)	Lowest recorded temperature of chronic hypothermia survivor, Chicago 1951
48.2°F (9°C)	Lowest recorded temperature of induced hypothermia in surgical patient with survival, 1958

about rewarming shock. Warm fluids, rebreathing air through a scarf or other wrap, and the careful application of wrapped, hot chemical packs or warmed rocks can also add heat. Care must be taken not to place a hot object in direct contact with skin. Cuddling with one, or preferably two, rescuers in a sleeping bag can also add considerable warmth.

5. AVOID REWARMING SHOCK. The victim who is unable to stand is so ill that if he/she were reheated too rapidly, he/she could be adversely affected. The dehydration of hypothermia causes a substantial decrease in fluid volume, so much so that a sudden rewarming can result in shock, even death. If sudden, large amounts of heat are given to the profoundly (core temperature lower than 90 degrees Fahrenheit) chronic hypothermic, the lack of adequate circulating blood supply, and its considerable alteration that takes place during the slow cooling process, can result in rewarming shock. A person who is obtunded should not be forced to drink fluids.

6. UNDERSTAND AFTERDROP. As a victim is being reheated, it will be noted that his core temperature continues to drop before starting to rise. This is called "afterdrop." It was originally thought to be a cause of death, but the significant reason for death in the chronic hypothermic is actually rewarming shock. All persons will have afterdrop, which is related to the rate of cooling that was taking place before the rewarming process started. In chronic hypothermia, afterdrop is caused by equilibration of heat from the warmer core flowing into the cooler surface tissues. The amount of this afterdrop is only a few degrees. Afterdrop is a serious problem in the treatment of acute (immersion) hypothermia, but is probably not of much concern in the chronic hypothermic. The acute hypothermic has extremely cold surface tissues. Both the equilibration process between the very cold mantle and warmer core, and any increase in blood flow through these tissues, can cause a prodigious afterdrop of many degrees, which becomes clinically significant.

7. ALLOW REST. The hypothermia patient is at or near exhaustion. Rest is mandatory to replace the high energy compounds that are required to shiver, work and otherwise generate heat. If the resting person is being adequately insulated from further heat loss, there is no reason why he/she cannot be allowed to sleep. It is therapeutic. Do not shake or slap a hypothermic individual (see item 3 above).

Deepening hypothermia will lead to a semicomatose state and worse. This victim needs to be evacuated to help. Provide a thermal wrap to prevent further heat loss and transport. Chemical heat packs, etc., can be added to the wrap to help offset further heat loss, but care must be taken not to burn the victim. If evacuation is not feasible, heat will have to be added slowly to avoid rewarming shock. Huddling with two lightly clad rescuers with the victim in an adequate sleeping bag may be the only alternative.

ACUTE HYPOTHERMIA

Acute hypothermia occurs within two hours and is usually caused by immersion in cold water. Whenever the sum of the air temperature and water temperature is less than 100 degrees Fahrenheit, there is a danger of acute hypothermia if a person becomes wet. Afterdrop is a problem in the "acute" or "immersion hypothermic" who has had a significant exposure to cold water. As a rule of thumb, a person who has been in water of 50 degrees or less for a period of 20 minutes or longer is suffering from a severe amount of heat loss. That individual's thermal mass has been so reduced that he/she is in potentially serious condition. He should not be allowed to move around as this will increase the blood flow to his very cold skin and facilitate a profound circulatory induced afterdrop; one that is so great as to be potentially lethal.

TREATMENT OF ACUTE HYPOTHERMIA IN THE FIELD

If an acute hypothermia victim is simply wrapped as a litter case and not provided outside heat, there is a real danger of his cooling below a lethal level due to the profound amount of total heat loss. The ideal treatment is rapid rewarming of the acute hypothermic by placing him in hot water (110 degrees Fahrenheit) to allow rapid replacement of heat. The patient may have an almost normal core temperature initially, but one that is destined to drop dramatically as his body equilibrates his heat store from the core to the very cold mantle. A roaring fire can be a life saver. If not available, huddling two sparsely clad rescuers with the victim in a large sleeping bag may be the only answer—the same therapy that might have to be employed in the field treatment of chronic hypothermia under some conditions.

OTHER COLD INDUCED INJURIES

The problems of prevention, recognition, and field treatment of frostbite, immersion foot, and treatment of cold-water near drowning are discussed in references Auerbach (1986), Forgey (1985, 1987, 1989), Goodman (1989), and Wilkerson (1985, 1986). These are important competencies for W.E.A. instructors, but are well addressed by the other references.

HEAT-STRESS INJURIES

Heat injury is the second leading cause of death among high school athletes, ranking only behind spinal cord injury. Its risk to the outdoor traveler mandates a thorough understanding of its prevention, recognition and treatment, particularly if the trip members are not heat acclimated. Heat-stress injuries are fully discussed by Auerbach (1986), Forgey (1987, 1989), Nelson et al. (1985), and Wilkerson (1985).

High environmental temperatures are frequently aggravated by the amount of work being done, the humidity, reflection of heat from rock, sand or other structures (even snow!) and the lack of air movement. It takes approximately five to seven days to become heat acclimated. Once heat adaptation takes place, there will be a decrease in the loss of salt in the sweat produced, thus conserving electrolytes. Another major change that occurs is the more rapid formation and production of larger quantities of sweat. Thus, the body is able to start its response to an elevation in the core temperature more rapidly and to utilize its efficient cooling mechanism, sweating, more fully and with less electrolyte disturbance to the body.

Salt replacement during the early days of acclimatization can generally be accomplished during meals. As thirst lags behind actual water requirements, people should be encouraged to drink more than thirst dictates to avoid dehydration.

Failure to properly handle heat stress can result in several disorders. While one may progress to another, these disorders are generally classified by increasing symptoms as heat cramps, heat exhaustion and heat stroke.

HEAT CRAMPS

Salt depletion can result in nausea, twitching of muscle groups and, at times severe cramping of abdominal muscles, legs, or elsewhere. Prevention, and treatment consists of stretching the muscles involved (avoid aggressive massage), resting in a cool environment, and replacing salt losses. Generally 10 to 15 grams of salt and generous water replacement should be adequate treatment.

HEAT EXHAUSTION

This is a classic example of SHOCK, but in this case encountered while working in a hot environment. The body has dilated the blood vessels in the skin, hoping to divert heat from the core to the surface for cooling. However, this dilation is so pronounced, coupled with the profuse sweating and loss of fluid—also a part of the cooling process—that the blood pressure to the entire system falls too low to adequately supply the brain and the visceral organs.

The signs and symptoms of heat exhaustion include a rapid heart rate and the other findings associated with shock: pale color, nausea, dizziness, headache, and a lightheaded feeling. Generally, the patient is sweating profusely but this may not be the case. The temperature is as usual in shock, namely it may be low, normal, or mildly elevated.

Treat as for shock. Have the patient lie down immediately and elevate the feet to increase the blood supply to the head. Also, provide copious water. Ten to 15 grams of salt would also be helpful, but water is the most important at a minimum of one to two quarts. Obviously, fluids can only be administered if the patient is conscious. If unconscious, elevate the feet three feet above head level, protect from aspiration of vomit and try to revive with an ammonia inhalant. Give water when the patient awakens.

HEAT STROKE (SUN STROKE)

Heat stroke represents the complete breakdown of the heat-control process (thermal regulation) in the human body. There is a total loss of the ability to sweat, core temperatures rise over 105 degrees Fahrenheit rapidly and will soon exceed 115 degrees Fahrenheit, resulting in death if this is not treated aggressively. There is an increase in the severity of the symptoms mentioned under heat exhaustion. In survivors serious permanent damage can result to kidney, brain and other vital tissues. The patient will be confused and rapidly become unconscious.

THIS IS A TRUE EMERGENCY. Immediately move into shade or erect a hasty barrier for shade. If possible employ immediate immersion in ice water to lower the temperature. Once the core temperature lowers to 102 degrees Fahrenheit, the victim is removed and the temperature carefully monitored. It may continue to fall or suddenly rise again. Further cooling with wet cloths may suffice. Intravenous solutions of normal saline are started in the clinical setting. In the wilderness, douse the victim with the coldest water possible. Massage limbs to allow the cooler blood of the extremities to return to core circulation more readily. Sacrifice your water supply, if necessary, to provide the best coolant effect possible.

This person should be evacuated as soon as possible, for his thermal regulation mechanism is quite unstable for an undeterminable length of time. He should be placed under a physician's care as soon as possible. Terminate the expedition, if necessary, to evacuate.

HIGH-ALTITUDE ILLNESSES

The high altitude-related illnesses can generally be avoided by gradual exposure to higher elevation, with the ascent rate not exceeding 1,000 feet per day when above 8,000 feet. Acclimatization results from physiological adaptation to low oxygen levels, or hypoxia. These complex changes are not fully understood, but include shifts in the acid-base saturation of the blood, changes in oxygen and carbon dioxide influences on respiration rates, increases in red cell concentration and shifts in plasma volume. The physiology is further discussed in references Hackett (1980), Houston (1987) and Wilkerson (1985). The three major clinical manifestations of this disease complex are outlined below:

ACUTE MOUNTAIN SICKNESS (AMS)

Rarely encountered below 6,500 feet (2,000 meters), AMS is common in persons going above 10,000 feet (3,000 meters) who have not taken the time to acclimatize for altitude.

Prevention, as with all of the high-altitude illness problems, is gradual ascent to an altitude above 9,000 feet and light physical activity for the first several days. For persons especially prone to AMS, it may be helpful to take acetazolamide (Diamox) 250 mg every 12 hours starting the day before ascent and continuing the next three to five days. This prescription medication would have to be provided by the individual's physician and should not be provided by the W.E.A. instructor or trip medic.

Symptoms beginning soon after ascent consist of headache (often severe), nausea, vomiting, shortness of breath, weakness, sleep disturbance and occasionally a periodic breathing known to physicians and mountaineers as Cheyne-Stokes breathing, which has the symptoms of rapid deep inspirations followed by periods of very shallow breathing.

Treatment is descent and relief can often be felt even if the descent is only 1,000 to 2,000 feet (300 to 600 meters). Full relief can be obtained by descending to below 6,500 feet (2,000 meters). Stricken individuals should avoid heavy exercise, but sleep does not help as the breathing is slower during sleep and oxygen deprivation is worse. Oxygen will only help if taken continuously for 12 to 48 hours. Aspirin may be used for headache. In addition to descent, Decadron (dexamethasone), another prescription drug, given 4 mg tablets every six hours until below the altitude at which symptoms appeared, has been shown to help mask the symptoms of AMS, but does not seem to correct the underlying pathology. Its use should be restricted in helping the stricken mountaineer in descending only.

HIGH-ALTITUDE PULMONARY EDEMA (HAPE)

This problem is rare below 8,000 feet (2,500 meters), but occurs at higher elevations in those poorly acclimatized. It is more prone to occur in persons between the ages of five and eighteen (the incidence is apparently less than .4% in persons over 21 and as high as six percent in those younger); in persons who have had this problem before; and in persons who have been altitude acclimatized and who are returning to high altitude after spending two or more weeks at sea level. Prevention is through gradual ascent, as described above.

Symptoms develop slowly within 24 to 60 hours of arrival at high altitude with shortness of breath, irritating cough, weakness, rapid heart rate and headache, which rapidly progress to intractable cough with bloody sputum, low-grade fever, and increasing chest congestion. Symptoms may progress at night. Climbers should be evaluated by listening to their chests for a fine crackling sound (called rales) and resting pulse rate checked nightly. A pulse rate of greater than 110 per minute or respirations greater than 16 per minute after a 20 minute rest is an early sign of HAPE. Respirations over 20 per minute and pulse over 120 per minute indicate a medical emergency and the patient must be evacuated immediately. Without treatment, death usually occurs within six to twelve hours after onset of coma.

Descent to lower altitudes is essential and should not be delayed. Oxygen may be of value if given continuously over the next 12 to 48 hours, starting at six liters/minute for the first 15 minutes, then reduced to two liters/minute. A snug face mask is better than nasal prongs. Oxygen may provide rapid relief in mild cases, however it should be continued for a minimum of six to 12 hours, if possible. Oxygen is not a substitute for descent in severe cases. A descent of as little as 2,000 to 3,000 feet (600 to 900 meters) may result in prompt improvement.

HIGH-ALTITUDE CEREBRAL EDEMA (HACE)

This is a less common event than AMS or HAPE just mentioned, but it is more dangerous. Death has occurred from HACE at altitudes as low as 8,000 feet (2,500 meters), but HACE is rare below 11,500 feet (3,500 meters). Prevention is through gradual ascent as described above.

The symptoms are increasingly severe headache, mental confusion, emotional behavior, hallucinations, unstable gait, loss of vision, loss of dexterity, and facial muscle paralysis. The victim may fall into a restless sleep, followed by a deep coma and death.

Descent is essential. Oxygen should be administered. Decadron (dexamethasone) should be given in large doses, namely 10 mg intravenous, followed by 4 mg every six hours intramuscular until the symptoms subside. Response is usually noted within 12 to 24 hours and the dosage may be reduced after two to four days and gradually discontinued over a period of five to seven days. Immediate descent and oxygen are recommended to prevent permanent neurological damage or death.

As can be noted from the above discussions of AMS, HAPE, and HACE, the symptoms progress rather insidiously. They are not clear-cut, separate diseases—they often occur together. The essential therapy for each of them is recognition and descent. This is life saving and more valuable than the administration of oxygen or the drugs mentioned. To prevent them it is helpful to "climb high, but camp low"—i.e., spend nights at the lowest camp elevation feasible. Treatment protocols for the high-altitude illnesses are discussed in references Auerbach (1986), Bowman (1988), Darvill (1985), Forgey (1987), Hackett (1980), Houston (1987), Lentz (1985) and Wilkerson (1985).

LIGHTNING

The four mechanisms of lightning injury are: (1) direct strike, (2) splash, (3) step current, (4) blunt trauma. To minimize the chance of lightning injury, the following should be noted about these mechanisms:

DIRECT STRIKES are most likely when in the open, especially if carrying metal or objects above shoulder level. Shelter should be taken within the cone of safety described as a 45 degree angle down from a tall object, such as a tree or cliff face.

SPLASH injuries are perhaps the most common mechanism of lightning hit. The current striking a tree or other object may jump to a person whose body has less resistance than the object the lightning initially contacted. Splash hits may jump from person to person when several people are standing close together.

STEP CURRENT is also called stride voltage and ground current. The lightning current spreads out in a wave along the ground from the object struck, with the current strength decreasing as the radius from the strike increases. If the victim's feet are at different distances from the point of the strike, and the resistance in the ground is greater than through his body, he/she will complete a circuit. Large groups of people can be injured simultaneously in this manner. Keeping feet and legs together, while squatting down, minimizes the chances of step voltage injury.

BLUNT TRAUMA, or the sledgehammer effect, results from the force of the lightning strike, or the explosive shock wave that it produces. It may occur with the victim being abruptly knocked to the ground. Over 50% of victims will have their ear drums ruptured in one or both ears. This may result from direct thermal damage, the thunder shock wave, or even skull fractures from the blunt trauma. Trauma to the ear drums may be reduced by keeping the mouth open during times of great danger.

Cardiopulmonary arrest is the most significant lightning injury. People screaming from fright or burns after an electrical bolt has struck are already out of immediate danger. Their wounds may be dressed later. Those who appear dead must have immediate attention as they may be salvaged. Generally, when dealing with mass casualties the wounded are cared for preferentially, while the dead are left alone. Not in this instance!

Without CPR, nearly 75% of those suffering arrest die. As the heart tends to restart itself due to its inherent automaticity, the heart beat may return spontaneously in a short time. The respiratory system, however, may be shut down for five to six hours before being able to resume its normal rhythm. The lack of oxygen this would cause will allow a person whose heart has started spontaneously to die.

While CPR is being performed, check for the pulse periodically. When the heart restarts, maintain ventilation for the patient until respirations also resume. Attempt to continue this as long as possible, for even after many hours the victim may revive with no neurological defects, but only if CPR or respiration ventilation has been properly performed. References: Auerbach (1986); Forgey (1987); Wilkerson (1985).

Competencies for Treatment of Traumatic Injuries

PLANNING EMERGENCY PROCEDURES

The ability to properly plan for prevention and subsequent management of a wilderness injury or illness is the most minutely examined portion of any outdoor program. Potential loss of life, discomfort for trip members, legal sanctions, and potential adverse publicity arise if this area of your outdoor program is deficient. The fact that a wilderness emergency occurs does not necessarily reflect a failure of proper pretrip preparation or planning, but actions taken after such an incident will certainly be minutely scrutinized. A plan for the proper care and potential evacuation of trip members is as important as any other aspect of your trip preparation.

THE NEED TO PREPLAN
Injuries due to an accident must be minimized. To avoid further damage a careful identification of the extent of all injuries must be obtained, preservation of life accomplished and a plan formulated for either dealing with the problem or obtaining additional help for the patient. The latter course of action may require evacuation.

PROPER MEDICAL TRAINING
Unconscious patients require a systematic examination and immediate intervention when necessary to treat life-threatening problems. W.E.A. instructors must be certified in CPR and certified at a level equal to Department of Transportation's First Responder or the American Red Cross Advanced First Aid. The proper sequencing of establishing level of consciousness, requesting help, positioning the victim, rescuer position, opening the airway, determining lack of respirations, performing rescue breathing, management of airway obstruction, determining lack of pulse, performing chest compressions with rescue breathing and management of choking emergencies must be proficiently learned.

PRIMARY AND SECONDARY SURVEY
Competency of preforming a head-to-toe examination must also be mastered by W.E.A. instructors. The majority of traumatic accidents produce a single injury. Detection of multiple injuries, however, requires an overall examination of the victim and assessment of the combined effect on the body. A head-to-toe examination must also be done whenever a patient is found unconscious, since it is impossible to tell what caused the unconsciousness and the patient cannot direct the examiner to specific problems.

THE RECORDER
A designated recorder must write down what happened, the examination findings, any condition changes and the treatment given. Indicate times with each notation. Rate of progression of symptoms and signs is very important information for medical personnel.

REFERENCES
Medical assessment, stabilization techniques, and evacuation considerations are covered by references Bechdel and Ray (1989), Bowman (1988), Goodman (1989), Setnicka (1980) and Wilkerson (1985). Self-care of minor wounds not requiring evacuation and prolonged care of injuries when evacuation is not feasible are covered by reference Forgey (1987).

Wilderness Medical Issues

There are several unresolved issues involving wilderness medical care of traumatic and environmental injuries of which the W.E.A. instructor should be cognizant. The considerations listed below are currently topics that are in flux, with differences of opinion among various authorities. Being aware of the basis of their opinions is necessary to devise an appropriate approach during implementation of the W.E.A. program.

ANAPHYLACTIC SHOCK TREATMENT: Provisioning and being able to use injectable epinephrine for the field treatment of anaphylaxis is essential if any course members are known to have an immediate type of hypersensitivity to insect stings. References: Auerbach (1986), Bowman (1988), Forgey (1987, 1989), Goodman (1989), Nelson et al. (1985), Wilkerson (1985).

ALTITUDE-RELATED ILLNESS: Proper acclimatization techniques for prevention of acute mountain sickness (AMS), recognition and treatment of high altitude pulmonary edema (Hape) and high altitude cerebral edema (HACE) are essential if trips are to be taken at elevations above 9,000 feet. References: Forgey (1987), Goodman (1989), Houston (1987), Wilkerson (1985).

BURN AND BLISTER MANAGEMENT: Use of Spenco 2nd Skin for these wounds is state of the art. References: Forgey (1987, 1989).

CPR USE IN THE WILDERNESS: Its use for cardiac causes in the wilderness is discouraged, but for treatment of near drowning, lightning victims, and—in certain cases—hypothermia, it is recommended. References: Forgey (1987), Wilkerson (1985).

DISLOCATED-JOINT MANAGEMENT: The ideal wilderness management of a dislocation includes reducing, or correcting, the dislocation immediately, if possible. References: Bowman (1988), Forgey (1987).

FRACTURE MANAGEMENT: Fractures must not be allowed to remain grossly angulated, but should be repositioned into a more natural alignment. References: Bowman (1988), Forgey (1987).

FROSTBITE: Frost nip and superficial frostbite must be distinguished from deep frostbite with field treatments of the first two and methods for field management of the latter understood. References: Bowman (1988), Forgey (1985, 1987), Wilkerson (1986).

HYPOTHERMIA: Instructors should recognize the difference between chronic and acute hypothermia and successfully execute prevention, diagnosis, and treatment protocols for each. References: Bowman (1988), Forgey (1985, 1987), Wilkerson (1986).

IMPALED OBJECTS: These must be removed if evacuation will take longer than 24 hours. References: Bowman (1988), Forgey (1987).

SNAKEBITE MANAGEMENT: Use of the "Extractor" is part of the basic first aid treatment, which also includes treatment for shock and proper wound management. References: Forgey (1987, 1989).

SPINE INJURY: These will require careful repositioning to allow evacuation. References: Bowman (1988), Setnicka (1980).

WOUND CLEANSING: Aggressive cleaning is essential to prevent infection. References Auerbach: (1986), Darvill (1985), Forgey (1987, 1989), Lentz et al. (1985), Wilkerson (1985).

Administrative Considerations

PRETRIP MEDICAL REQUIREMENTS FOR COURSE PARTICIPANTS
Due to the exertion required to traverse wilderness terrain under various weather conditions that will be encountered during W.E.A. training, trip participants must be free of medical conditions that would place them at danger or cause other trip members significant educational compromises. The course is a leadership laboratory and not simply an outdoor experience for participants. The entire group must be able to benefit from the time in the field.

Participants must be free from orthopedic problems that would hinder full participation. This particularly includes problems with foot, ankle, knee and back. Participants should not have infirmities or medical or mental conditions that might deteriorate in the wilderness and potentially require medical evacuation. All trip members should be in good physical condition and be able to perform adequate aerobic exercise at intended altitudes of course operation.

A medical history form must be used that identifies any of the above problems. If a student history form is flagged with a possible deficiency, the course director must decide the feasibility of allowing the student to enroll. Questionable cases should be referred to a physician who can indicate that he/she feels there is no disqualification, or recommend disqualification from course participation, or perhaps recommend a physical examination for additional information upon which to base a decision.

Immunizations must be current. Tetanus-diphtheria prophylaxis must be current (within 10 years). If foreign travel is involved, immunizations must be obtained that are required and those that the individual participant's physician recommends.

THE WILDERNESS MEDICAL KIT

Instructors must be able to assemble medical kits that are appropriate to support the proposed trip. Several criteria for design of medical kits must be considered. They include purpose of the trip, level of medical training of participants, destination, length of trip, interval of time until outside medical help can be reached, size of the party, bulk and weight that can be carried and cost of components. A discussion of these aspects of general kit design can be obtained from the position paper on medical kits published by the Wilderness Medical Society, Box 397, Point Reyes Station, CA 94956. Examples of medical kits can be found in references Auerbach (1986), Bowman (1988), Darvill (1985), Forgey (1987, 1989), Goodman et al. (1985), Goodman (1989), Lentz et al. (1985) and Wilkerson (1985).

The number of items chosen for a medical kit should be minimized. This may be accomplished in various ways. One technique is to attempt to use multifunctional components. Providing a codeine containing preparation— such as the prescription product Tylenol 3—for treatment of cough, diarrhea and pain would be an example. A nonprescription example would be the use of Percogesic for treating pain, muscle spasm, itch and congestion. A Sam Splint with its multiple uses would make an ideal general purpose splint, if its four ounce weight is justified for inclusion. Spenco 2nd Skin is a multipurpose dressing for friction blisters, first through third degree burns, abrasions and weeping wounds of all sorts which eliminates the need for various ointments, pain medications, and gauze bandaging. A discussion of multifunctional components is found in reference Forgey (1987).

If the organization outfits a variety of trips, a general formulary may be approved, with various items being chosen depending upon the criteria listed above. An example of such a system is the "wilderness medication index" as described in reference Goodman et al. (1985).

For the routine expedition medical kit a formulary should be constructed that would cover the required prophylactic medications and treat anticipated illness and injuries with the least number of line items of medications.

An example of a medical kit designed for the W.E.A. five-week field trip follows.

State-of-the-art dressings, wound closure tapes, and very useful nonprescription medications allow the construction of a very useful first aid kit for general outdoor use.

Very often treatments can be improvised with other items on hand, but prior planning and the inclusion of these items in your kit will provide you with the best that modern medical science can offer.

Quantity	Item
2 pkgs	Coverstrip Closures 1/4" x 3" 3/pkg
2	Spenco 2nd Skin Dressing Kit
1	Bulb irrigating syringe
5 pkgs	Nu-Gauze, high absorbent, sterile, 2 ply, 3" x 3" pkg/2
4	Surgipad, Sterile, 8" x 10"
2	Elastomull, Sterile Roller Gauze, 4" x 162"
2	Elastomull, Sterile Roller Gauze, 2 1/2" x 162"
10	Coverlet Bandage Strips, 1" x 3"
1	Tape, Hypoallergenic, 1/2" x 10 yd
1	Hydrocortisone Cream .5%, 1 oz tube (allergic skin)
1	Triple Antibiotic Ointment, 1 oz tube (prevents infection)
1	Hibiclens Surgical Scrub, 4 oz (prevents infection)
1	Dibucaine Ointment 1%, 1 oz tube (local pain relief)
1	Tetrahydrozoline Ophthalmic Drops, (eye irritation)
1	Starr Otic Drops, 1/2 oz bottle (ear pain, wax)
1	Micronazole Cream, 2%, 1/2 oz tube (fungal infection)
24	Actifed Tablets (decongestant)
24	Mobigesic Tablets (pain, fever, inflammation)
24	Meclizine 25 mg tab (nausea, motion sickness prevention)
2	Ammonia Inhalants (stimulant)
24	Benadryl 25 mg cap (antihistamine)
10	Bisacodyl 5 mg (constipation)
25	Diasorb (diarrhea)
25	Dimacid (antacid)
12 pkg	Q-tips, sterile, 2 per package
1	Extractor Kit (snakebite, sting, wound care)
6	1 oz vials for repackaging the above
1	Over-pak Container for above

Consideration should be given to a dental kit. As a minimum, a small bottle of oil of cloves can serve as a topical toothache treatment or a tube of toothache gel can be obtained. A fever thermometer should be included on trips. People wearing contact lenses should carry suction cup or rubber pincher device to aid in their removal. An adequate means of water purification must also be arranged.

Additional modules to this kit are described in detail in reference Forgey (1987), some of which include prescription-level medications. The above kit, and the advanced treatment modules can be purchased prepacked, or the individual items may be purchased separately from Indiana Camp Supply, Inc., PO Box 2166, Loveland, CO 80539, telephone 800-759-4453. Various other medical supply houses also carry these components. University Health Centers are a source for the catalogs or contacts for these supplies.

REFERENCES

Auerbach, P. (1986). *Medicine for the outdoors.* Boston: Little, Brown and Co.

Bechdel, L., and Ray, S. (1989). *River rescue* (2nd ed.). Boston: AppalachianMountain Club Books.

Bowman, W. D., Jr. (1988). *Outdoor emergency care.* Denver: National Ski Patrol System.

Darvill, F. (1985). *Mountaineering medicine* (11th ed.). Berkeley: Wilderness Press.

Eisenberg, M. and Copass, M. (1978). *Manual of emergency medical therapeutics.* Philadelphia: W. B. Saunders Company.

Forgey, W. W. (1989). *Basic essentials of outdoor first aid.* Merrillville, IN: ICS Books.

Forgey, W. (1985). *Hypothermia: Death by exposure.* Merrillville, IN: ICS Books.

Forgey, W. (1987). *Wilderness Medicine (3rd ed.).* Merrillville, IN: ICS Books.

Goodman, P. H. (1989). Wilderness equipment and medical supplies. In P. S. Auerbach and E.C. Geehr, (Eds.). *Management of wilderness and environmental emergencies* (pp. 289-320). St. Louis: C. V. Mosby Company.

Goodman, P. H., Kurtz, K. J. and Carmichael, J. (1985). Medical recommendations for wilderness travel: 3. Medical supplies and drug regimens. *Postgraduate Medicine.* 78 (2). 107-115.

Hackett, P. H. (1980). *Mountain sickness: Prevention, recognition, and treatment.* New York: The American Alpine Club.

Houston, C. S. (1987). *Going higher: The story of man and altitude* (rev. ed.). Boston: Little, Brown and Company.

Lentz, M. J., Macdonald, S. C, and Carline, J. (1985). *Mountaineering first aid* (3rd ed.). Seattle: The Mountaineers.

Nelson, R. N., Douglas, A. R. and Keller, M. D. (1985). *Environmental emergencies*. Philadelphia: W. B. Saunders Company.

Setnicka, T. J. (1980). *Wilderness search and rescue*. Boston: Appalachian Mountain Club Books.

Wilkerson, J. A. (Ed). (1986). *Hypothermia, frostbite and other cold injuries*. Seattle: The Mountaineers.

Wilkerson, J. A. (Ed). (1985). *Medicine for mountaineering* (3rd ed.). Seattle: The Mountaineers.

9.

COURSE ADMINISTRATION

by Mark Wagstaff
Wilderness Education Association
and David Cockrell,
University of Southern Colorado

Proper administration of the W.E.A. course establishes the overall tone and directly contributes to the success or failure of the program. Developing an administrative plan should be the first order of business in mounting a National Standard Program for Outdoor Leadership Certification (N.S.P.). An administrative plan serves as a tool for program development, implementation, and evaluation. The basic ingredient of a comprehensive plan is a detailed checklist of tasks organized into a realistic timetable. Each institution offering the N.S.P. faces the challenge of carefully considering factors unique to the institutional setting, course environment, staff and resources availabile. The ultimate organization of program specifics will be unique to each institution. The present discussion summarizes the fundamental elements of course administration and provides basic guidelines for developing and implementing an administrative plan.

Chapter 9 also describes, as course administration tasks, two program components: 1) The W.E.A. Shakedown and 2) the W.E.A. Evaluation Process. The shakedown occurs during the first week of the N.S.P. and is designed to be an intense philosophical orientation and skills preparation for the remaining time in the field. The W.E.A. evaluation process formally begins on the first day of a course and is completed upon submission of all evaluation forms to the W.E.A. administrative office. Certification decisions are based on the evaluation process; therefore, knowledge of the evaluation process and its proper implementation are quite important.

Before a course administrative plan is developed, it is assumed that all the necessary requirements to sponsor a W.E.A. course described in chapter 1 have been met. This assumption aside, the first priority consists of dividing the planning process into five phases:

Five Phases of an Administrative Plan

I. **Initial Preparation and Marketing**—Administrative tasks to be initiated seven to eight months before the course starts.

II. **Early Course Preparation**—Administrative tasks to be initiated at least three months before the course starts to reduce stress and meet time constraints.

III. **Pre-course Preparation**—Administrative tasks to be finalized immediately before the course starts.

IV. **Primary In-Course Administrative Activities**—Administrative and program tasks to be completed during the course.

V. **Course Evaluation and Wrap-up**—Administrative and program tasks to be initiated during the course, and tasks to be completed after the course.

These phases help to create structure for a realistic timetable thereby ensuring ample time to complete all tasks and allowing for unforeseen problems. No distinct division lines exist between the phases, and in most cases they overlap. Detailed organization of the task list within the structure of the five phases outlines the administrator's duties and time constraints. The following five sections are designed to guide administration by explaining various tasks, program components and considerations for the development and implementation of an N.S.P. administrative plan.

Preliminary Preparation and Marketing

Several responsibilities must be executed in the initial stages of planning well in advance of the course start. For instance, begin in early fall for an offering the following summer. Objectives of the preliminary preparation focus on finalizing the curriculum, developing a tentative course plan and actively recruiting participants.

FINALIZE THE CURRICULUM

A finalized curriculum provides the administrator a written resource containing important program components and other information needed to actively promote the program. The substance of any W.E.A. program, of course, comes from the 18 point standard curriculum, but there are many decisions to be made concerning sequencing, travel modes, adventure activities, and emphasis areas. To some extent each course becomes a unique program. Goals and objectives can then be taken from the curriculum outline and applied to marketing campaigns. A well-thought-out W.E.A. curriculum coinciding with the institution's degree programs enables the administration, faculty and students to accept, understand, and help sell the program. Specifics of the curriculum aid the course administrator in determining instructional sites, course activities, specialized staffing needs and equipment considerations. Early recognition of these issues offers the administrator more substance when developing a course description necessary to sell the program.

SELECT A COURSE AREA

Early decisions designating a course area give prospective participants specific reference to form initial expectations guided by the description of the area. Students respond more favorably to the time and cost commitment of a field experience with advance notice. The W.E.A. administrative office advertises all affiliate-sponsored courses and requires basic course information by fall for the following year. Early determination may help attract students from other colleges and universities around the country to fill available space.

RECRUIT PARTICIPANTS

The number of responses to a recruiting effort is directly proportional to the administrator's creativity and the amount of effort put into recruiting. Once responses roll in, personal contact and individual attention given to each response ultimately sell the number of spots available. Marketing the course aggressively involves using a variety of methods such as:
(a) Flyers or other on-campus media
(b) Approaching other programs on campus with an interest in leadership training
(c) Regional newsletter advertisements
(d) Personal invitations to staff of outdoor programs in the area
(e) Presentations (slides, talks, special events, etc.)
(f) Submitting course information to the W.E.A. office for advertising

DEVELOP A TENTATIVE BUDGET

A budget must be developed to give prospective participants an idea of cost. Administrators will find themselves in one of two positions:
1. Resources and information are available to accurately calculate the cost per participant.
2. The program is new or time does not allow for exact calculation of cost per participant.

Position two requires the administrator to calculate a price to the best of his/her ability using the following considerations as a guideline for expenditures:
1. Food (Prices average $3.00 to $5.00 per person per day using standard W.E.A. rations)

2. Transportation (All vehicle use and driver salary)
3. Equipment (Rentals, Acquisition Cost)
4. Field Supplies (Stove fuel, journals, film, etc.)
5. Administrative Costs (Photocopying, paper, mailings, phone, etc.)
6. Academic fees (Cost of credit hours)
7. Special Events (i.e., Postcourse banquet)
8. Contractual Services (Outfitters, special instruction, and equipment)
9. Fees for course area permits
10. W.E.A. certification fee
11. Instruction salaries
12. Miscellaneous

Early Course Preparation

Early course preparation typically begins about three months before the course starts. Early preparation reduces stress and alleviates last minute rushes. The administrator should have an estimate of the approximate number of students in order to finalize the budget and then develop a fee collection schedule. Details such as outfitting, course area reconnaissance, equipment lists, course policies and course forms are all items that cannot wait until the last minute. Early preparation includes contacting the resource managers or private land owners for permit application or permission. If the administrator is not the course instructor, final negotiations and plans must be initiated for contracting with a certified W.E.A. instructor.

FEE-COLLECTION SCHEDULE AND PAYMENT POLICY

Many W.E.A. affiliates recommend at least a $100 deposit, $50 non refundable, be required three months before course start. The participant's financial commitment enables the administrator to finalize the budget and begin relaying paperwork to participants. Cost of food and transportation, two major costs, are no longer a mystery once that financial commitment happens. A detailed budget can be created listing specific line-item expenditures as details come together. Early communication with participants describing the payment schedule and detailing the basic content of the course is critical. After the initial deposit, one half of the remaining tuition may be due three months before the course starts. The remaining tuition can be due one month before the course starts.

COURSE POLICIES

An effective approach to creating a professional tone and properly guiding expectations involves sending each student a W.E.A. program policy and agreement to participate. Establish course policies early and give this considerable thought to avoid problems in or out of the field. Take into consideration the course area, the participant, and local culture and norms of the course area inhabitants when developing course policies. Instructors are trusted to use good judgment and are expected to consider factors unique to each course environment to ensure a smooth trip. Several policies should be considered that potentially have important impact on the individual, the affiliate, W.E.A., or the course experience. The following are general areas of concern that could have adverse effects on many levels if not addressed in a policy format:

1. **Alcohol, Drugs and Tobacco**—W.E.A. acknowledges that these items have no place during an outdoor experience. W.E.A. trains leaders and if leaders cannot refrain during the experience then the participant comprises his/her certification.

2. **Emergency Rescue Payments**—A determination must be made by each instructor concerning how the costs of rescues will be paid.

3. **Co-Ed Tenting**—This is up to the discretion of the instructor, keeping in mind that this may not be acceptable in some local areas and may bring bad public relations.

4. **Early Course Departures**—A course policy should address reimbursement of fees to students who depart from a course before the end, either due to factors beyond their control or by personal choice.

5. **Nudity**—This is sometimes offensive to group members and other people using the course area. This could also cause poor public relations with local residents.

6. **No-shows**—W.E.A. recommends that students who do not show up for course start should not be refunded course tuition.

7. **Swimming**—Swimming in water over head level unless participating in water activities is strongly discouraged. (This policy is recommended based on statistics concerning water-related accidents in the outdoors.)

8. **Physical Examinations and Health Insurance**—Typically, students are required to have a physical examination by a doctor within twelve months of the course and provide their own medical insurance.

These eight considerations do not exhaust the number of policies the administrator and instructor must consider. Policies deemed important should be recorded and written in a clear, concise manner and distributed to all students. The Association for Experiential Education's publication "Common Practices in Adventure Programming" (Johanson, 1984) serves as an excellent source for developing guidelines and policies for specific adventure activities and modes of travel found in a W.E.A. course. The W.E.A. administrative office acts as a resource for affiliates developing course policies. Administrators should carefully consider all policies and steer toward conservative viewpoints realizing these policies serve as a model for aspiring leaders.

BASIC FORMS AND INFORMATION SHEETS
1. Statement of acknowledgement of risk
2. Student medical and insurance information
3. Equipment list and check-out procedures
4. Course itinerary

Early preparation of these forms allots participants enough time to complete forms and allows the administrator time to follow up on incomplete student paperwork. Student medical forms sent out as early as possible give students a fair chance at making appointments with heavily scheduled doctors who put such items low on the priority list.

PRECONDITIONING RECOMMENDATIONS

While the W.E.A. course is not known as a strenuous, hard physical push, preconditioning will make the experience more enjoyable. Historically, W.E.A. students have expressed, through evaluations, that their course was not as physically demanding as they had anticipated. The W.E.A. course format is one of teaching and learning along the way and does not emphasize clocking miles that takes away from teaching time. However, the instructor may schedule several strenuous days if this accomplishes predetermined objectives involving the outcomes of a hard push. The physical nature of expeditions requires that outdoor leaders maintain a reasonable level of physical fitness to handle emergencies and maintain a healthy mental state.

Encouraging exercise prior to a W.E.A. course varies among affiliates depending on personal philosophies and the type of course offered. Many W.E.A. instructors begin courses slowly with minimal movement from camp to camp and students acclimatize to increasing physical challenge as the course progresses. The progression of physical challenge increases under certain environmental conditions and increases during specific adventure activities.

A thoughtful primer on conditioning for physical outdoor activities is Steve Ilg's (1987) book, *The Outdoor Athlete*. For "preseason" training, he suggests a mixture of resistance (weight) training, aerobic activity and sports-specific workouts. For example, one basic preseason regimen includes upper and lower body resistance routines on day one, a 40-60 minute aerobic workout on day two (running, cycling, swimming, brisk walking), sport-specific training on day three, and stretching, kinesthetic and centering activities on day four. The balance shifts toward sport-specific training in-season, and Ilg provides a number of specific training activities for backpacking, mountaineering, backcountry skiing, kayaking, etc. The basic idea is to acquire principal strength in the gym and build more specific strengths through the sports themselves. Ilg notes, however, that absolute strength levels increase approximately 1 to 3 percent per seven days of training, so it is important to start early.

It is also recommended that students start eating similar types of food that will be eaten during the course. For example, participants who are meat eaters should begin consuming more grains and pasta to acclimate the digestive system. By cutting down on sugars and coffee consumption, the participant's system may not experience the withdrawal symptoms (headaches, dramatic mood swings) that many participants experience. (This applies to instructors/affiliates that do not provide coffee and foods containing large amounts of sugar normally encountered in most American diets.) Establishing a pattern of going to bed early and rising early before the course starts also helps participants adjust more easily to a normal outdoor schedule. A W.E.A. course is not the time to stop smoking, particularly if withdrawal symptoms may cause severe mood swings. Students should be encouraged to stop long before the course and give the body time to adjust.

OUTFITTING NEEDS AND SUPPORT SERVICES

Early preparation and inquiries to obtain support services occurs during the early planning phase. Many commercial outfitters require advance notice in the form of a reservation accompanied by financial commitment in order to provide services. Outfitting needs for W.E.A. courses entail a variety of services ranging from logistical support and equipment rentals, to technical skill training. Technical skill training support includes agencies specializing in activities such as whitewater paddling, technical rock climbing, or salt water sailing. The course administrator should shop around and choose reputable agencies with safe track records and highly trained and experienced staff who understand outdoor leadership training as opposed to only traditionally guided trips. The time spent educating contract help on W.E.A. philosophy and program goals may prevent nonproductive time in the field. Overreliance on outside consultants might suggest problems in course staffing or an inadequate understanding of W.E.A. philosophy.

Also, outfitters or support staff may be needed for food drops or pickups. An overall plan for logistical support should be formulated. Time spent acquiring dependable people and prior planning enables the instructor to do his/her job without undue stress. There should be a system of instructions and expectations for logistical and program support that can be implemented without direct supervision. For example, after the details are worked out, develop instructions that are self-explanatory and easy to initiate. The idea is to reduce the margin of error so that during a food drop or meeting time the support staff have all the information at their finger tips. Basic instructions for food drops, pickups, and rendezvous include:

1. List of contents to be dropped off and their location;
2. Well-marked containers listing contents, the time and date to be dropped off;
3. Map and specific directions for meeting point;
4. Driving, hiking, or packing time to meeting point;
5. Back-up plan and instructions if anticipated problems were to occur;
6. Specific information concerning vehicles, parking, gas, or other miscellaneous details.

CONTACTING RESOURCE MANAGERS AND LANDOWNERS

Acquiring permits and permission to utilize course areas must begin well before the course. It is important to contact and inform resource managers of the program. Resource managers appreciate being informed and tend to feel much more comfortable with extended programming when this communication occurs. Communication should go beyond acquiring the necessary permits and permissions, and should be carried out even when backcountry use permits are not required. The resource manager should receive an itinerary with emergency procedures for his/her review and general information. Many resource managers have expressed great appreciation over the years when W.E.A. affiliates share plans and scheduled activities on public lands. The itineraries and emergency procedures are usually kept within easy reach by resource managers to be used at a moment's notice for any situation that might arise.

Private land owners are also a population that must be contacted when expeditioning in many parts of the country. Good public relations with private land owners, informing them of activities and proper environmental practices, open the door to land use and provide contact with colorful natives rich in local culture. W.E.A. recommends personal contact with private land owners based on the premise that people naturally trust one another after a face-to-face conversation resulting in mutual understandings.

One more population often forgotten, depending on the low or high use of an area, is other outdoor programs utilizing the same course area. During peak season use, many areas such as climbing sites, camping spots, hiking trails and water sources may be used by outdoor groups involved in similar programming. It is important to establish early communications with other programs to coordinate the use of course areas and to avoid overuse and unwanted group-to-group interaction. This contact becomes more important as participation increases in popular areas. Outdoor educators should embrace this as normal procedure during the early planning stage.

RECONNAISSANCE OF COURSE AREA
Instructors/administrators unfamiliar with a course area have sufficient time during early preparation to familiarize themselves with the area. While it may not be necessary to cover the entire area, a significant portion should be scouted in order to maximize the learning experience for the participant. Reconnaissance can be augmented through reference to guidebooks, local publications and other people familiar with the area. Familiarity with the course area allows the instructor to utilize areas conducive to planned activities and reduces preoccupation with the unknown. Predetermined rock sites or river crossings reduce searching and inspection time, and in return, programming opportunity increases. Scouting a significant portion of the course area is possible because W.E.A. crews do not usually travel long distances. Evacuation routes and questionable areas of safety can be inspected and documented in order to develop a quality emergency plan and evacuation procedures that will be part of the risk-management plan.

Precourse Preparation

Precourse preparation is the high-pitched period of precourse activity during the last few weeks before a course begins. This period includes the final preparations necessary to ensure a smooth course start. Early preparation details must be finalized, and final tasks are completed that include personal matters involved in preparing for an extended field experience. Precourse preparation usually includes:

1. Developing and documenting a risk-management plan
2. Finalizing permits
3. Purchasing supplies (i.e., cooking supplies, stove fuel, maps, food bags, first aid supplies, student journals, etc.)
4. Arranging with local merchants for food purchases
5. Purchasing dried and nonperishable items. Plastic five gallon buckets with lids are particularly good for storing food. Perishable items such as dairy products may be purchased if freezer space is available.
6. Making final transportation arrangements
7. Preparing student packets containing evaluations, itineraries, emergency procedures, equipment and clothing lists, and general handouts
8. Sending student registration forms and retail orders to the W.E.A. office
9. Collecting necessary forms from students and following up on any questionable medical problems
10. Defining roles and responsibilities among instructors and apprentices
11. Obtaining emergency money before course start (The amount of emergency money should reflect a conservative estimation of the worst possible case requiring cash—this is largely contingent upon nature of the course and course area.)
12. Securing parking for participant vehicles if applicable
13. Making arrangements for a final budget

DEVELOPMENT AND DOCUMENTATION OF A RISK-MANAGEMENT PLAN

For those of us working in universities, it can be tempting to assume that risk management is someone else's issue. University systems often include fairly large, well-established professional liability insurance policies and may not demand or even understand the basic steps for risk reduction in outdoor programs. We are, however, personally familiar with several negligence suits against university outdoor leadership training programs in the last decade, involving expert witness testimony and in-court settlements. It is important for W.E.A. instructors to understand their professional liability insurance coverage, and even more important to implement a standardized plan of risk reduction and emergency procedures.

Fortunately, there are now a number of good references for risk management in adventure programs. The American Camping Association (1988) recommends three basic steps in the risk-management process: (1) Identification of risks specific to your site, program and operation; (2) determination of the extent of the risks you face; (3) selection of a method or approach to handling the risks. The four basic approaches to handling risk are to retain it and budget for it, to transfer it to another party through insurance, to reduce it, or to avoid it. As the primary risk an instructor is exposed to in a W.E.A. course is injury due to negligence, it is imperitive that instructors understand the standard of care that is required of prudent professionals in the field.

As summarized by Van der Smissen (1982), Christiansen (1986), McEwen (1983), Ford and Blanchard (1985) and others, there are three principal elements of the required standard of care that must be addressed in a risk management plan. First, there must be a plan of supervision. Staff must know their responsibilities and the plan should be discussed in pre-course planning. The instructors must be accessible to students, aware of potentially dangerous situations and competent in first aid procedures necessary for specific anticipated problems. A differentiation should be made between general supervision and situations requiring specific supervision. In specific supervision, instructors must communicate on the level of the student, make sure that students understand and adhere to safety policies and pay attention to changing conditions in students and the environment.

Second, instructors must conduct instructional activities professionally. This means executing a progression of instructional activities appropriate to the ability levels of students, including adequate instructions. Instructors must understand students biologically and plan activities appropriate to their age, skill and maturity levels.

Finally, instructors must understand and plan for the instructional environment. Instructors are not responsible for "acts of God" but they are responsible for knowing of predictable "hidden perils." Thus, if a leader leads students into predictable hazardous conditions, then the leader is liable. Students do not assume the risks of faulty equipment, so a system of preventative equipment maintenance must be executed. Also, instructors must check the layout or design of a course route, including trails, trailheads, emergency access routes at various points, telephone access points, ranger stations and sources of emergency assistance.

Documentation is the hallmark of risk management. Plans should all be written, and course activities should be documented through an instructor's journal and a variety of standardized forms. Typical forms include acknowledgement of risk forms, itineraries with emergency contact information, health and medical information sheets, course report forms, equipment log and maintenance records, accident and near-miss report forms (Johanson, 1984). All the issues summarized here are addressed in more detail in the references listed.

STUDENT HANDBOOK

W.E.A. affiliates employ an assortment of methods to disseminate final information and forms to students. One effective method consists of generating student handbooks containing information needed throughout the course. The physical design of the handbook should provide students a writing surface and the ability to detach forms and homework assignments. A plastic cover protects the contents from the elements and helps reduce crumpling and abuse caused by a backpack. Keeping paperwork clean and neat must be a priority primarily because student evaluations go to the W.E.A. office where this information may be shared with future employers if the student desires. The following list describes likely contents to be included in a student handbook:

1. Student and Instructor Evaluations
2. Course Policies
3. Equipment and Clothing Lists
4. Food and Rationing Lists
5. Emergency Procedures and Emergency Contacts (phone numbers)
6. Itinerary
7. Student Names and Addresses
8. Course Objectives and Explanation of Criteria for Certification
9. Natural and Cultural History of the Area
10. Contents of First Aid Kit and Repair Kit
11. Student Skill Check List (Instructor-generated check lists for students to document specific skills demonstrated)
12. Accident Report Form
13. Homework Assignments (problem-solving scenarios)
14. Patient Assessment Survey (survey used in Wilderness First Responder Courses)
15. Rules and Regulations of Course Area
16. Schedule of Logistical and Outfitting Support

Affiliates are encouraged to be creative with student handbooks so that the information enhances the experience. A well-done handbook can serve as a valuable tool during the course and serve as an excellent resource for W.E.A. students long afterwards. Student handbooks also function as a resource for logistical personnel, resource managers, and emergency contacts.

Primary Incourse Administrative Activities

The primary in-course administrative and program activities occur after the course start and through the shakedown component of the course. Responsibilities associated with this phase should not interfere with teaching time; therefore, careful coordination with fellow instructors reduces individual responsibility loads. Responsibilities primarily consist of implementing tasks planned during the first three phases of the administrative plan. Typical responsibilities include:

1. Purchasing perishable and last-minute food items
2. Accounting for money spent and retaining receipts in an organized fashion.

3. Administering the transportation plan, including shuttles and food drops

4. Final communications with resource managers if necessary

5. Executing any emergency procedures required

6. Delegating such roles as course photographer, medical officer, etc.

7. Executing the shakedown component of the W.E.A. course

The above list varies according to the level of completion each responsibility received during prior phases of planning. Most in-course tasks are straightforward. For example, developing a system for retaining receipts and accounting for expenditures does not necessarily require sophisticated accounting procedures. Be sure to neatly document expenditures and safely store receipts to avoid problems once the course ends weeks later and memories falter. Be prepared for last-minute participant personal needs such as phone use, lack of or improper clothing and gear, and insufficient personal items, i.e., sun block, insect repellent, etc. Seasoned outdoor leaders agree, once the course is in the field there is great relief from the administrative and logistical barrage.

THE W.E.A. SHAKEDOWN

The W.E.A. approach to teaching emphasizes trail teaching, opportunity teaching and the grasshopper method—flexible approaches to instructional sequencing based on unpredicted learning opportunities, weather, etc. However, the first six to nine days of a course are scheduled with more structure to make certain that basic topics are covered in a somewhat orderly fashion. Petzoldt's (1984) description of the first seven days of a course remains the guiding philosophy. Briefly, the organization of the curriculum elements should look something like the following:

1. Orientation
   Expedition Behavior
   Clothing and Equipment
   Nutrition and Rations Planning
   Pack Packing
   Leadership and Judgment

2. First Day
   On the Trail:
      Blister Control
      Human Waste Disposal
      Map Reading

   In Camp:
      Expedition Behavior
      In-camp Conservation Practices
         Basic Cooking

3. Second Day
   In Camp:
   Personal Hygiene and Sanitation
   Water Pollution
   Second Cook Class
   First Map and Compass Class

   On the Trail:
   Map Work
   Time Control

4. Third Day
   In Camp:
   Review of Curriculum So Far
   Introduction to Specific Activity (fishing, climbing, etc.)
   Breaking Camp
   Second Map and Compass Class
   Campsite Selection

   On the Trail:
   Time control Plans
   Map Reading

5. Fourth Day:
   In Camp:
   Energy control Plans
   Third Cook Class (baking)
   Time control plans (formal development)
   Natural History

   On Trail:
   Time and Energy Control

6. Fifth Day (layover day):
   Baking
   Bathing and Sanitation
   Debriefing Time-control Plans
   Group Dynamics and Leadership
   Natural History

7. Sixth Day
   Time-control Plans
   Third Map and Compass Class
   First Aid Class
   Potluck Dinner

8. Seventh Day
   Expedition Planning
   Rations Planning
   Tyrolean Traverse

Course Evaluation and Wrap-up

Evaluation should be embraced as a significant program component and curriculum area rather than tolerated as an administrative necessity. The W.E.A. evaluation process is formative as well as summative. It includes self-evaluation, peer evaluation, instructor evaluation of students and student evaluation of instructors and courses. Evaluative media include journals, rating scales, narratives, individual conferences and group debriefing. The process includes many different approaches to performance evaluation because the ultimate decisions are serious: certification by the instructors that students have demonstrated good judgment and a basic national standard of outdoor leadership. In order to make sound certification decisions, instructors must have clear conceptions of what good judgment and leadership consist of, and behaviors they believe must be exhibited in order to demonstrate certifiability. These issues have been discussed throughout the book, but perhaps most directly in chapters 2, 3 and 8.

The evaluation process occurs in three phases. First, at the beginning of a course, the entire evaluation process must be made clear to all students. This should include a formal presentation of course objectives, a discussion of the evaluation process and its purpose, and an explanation of the expedition journal.

The journal is a reflective tool designed to aid in the process of integrating new information and experience into one's conceptual framework. W.E.A.'s use of the journal is not unlike its use in other areas of experiential education, and it is considered a key vehicle in the development of good judgment. In addition to narrative reflection on changes in perspectives through new experiences, students also use the journal for notes from structured classes, time, energy and climate-control plans and daily schedules. Some instructors ask students to solve expedition planning exercises in their journals, for example, developing a rations plan for a long trip. But the primary emphasis should be on verbalizing new lessons and experiences that have prompted changes in thinking, values and philosophy and will have impact on future decisions.

We usually spend some time on evaluation at the initial course meeting and then devote several hours to it on the morning of the second day. A presentation of each student's personal course goals and a discussion of how judgment is taught and learned can also be combined with this class. As the course progresses students should be encouraged to familiarize themselves with the course objectives and to reflect on their abilities and limitations in regard to the objectives. They should practice a daily habit of writing in journals.

Within a few days the "leader-of-the-day" process is initiated. Each day one student is assigned leadership responsibility for that day. The leader of the day facilitates the daily debriefing, schedules events, coordinates decisions and organizes travel activities. If there are unexpected crises, the leader of the day participates with the instructors in a leadership team. Each day the previous day's leader of the day is debriefed. He/she is then encouraged to write about the experience in his/her journal, and further feedback is given in conferences with the instructors.

The second stage of the evaluation process is the midcourse evaluation. The backbone of this formative exercise is the W.E.A. Student Evaluation Form. Using this form students are rated on seven categories of quality judgment-related activity:

1. Knowledge of abilities and limitations
2. Expedition planning
3. Expedition behavior
4. Environmental ethics
5. Safety systems
6. Fun and enjoyment
7. Group handling skills

Each of these curriculum areas is, of course, defined on the form and taught through classes and course activities daily. The form is completed on each student by small groups of peers and by the instructors. Then instructors hold individual conferences with each student to: 1) Review the peer evaluations; 2) review the instructors' midcourse evaluation; and 3) review the expedition journal. This is also a good time for instructors to receive evaluative feedback about the course and their leadership.

The final summative stage of the evaluation process begins several days before the course ends. Students complete a personal Ability Assessment Form. This self-evaluation instrument asks students to describe the kinds of outdoor experiences they would and would not feel qualified to lead. Dimensions addressed are clientele populations, trip size and length, environments, seasons and activities. In a final exit interview instructors review with each student: 1) the Ability Assessment Form, 2) the expedition journal; and 3) the instructors' final evaluation as recorded on the Student Evaluation Form. A final section of the Ability Assessment requests a narrative evaluation of the student by instructors. Instructors must recommend positively or negatively on certification of the student. Both the student and the instructor must sign this form.

Finally, students complete the Course Evaluation Questionnaire, rating the course and instructors on a number of dimensions. These forms may be mailed to the W.E.A. office separately or (preferably) all together as an independent packet. Instructors must file the final Student Evaluation Forms, the Ability Assessment forms and the instructor's Course Completion Questionnaire. Files are maintained by W.E.A. for each student, and copies of course evaluations may be sent to prospective employers or others at a student's request only.

POSTCOURSE WRAP-UP

Postcourse wrap-up duties, in addition to completing evaluations, entails several other responsibilities. After a long course, care must be taken to tie up loose ends and ensure equipment and supplies are properly stored. An organized cleaning system, sufficient cleaning space and supplies, and proper drying area ensure a quality clean-up job. Administrators control paperwork by setting deadlines and stressing the importance of each form. Many times instructors and participants alike leave the course, in a mental sense, before it is actually over. Organized clean-up procedures, final completion of forms and final preparation for the banquet deserve as much energy as activities on day one of the course.

A final closing of the experience through a banquet and ceremony aides participants in personal transition. Administrators are encouraged to plan and provide this vital transition tool to ease participants back into normal routine. Many students undergo stress and personal growth inherent in a long expedition; therefore, transition activities and inclusion of transference issues in debriefings begin long before the banquet. The banquet merely acts as a formal closing and opportunity for final sharing.

The following list suggests responsibilities to consider in order to complete final tasks:

1. Follow up on any incomplete near miss and accident report forms

2. Inventory and inspect equipment for repair and replacement

3. Pay any outstanding bills, collect debts, and finalize the accounting summary

4. Arrange for disposal of extra food and supplies

5. Write thank you letters to landowners and significant supporters of the program

6. Conduct appropriate public relations activities (slide shows, news releases, T-shirts, etc.)

7. Submit evaluation materials and near miss/accident report forms to the W.E.A. administrative office

Conclusion

For most W.E.A. instructors, course administration is not the most enjoyable of our responsibilities. Many of our rewards come from teaching, and it is the contact time with students that motivates us to go on. The important point to remember about administrative responsibilities in this particular context, however, is their unique role in experiential education. As experiential educators, often we claim to design specific learning experiences in circumscribed environments and let the experiences do the teaching. Much of this book has described methods for enhancing the significance and transference of lessons from specific situations to general principles.

If the administrative arrangements for experiential lessons are not handled properly, the effectiveness of the W.E.A. approach can be greatly compromised. If a course budget is underestimated and money is gone before the end, if course policies are unclear, if permits are not properly secured or a food drop doesn't materialize—if any number of administrative details are not handled properly, the lesson may be how not to handle it next time. The learning opportunity and the instructor's credibility are sacrificed. On the other hand, there is considerable satisfaction to be drawn from a well-orchestrated, well-executed expedition, reasonably safe but full of adventure. Perhaps the moral is: Plan well and stay loose!

REFERENCES

American Camping Association (1988). *Camp Standards with Interpretations.* Bradford Woods, IN: American Camping Association.

Christiansen, M. L. (1986). How to Avoid Negligence Suits: Reducing Hazards to Prevent Injuries. *Journal of Health, Physical Education, Recreation and Dance,* 57 (2), 46-52.

Ford, P. and Blanchard, J.L. (1985). *Leadership and Administration of Outdoor Pursuits.* State College, PA: Venture Books.

Ilg, S. (1988). *The Outdoor Athlete.* Evergreen, CO: Cordillera Press.

Johanson, K. (Ed.) (1984). *Common Practices in Adventure Programming.* Boulder, CO: Association for Experiential Education.

McEwen, D. (1983). Being High on Public Land: Rock Climbing and Public Liability. *Parks and Recreation,* 18 (10), 46-48.

Van der Smissen, B. (1982). Minimizing legal liability risks in adventure programs. *Journal of Experiential Education,* 4, 10-17.

ABOUT THE AUTHORS

Kelly Cain is an assistant professor in resource management at the University of Wisconsin-River Falls. He has been a W.E.A. instructor since 1979 and has taught a variety of national standard and professional courses, including the first formal Instructor's Certification Course in 1984. Kelly holds a Ph.D. in education (Park & Recreation Administration) from the University of Minnesota. His current academic interests besides outdoor leadership include environmental ethics and sustainable earth lifestyles.

Jerry Cinnamon has thirty years experience in high-adventure outdoor pursuits that has led to an interest in safety management. A member of the pilot W.E.A. instructors course, he teaches experientially focused earth-science courses and mountaineering. Dr. Cinnamon is Professor of Outdoor Recreation at Unity College of Maine.

David Cockrell is Assistant Professor and Director of the Leisure Studies Curriculum at the University of Southern Colorado. He holds a Ph.D. in wildland recreation management and an M.S. in psychological services in education. His research and writing interests focus on psychological issues in outdoor adventure education and outdoor recreation policy. Dr. Cockrell has taught W.E.A. national standard courses since 1981.

Jack Drury is Associate Professor and Director of Wilderness Recreation Leadership at North Country Community College, a unit of the State University of New York (SUNY) in Saranac Lake, New York. He is a W.E.A. instructor having taught W.E.A. N.S.P. courses annually since 1979. He is currently president of the Wilderness Education Association and holds a B.S. in recreation education from SUNY, Cortland and a M.S. in education administration from SUNY, Plattsburgh.

William W. Forgey, M.D. is a family practitioner in Merrillville, Indiana. In addition, however, as a popular lecturer and author of *Wilderness Medicine* and *Hypothermia: Death By Exposure,* Bill has played a significant role in upgrading the now sophisticated field of wilderness medicine. Bill is a highly experienced backcountry expeditioner.

Frank Lupton is a professor in the Department of Recreation, Park and Tourism Administration at Western Illinois University. He is a founder and past president of W.E.A. He has taught several national standard courses for Western's ECO Education Expedition, which he founded in 1976. His Ph.D. is in recreation and park administration from the University of Illinois.

Cynthia A. Phipps holds an M.S. in community counseling from Mankato State University in Minnesota and a B.A. in psychology from the University of Minnesota at Morris. Cindy co-led both therapy groups and educational wilderness groups. She has served as the director of a mental health center and focuses much of her training on the management of groups.

Maurice Phipps has a Ph.D. in education with an emphasis in parks, recreation and leisure studies from the University of Minnesota. He has a background in outdoor recreation from the United Kingdom, Australia and North America. He has worked in public, private and nonprofit agencies, including outdoor pursuits centers, schools and universities. Maurice's research interests include leadership, group dynamics and psychology in relation to the outdoors. He is the author of the book *Canoeing in Australia*.

Ed Raiola is the coordinator of the Unity College Outdoor Recreation Department. He has been a W.E.A. instructor since 1981. He holds a Ph.D in wilderness-based outdoor recreation. His research and publications have focused on communication, outdoor leadership education and the philosophy and foundations of experiential education.

Mark Wagstaff is the executive director of the Wilderness Education Association. Mark's past experience includes former river manager of Wildwater Ltd. on the Chattooga River, and a teaching position at North Carolina State University (NCSU) with the Department of Recreation Resources. He has served as a field instructor for W.E.A. and the North Carolina Outward Bound School. Mark received a M.S. degree in recreation resources from NCSU.

INDEX